LIGHTNING
OUT OF
LEBANON

LIGHTNING
OUT OF
LEBANON

HEZBOLLAH TERRORISTS
ON AMERICAN SOIL

TOM DIAZ AND BARBARA NEWMAN

PRESIDIO
PRESS

BALLANTINE BOOKS
NEW YORK

A Presidio Press Book
Published by The Random House Publishing Group

Copyright © 2005 by Gregory T. Diaz and Barbara Newman

www.presidiopress.com

Library of Congress Cataloging-in-Publication Data

Newman, Barbara.
   Lightning out of Lebanon : Hezbollah terrorists on American soil / Barbara Newman and Tom Diaz.
     p. cm.
   Includes index.
   ISBN 0-345-47568-2
    1. Terrorism—United States.   2. Hezbollah (Lebanon)   3. Terrorism—Religious aspects—Islam.   I. Diaz, Tom.   II. Title.

   HV6432.5.U62H596 2005
   303.6'25'0899275692073—dc22   2004057388

Manufactured in the United States of America

9 8 7 6 5 4 3 2 1

First Edition: March 2005

Text design by Joseph Rutt

In memory of BG and JPO.

To Paola Sara Czyzewski and the thousands of other innocent
victims of Hezbollah violence—"no pudo ser."

ACKNOWLEDGMENTS

The names of many who helped us in researching this book must of necessity remain unwritten. They are men and women, Americans and citizens of other friendly nations, who have devoted their lives to anonymous public service fighting terrorism, too often maligned, and hardly ever properly acknowledged. To these silent soldiers we all, and the authors in particular, owe a debt of gratitude. The list of others who helped in many ways, great and small, would be too lengthy to recite without fear of inadvertently overlooking one.

We would, however, like to acknowledge the excellent guidance of our editor, Ron Doering. Ron's steady hand and gentle, but firm, suggestions are evident in the ideal writer's result—it is difficult for us to tell where lie the seams between his thoughts and ours. The staff of The Washington Institute for Near East Policy in Washington, DC, in particular senior fellow Matthew Levitt, early on provided invaluable background information that pointed us in the right direction. Rex Tomb of the FBI's Office of Public Affairs was always helpful, as were others within the FBI and a number of career attorneys in the U. S. Department of Justice, including especially the offices of the United States Attorneys in Charlotte, North Carolina, and Detroit, Michigan. Federal court reporters Theresah Sorensen in Washington, DC, and Joy Kelly in Charlotte were quite helpful in our obtaining key court records. Mehsah Tariy was a constant friend and unfailing source of wisdom. Our families endured much and provided support and inspiration throughout, so to them a special thanks.

CONTENTS

INTRODUCTION

When I was running the Voice of America (VOA) during the last years of the Cold War, the primary focus of our 24-hour-a-day broadcasts in English, and 50 other languages, was on the vast Soviet Union, its surrogates in Eastern Europe, and its allies in countries such as China, Cuba, North Korea, Vietnam, Mozambique, etc. Our broadcasts were listened to by tens of millions of people in tightly closed societies, many of them in secret, fearful of reprisal by authorities. We also had other geopolitical considerations and audiences, not all of them behind the Iron Curtain.

In 1985, one listener we hoped to reach was William Buckley in Beirut, Lebanon. Buckley had volunteered for the dangerous posting there as CIA station chief and was soon kidnapped by Hezbollah terrorists, disappearing with his captors into the maw of the Beirut slums. Periodically, the VOA sent coded messages to Buckley in broadcasts to the Middle East. Our hopes of contacting him depended on his captors listening to the radio within his hearing. We never learned whether we reached Buckley, who died from imprisonment and torture that lasted for more than a year.

Back when Osama bin Laden was just another wealthy young

Saudi and al Qaeda had not yet inflicted its terrible wounds on the world, Hezbollah was torturing and murdering Americans. Until the al Qaeda attacks of September 11, 2001, the self-described "Party of God" had killed more U.S. citizens than any other radical Islamist group and, for the most part, they had gotten away with it. Three of the early attacks occurred almost twenty years ago. One of the first victims was Robby Stethem, a U.S. Navy deep-sea diver. Robby was raised in a military family. His father is a retired Navy chief petty officer and his mother was a longtime clerk at the U.S. Court of Military Appeals in nearby Washington, D.C. They raised Robby, his brother Kenneth, who became a Navy SEAL, and his brother Patrick, also a U.S. Navy diver, in rural Waldorf, Maryland.

Robby Stethem, 23 years old, athletic and clean-cut, was returning with five other American sailors to their base in Little Creek, Virginia, in the summer of 1985, after a diving assignment in Athens, Greece. At the time, the Athens airport was notorious for lax security. The Greek government and left-wing Prime Minister Andreas Papandreou were more than willing to accommodate terrorists. Three years earlier, Papandreou successfully pressured Athens' airport managers to give jobs to Palestinian extremists fleeing the Israeli army in Lebanon. In May 1985, a U.S. aviation magazine warned readers that Athens is the airport from which "you are most likely to be hijacked."

On June 14, at 10 A.M., a few minutes after taking off from Athens for Rome, TWA Flight 847, carrying 143 passengers, the majority of them American tourists, was hijacked by two Hezbollah terrorists waving guns and hand grenades. Passengers were terrorized as the men ran through the cabin striking them with the butts of their guns. An elderly American woman was kicked in the face, her glasses smashed. With a cocked pistol held against his head, the pilot was forced to land in Beirut, made to take off for Algiers, and finally forced back again to Lebanon where the passengers endured sixteen terror-filled days before it ended.

Robby Stethem was singled out after the terrorists saw his U.S. Navy ID. His hands were tied behind his back with a bungee cord and he was savagely beaten. As sobbing passengers watched, he was punched to the cabin floor, and one of the terrorists, wearing boots, jumped up and down on his chest, breaking all of his ribs. Unable to walk or even stand, Robby was dumped into a seat next to Rosemary Henderson of Australia and her young daughter. Stethem told Mrs. Henderson that if any one of the American sailors on the flight were killed he hoped it would be him because the other men were married and had families. A few minutes later, Robby was dragged to the front of the plane and shot in the head by Mohammed Ali Hammadei. Still alive, he was thrown onto the tarmac where he lived for a few more minutes.

In 1987, Mohammed Hammadei was captured in Frankfurt, Germany, as he carried explosives into the airport. The Germans refused to extradite him to the United States, ostensibly because he would face the death penalty. Hammadei was convicted by a trio of West German judges of Robby Stethem's murder, of air piracy, kidnapping, and beating of the other passengers on Flight 847, and given the toughest of German sentences—a minimum of fifteen years in prison. The Bush administration of 1988 claimed they were satisfied with the Mahdi's conviction as a demonstration "of the effectiveness of the rule of law against terrorism."

A month after the attacks of September 11, 2001, a new guided missile destroyer, one of America's most advanced warships, employing lasers and sophisticated computer systems to be used in the war against terrorism—the USS *Robert Stethem*—was commissioned in San Diego. Robby's brother Kenneth, now a decorated U.S. Navy SEAL was the guest speaker at the ceremony.

The week before Robby Stethem died in Beirut, another American, arms and legs fettered with iron shackles, in grimy captivity, had died in the hands of Hezbollah terrorists. Bill Buckley had been held for 444 days and died at the age of 57. During that time, he was taken secretly by car to Syria and then flown from Damascus to Tehran for interrogation and torture by Iran's Islamist government. After returning to imprisonment in Beirut, he died on June 3, 1985, a week before the TWA flight was hijacked.

Imad Fayez Mugniyah is a senior operator of Hezbollah and is responsible for the deaths of Bill Buckley and Robby Stethem, and the kidnappings of Americans in Beirut including Associated Press reporter Terry Anderson. Mugniyah, 43, is an ally of Osama bin Laden and al Qaeda and helped plan the bombing of the U.S. Marine barracks in Beirut that killed 241 American servicemen in 1983, the largest number of U.S. military deaths since the Vietnam War.

Mugniyah and the Iranian security services planned and carried out the 1996 Khobar Towers attack in Dahran, Saudi Arabia, that killed nineteen American soldiers, as well as the bombings of the U.S. embassies in East Africa in 1998. Still unpunished by the United States after two decades of terrorism, he currently resides in Iran, where he is protected by its government. From the safety of Iran, Mugniyah presently directs terrorist enterprises in Iraq.

In 1982, Hezbollah was formed in the Bekaa Valley of Lebanon by Shiite Muslims like Mugniyah with the financial support of the Iranian government, and the training efforts of the Islamic Revolutionary Guard. Iran has since supplied as much as $100 million a year to Hezbollah. Hezbollah gave Iran a further foothold in Middle East politics by its use of terror against the Israeli army and the U.S. peacekeeping forces then in Lebanon. Truck bombings of the U.S. Marine barracks, the U.S. embassy and its annex, and the violent kidnappings and murders of British, French, and American citizens forced the withdrawal of Western forces during the civil war between Christian and Muslim factions ("The first Arab victory in the history of the Arab–Israeli conflict," a spokesman for Hezbollah said at the time). The last of the Western hostages were not released until 1992.

Syria and Iran both continue to use Hezbollah as their agent in efforts to hurt Israel and the West, although Hezbollah has its own leadership and increasingly acts independently. Sheik Hassan Naserallah, Hezbollah's charismatic leader, recently told a cheering throng of 150,000 in Beirut that the United States will suffer greatly for its current presence in Iraq. " 'Death to America!' was, is, and will stay our slogan," he said. Hezbollah is very popular and has at least 50,000 members and millions of supporters of varying enthusiasm in the Muslim world. It currently holds nine seats in the Lebanese parliament and controls three others.

Hezbollah is now at work on four continents. The Kuwaiti daily newspaper *Al-Seyassah* recently reported that Syria and Iran are closely cooperating in developing a missile earmarked for delivery to Hezbollah. Iranian diplomats were present at a Syrian airfield in north Damascus in August 2004 when a "significant number" of surface-to-surface missiles were given to Hezbollah by Islamic Revolutionary Guard (IRG) members who had flown them in from Iran. In addition, 220 missiles were delivered by truck to three Hezbollah military facilities in Lebanon near the Syrian border.

To Hezbollah, Israel is the "Little Satan" and the United States is the "Great Satan." America and the American people are targeted, and Hezbollah now has cells in more than two dozen U.S. cities. The threat against our vulnerable society is very real. Barbara Newman and Tom Diaz know exactly what they are writing about. They have performed an important service by offering us a significant warning about the nature and operational capacity of the enemy we now face.

Richard W. Carlson

LIGHTNING
OUT OF
LEBANON

"YOU'VE GOT TO BE TAUGHT . . ."

You've got to be taught . . .
Before you are six or seven or eight.
        —Rodgers and Hammerstein
        lyrics from South Pacific

Mohammed Ghandour is a child of Lebanon, born into the desperately poor slums of south Beirut. Packed with Palestinian refugees and Shiite Muslim migrants from the south, the area is called the "Belt of Misery." But when Mohammed was four years old, his bedtime routine was like that of millions of kids in the comfortably affluent suburbs of the United States. Mohammed took out the same video every evening. And after he put the cassette into the video player, he called his baby sister to join him. The two children sat side by side before the television every evening and watched a story that soon enough was not only familiar, but thoroughly ingrained in their young minds.

What parent's heart wouldn't be touched by this image of tender childhood? Who would not want to reach into this charming picture, tousle the moppets' hair, and pull them close for a kiss? But Mohammed and his sister weren't watching visual lollipops served up by the likes of Barney, the Teletubbies, or Baby Einstein. They weren't learning the joys of playground toysharing, the mysteries of counting, or the thrills of reading. In the flickering blue light of the tiny television in a small room deep in the winding alleys of a fetid slum, Mohammed and his baby sister watched a suicide bombing, a real suicide bombing—a five-minute film of Mohammed's father, Salah Ghandour, ramming a car stuffed with 990 pounds of explosives into an Israeli convoy in south Lebanon.

"There's my daddy," Mohammed proudly exclaimed to a visitor at the climactic moment when the image of the crudely produced film flashed into the rolling orange and black ball of a terrible explosion. That massive blast ripped Mohammed's father to shreds and killed a dozen Israeli soldiers.[1]

"There's my daddy." What seems horrible to Western sensibilities is not only glorified as the holiest of acts within radical Islam, but is taught to children with the same facility and intensity that MTV teaches American kids the latest music and language trends. In a thousand ways every day children like young Mohammed are taught that the suicide bomber not only offers self-sacrifice in the service of an excruciatingly grim God, but has an express ticket to the highest rewards of Heaven. Public processions at the funerals of Islamic terrorists and the demonstration marches of radical Islamic groups feature children carrying AK-47 rifles and wearing belts of fake explosives—belts just like those worn by real suicide bombers not much older than they. Nothing more sharply defines the vast chasm between Islamic extremism and the West, their different views of the value of life itself, than these poignant images of children playing at martyrdom.

Salah Ghandour's self-immolation was an act of terrorism committed—and recorded in progress for a sophisticated program of media and propaganda use—by an organization that terrorism experts call the "A-Team" of international terrorism: Hezbollah, the "Party of God." Founded in 1982 with the help of Ayatollah Khomeini's Islamic Revolutionary Guard (IRG), headquartered in Lebanon, closely allied with and supported by Iran, Hezbollah held the record for terrorist murders of Americans before al Qaeda seized that grisly distinction with the catastrophic events of September 11, 2001. Hezbollah, constituted as a political party in Lebanon, is known to have warm links with al Qaeda. According to the *Final Report of the National Commission on Terrorist Attacks Upon the United States* ("9/11 Commission Report") issued in July 2004, "Al Qaeda members received advice and training from Hezbollah." This statement confirms information documented elsewhere in this book. The 9/11 Commission Report also describes the contacts of senior Hezbollah members with the hijackers who attacked the United States on September 11, 2001, and advises that "this topic requires further investigation by the U.S. government."

Hezbollah still holds the record for terrorist killings of U.S. military personnel—the murder of 241 U.S. marines, sailors, and soldiers when a 12,000-pound Hezbollah truck bomb leveled their barracks in Beirut on October 23, 1983. It is operating in Iraq.

Just as Henry Ford did not invent the automobile but made it a mass-produced fact of modern life, so Hezbollah did not invent the suicide car bomb. But Hezbollah ruthlessly elevated this horrifically indiscriminate device into the first choice of weapons in the sinister toolbox of Middle Eastern terrorism. Large-scale suicide bombing, often coordinated in multiple attacks, is a Hezbollah trademark. Some counterterrorism experts believe that a man named Imad Mugniyah—Hezbollah's operations chief, wanted by the United States—taught this concept of rolling destruction to Osama bin Laden in 1994, seven years before the al Qaeda attacks of September 11, 2001. Sanctioned suicide pioneered by Hezbollah has made mass murder by explosive numbingly routine, not only in the Middle East, but around the world.

Hezbollah is neither a remote curio of Lebanon nor an organization whose activity is limited to the Middle East. The Party of God has intertwined itself like a noxious vine around the vast Lebanese diaspora, a worldwide expatriate community of traders and merchants. Silently, deliberately, and all but invisibly, its cohorts have infiltrated the United States and its neighbors, Canada and Latin America. Hezbollah is here, now. Hezbollah cadres are known to have been planted in at least fourteen cities in the United States, places as unlikely as Houston, Texas; Louisville, Kentucky; and Charlotte, North Carolina. Its American cells are led by dedicated, coldly calculating men who grew up on the same stark diet of fanatical hatred of the West that is fed daily to millions of children like young Mohammed Ghandour. Carefully—but sometimes audaciously, a measure of their contempt for U.S. law enforcement authorities—Hezbollah's operatives have woven themselves into the American tapestry.

These hidden agents of hatred have taken advantage of America's cultural openness and exploited our civil liberties to raise funds and acquire military equipment illegally shipped abroad to support Hezbollah's war of terror against the West. They have engaged in military training and raised millions of illicit dollars through a ruthless catalog of criminal enterprises, including large-scale cigarette smuggling and tax evasion schemes, credit card fraud, drug running, gun trafficking, Internet pornography, and an array of other criminal schemes. Lying effortlessly and continuously, they have cynically duped ordinary Americans into unknowingly aiding their terror operations, often by appealing to simple greed and a willingness to dismiss low-level criminal acts as "not really that bad."

Most ominously, Hezbollah's minions lurk in sleeper cells, willing, able, and waiting only for the command of their masters in Beirut and Tehran to commit acts of violent terror on American soil. No one who understands Hezbollah's history doubts for a second its ability to inflict horrible damage should it choose to do so. According to FBI officials, serious credence was given to fears of a Hezbollah plot to assassinate President Clinton's National Security Adviser, Anthony (Tony) Lake. In 1995 there was enough concern to have Lake move out of his home into the more secure quarters of Blair House, the nation's official guest residence opposite the White House.

The threat is not theoretical. Hezbollah's dark talents have been gruesomely demonstrated in the Western Hemisphere by sophisticated bombing attacks in Argentina. Hezbollah sleeper cells—constituted much like those in the United States—are known to exist in an area of South America known as the Tri-Border region of Brazil, Argentina, and Paraguay. These cells cooperated with the Iranian secret service to carry out two horrific signature bombings in Argentina. On March 17, 1992, the Israeli embassy in Buenos Aires was struck by a suicide bomber, killing 29. And on July 18, 1994, another powerful bomb destroyed the main building of the Asociación Mutualista Israelita Argentina (AMIA) on a busy street in downtown Buenos Aires. That bomb killed 86 and wounded 300, the greatest loss of Jewish life in a terrorist incident outside Israel since the Second World War. A senior staff member of a committee of the U.S. Congress regards the Argentine bombings as, in part, a not-so-subtle Hezbollah signal to the United States. "The message is," he said, "we did it there. We can do it here."

Just as distant thunder warns of the fury of a coming storm, the presence of these Hezbollah cells in America warns of a frightening potential from a body of killers said by one American intelligence expert to make Osama bin Laden's al Qaeda "look like a bunch of kindergartners." Fortunately, a small band of extremely talented men and women from the ranks of local and federal law enforcement, together with a team of equally talented prosecutors, have dedicated much of their lives to rooting out Hezbollah's weeds in America. The almost serendipitous coming together of a handful of these able men and women exposed and successfully prosecuted one major Hezbollah cell in the most unlikely of places—Charlotte, North Carolina. They continue working to unravel a tangle of other cells rooted deeply in other unsuspecting American communities.

This is the story of Hezbollah's invasion of America, and of the thin line of defense upon which American lives depend. It describes in microcosm virtually all of the issues raised by and investigated by the 9/11 Commission—with one major difference. These extraordinary men and women overcame the obstacles that blinded America to the coming attack by al Qaeda, and succeeded in exposing Hezbollah's operations. But one part of this story cannot be told, because it remains unknown—and that is whether even more hidden layers of Hezbollah's dark enterprise lie undetected, coiled to strike in America.

The Bourj al-Barajneh neighborhood lies about ten miles to the southeast of downtown Beirut, not far from the headquarters of Hezbollah. What strikes many visitors first is the pervasive stench from the vast heap of an open garbage dump, swarming with dark clouds of flies, at the entrance of an eponymous refugee camp for Palestinians. The Bourj al-Barajneh refugee camp, established after the creation of Israel and the partition of Palestine in 1947–48, blends into the surrounding Lebanese neighborhoods. Its borders are indistinguishable to the visitor, although Palestinians and Lebanese know precisely where the boundaries lie. In any case, the camp and the surrounding neighborhoods are grindingly poor warrens, labyrinths of narrow paths barely deserving to be called alleys, rank with open sewers and the acrid smell of stale urine, littered with garbage, spiderwebbed with makeshift electrical connections, drunken with bootleg utility piping, and above all, dark with despair. The encamped Palestinians have been virtually ignored by Arab governments for more than fifty years, with the exception of the occasional trotting out of refugee misery for purposes of international incitement. Their children are regularly rallied to dance and cheer upon news of the latest suicide bombing in Israel.

The other residents of Bourj al-Barajneh, packed cheek by jowl with the Palestinians, are poor Shiite Muslims, émigrés from Lebanon's rural south. The Shiites are a minority Muslim denomination that broke off from the majority Sunni faithful in the seventh century, persecuted ever since as a heretical sect. Shiites, however, are the majority in Iran. They are also strongly represented in Iraq, where they were viciously suppressed by its erstwhile dictator, Saddam Hussein, and remain ungratefully and violently rebellious in the wake of the American invasion of Iraq in 2003. In Lebanon, most Shiites were farmers, living for centuries in numbing medieval rural servitude in the south. Desperately poor, badly organized, and long-suffering under the dominant Sunnis—Islam's majority wing—the Shiites in Lebanon were traditionally friendly with Israel, Lebanon's southern neighbor. During the 1970s some Shiites even fought alongside Israeli soldiers against the Palestinian Liberation Organization (PLO) as members of the Israeli-backed South Lebanon Army (SLA).

The Shiites began immigrating to the city's suburbs in the 1970s, under pressure from the successive invasions of Yasser Arafat's PLO—expelled from Jordan in 1970—and an Israeli army determined in 1982 to eradicate the PLO after suffering a decade of cross-border terrorist raids and rocket attacks mounted by the PLO from Lebanon. The Israelis' heavy-handed treatment of the Shiites played into the agenda of Israel's radical Islamic foes. The occupation of the south soon destroyed the earlier amicable relations and turned Lebanon's Shiites into implacable enemies. Israeli officers and soldiers who once motored leisurely home through south Lebanon on weekend passes found themselves the targets of Shiite ambushes and suicide attacks, like that committed by Salah Ghandour and enshrined by his son.

Like many such centers of rural-to-urban emigration in less developed parts of the world, Bourj al-Barajneh became a hellhole of futility, its residents trapped in endless poverty, the victims of and participants in rolling waves of violence over the beginnings and ends of which they had no control. The chronic cancer of despair thrived. The male children born into these hopeless streets quickly became willing grist for the mills of an array of armed militias that succeeded one another in archaeological layers of violence. The violent process culminated with the Hezbollah terror machine controlling the area.

Mohammed Youssef Hammoud came kicking and screaming into the pitiless world of Bourj al-Barajneh on September 25, 1973. The Hammoud family was devoutly religious, one to whom Shiite clerics and saints, and some lay leaders, were figures of reverent authority. The hand of centuries of Islam and Shiite doctrinal history touched the infant Mohammed at his birth. Like many such families, the Hammoud family grew large beyond the means of its poverty. Mohammed Hammoud was one of five brothers and seven sisters. In addition to the ties of his immediate family, young Mohammed was born into the intense bonds of a network of clan and extended family. The physical and social closeness of Bourj al-Barajneh creates a world in which one's business is at once both no one's and everyone's. Cousins and close friends would turn up time and again in Mohammed's life, far from Lebanon.

The tumult of the larger Middle East conflict marked every milestone in Mohammed's young life. On October 6, 1973, scarcely two weeks after his birth, Syria and Egypt struck Israel in a surprise attack on Yom Kippur, the holiest day of the Jewish religious calendar. Only emergency aid from the United States saved Israel from a military setback that could have threatened the Jewish state's existence. Discussion of the war, its impact, and America's role burned hotly through Bourj al-Barajneh, as it did everywhere on the "Arab street." In the United States, however, ordinary

Americans were more focused on relief over the end of the Vietnam War—the Paris Peace Accords had been signed only in January—and frustration over the impact of an oil embargo that the Organization of Petroleum Exporting Countries (OPEC) imposed on the West in retaliation for aid to Israel. The Arab embargo set off a recession, and the price of gasoline soared in America from 30 cents a gallon to about $1.20 in the worst days. Those events generated a brief flurry of crudely stereotypical ethnic attacks on the Arabs. But the subtleties of the longer term implications of the Arab-Israeli struggle simply failed to interest most Americans.

For the residents of Bourj al-Barajneh, the Arab-Israeli struggle was no subtlety but a reality that pressed every day like a razor's edge against their throats. Battered and dispossessed by war, bitter and angry due to their lack of power, young Shiites like Hammoud grew up fueled by stories of alleged Israeli atrocities and nurtured on a psychology that preaches retribution as the only path to regaining dignity. They grew up hating the United States as much as Israel. To them, there is no difference between the two. The Great Satan of the United States is the world superpower that supports the Little Satan of Israel, and Israel is the Middle Eastern regional superpower responsible for their endless misery.

A steady succession of violence accompanied the passages of young Mohammed Hammoud's life. At his birth the swaggeringly armed minions of the PLO—who virtually overran the country after being expelled from Jordan in 1970—exercised de facto control over much of Lebanon and certainly over Bourj al-Barajneh. The arrogance of the PLO's de facto government led inexorably to a clash with the armed militias of the Christian Maronites of Lebanon in 1975. That clash set off an exceedingly violent fifteen-year-long civil war, which metastasized into intra-Muslim fighting as well. Neighboring Syria promptly seized on the war as an excuse to send armed troops into Lebanon, further complicating the increasingly unstable situation.

In Hammoud's neighborhood, armed PLO militia were eventually succeeded in the 1980s by the armed militia of Amal ("Hope"), an Arab group with a more secular orientation than Hezbollah. Amal in turn was gradually succeeded by Hezbollah, the more sectarian group.* In the intervening process, a three-year "war of the camps" erupted in 1985, when Amal sought by violence to break the hold of the PLO over refugee camps, including that at Bourj al-Barajneh. Residents suffered terribly.

In short, violence and its effects were neither remote nor academic to Mohammed Hammoud, his family, and his young friends, some of whom chose the short path to eternal glory of the suicide bomber. Like many other families, the Hammouds kept a Kalashnikov automatic rifle at hand—the famed AK-47, the most widely distributed rifle in history. Israeli bombs, rockets, and shells fell nearby during the 1982 invasion and assault on Beirut, when Mohammed was a student at the al-Sadiq elementary school, named after a revered Shiite holy figure, Imam Jafar ibn Mohammed al-Sadiq, the sixth Imam. According to Mohammed, he was knocked unconscious when an Israeli rocket fell on a party of children celebrating the last day of school in 1982. He says that he awoke in the hospital to learn that the rocket had killed a young friend.

A similar maelstrom of violence erupted during the sieges mounted by Amal against the camps beginning in 1985. Mindless street violence also sometimes erupted between heavily armed men with no discernible purpose other than the ancient one of bloodily asserting petit tribal power over one another. As a teenager, for example, Mohammed witnessed an Amal militiaman pump half a dozen rounds from an AK-47 rifle into the chest of a man with whom he was arguing on the street. No apparent consequence followed the murder.

In spite of its apparent chaos, however, a pattern was emerging in Mohammed Hammoud's neighborhood, just as iron filings on paper are drawn into a pattern when a magnet is held underneath. In this case, the invisible magnet was a once-obscure Shiite cleric named Ayatollah Ruhollah Khomeini. In 1979 Khomeini led an Islamic revolution that overthrew the Shah of Iran and put into power an intensely narrow-minded clique of Shiite clergymen. On November 4 of that year, Iranian radicals seized the U.S. embassy

---

* This history and the rise of Hezbollah is discussed in detail in Chapter Two.

in Tehran and took 66 American diplomats hostage. Thirteen hostages were soon released, but the remaining 53 were held until their release on January 20, 1981.

The shock waves of Khomeini's revolution and ascendant Shia power, combined with the humiliation of an apparently helpless United States, rippled powerfully through the Muslim world, nowhere more so than in battered Lebanon. The intensely religious men of Hezbollah, a new militia formed with the help of Khomeini's Revolutionary Guard in 1982—when Mohammed was nine years old—began to win converts from the more secular Amal. It appeared that radical Islamic faith was winning more battles than the leftist and vaguely pan-Arabic political doctrine affected by the elite who controlled Amal. No small part of Hezbollah's mystique was its demonstrable and violent humiliation of the United States, the "Great Satan" of Khomeini's virulent anti-Western rhetoric: On April 18, 1983, seventeen Americans— among whom were six of the CIA's top Middle East experts, including the spy agency's station chief—were killed when the U.S. embassy was devastated by a 400-pound Hezbollah suicide truck-bomb attack. Scarcely six months later, on October 23, 1983, Hezbollah mounted simultaneous suicide truck-bomb attacks on American and French military compounds. A 12,000-pound bomb destroyed the U.S. Marine Corps barracks, killing 241. Soon thereafter, President Ronald Reagan withdrew American forces from Beirut. The Great Satan's enemies exulted. Few Americans—in or out of government—grasped then the enormous significance of the American superpower's withdrawal under pressure from an obscure band of terrorists. Hezbollah's stock soared in the radical Muslim world.

These and other Hezbollah affronts—the kidnap murders of the CIA station chief and a U.S. Marine colonel on UN peace-keeping duty—to American and Israeli power were trumpeted in the mid-1980s by a charismatic cleric whose star was rising in Beirut, Sheik Sayyid Mohammed Hussein Fadlallah. The humbling of America, combined with Fadlallah's incendiary ranting, drew many young men from Bourj al-Barajneh to the nearby Hezbollah Center. By the time he was a mature-looking sixteen-year-old, Mohammed Hammoud had been photographed at the center, brandishing an AK-47, looking determined to use it.

Hammoud is exceptionally bright, extraordinarily personable, and deeply religious. He has the confident air of the natural leader. No wonder, then, that Mohammed Hammoud drew the attention of those in the highest ranks of the Hezbollah structure. Here was a young man with precisely the characteristics needed for the delicate, difficult, and important undercover work they had in mind. Although much remains veiled about the details of his grooming within the terror organization, before he was out of his teens he was on an intimate basis with senior military and political figures of the Party of God in Lebanon. In his early twenties he was able to place direct calls from the United States to Hassan Naserallah, secretary-general and secular head of Hezbollah. This was roughly the equivalent of placing a call to the White House—and having it taken. Fortune and those in power clearly favored young Mohammed.

Much is expected of those to whom much is given. It is clear that Hezbollah's master terrorists expected much of Mohammed Youssef Hammoud. America in the 1990s was a soft and tempting target for terrorists. Many experts thought American soil was immune to international terrorism. But one of Hezbollah's highest-ranking commanders, Sheik Abbas Harake, knew otherwise and chose to entrust young Hammoud with a special mission: Get inside the United States, exploit its vast wealth and comfortable complacency, and help create a hidden network ready to spring into action when ordered.

Thus, Hammoud, while still a teenager, began his quest to get inside the United States. He made repeated trips to the American embassy in Syria to request an entry visa. Thanks to Hezbollah's earlier violent ministrations, the American embassy in Beirut had been effectively shut down, and in any case it was not issuing any visas to Lebanese nationals. After the embassy in Damascus rejected three successive visa applications, the frustrated Hammoud took a different tack, and one that illustrates the long reach of the worldwide Hezbollah network.

In 1992 Mohammed Hammoud abruptly gave up his local attempts at obtaining a visa. He flew to the improbable destination of the tropical Caribbean island of Margarita, 25 miles off the coast of Venezuela. Hammoud's choice of Isla Margarita was no accident. The island's miles of stunningly white palm-lined beaches, like Playa el Agua and Playa Parguito, and its mountainous back-drop, make it a popular resort for Venezuelans and the cruise ship trade. On average, the sun shines more than 320 days a year, and the temperature is always moderate. The island was briefly in American news in 1999 when a group of aging Cuban exiles were accused, and acquitted after trial, of plotting to assassinate Cuban dictator Fidel Castro with a .50 caliber sniper rifle when he attended an international conference on the island.

But Mohammed Hammoud did not fly to Margarita Island to enjoy its lush contrast with the stinking slum of Bourj al-Barajneh. Western intelligence officials know Isla Margarita as one of several strongholds of the Hezbollah infrastructure in Latin America. For example, Hezbollah operatives fleeing scrutiny in the Tri-Border region after the Argentine bombings passed through Margarita Island, where via the Hezbollah network they obtained visas to enter a variety of countries. Hammoud spent some 40 days on the island in the home of an uncle, where he linked up with two cousins, Mohammed Atef Darwiche and Ali Hussein Darwiche. Hammoud and the Darwiches also acquired fraudulent visas to enter the United States.

The business of acquiring false visas, an American intelligence expert explains, is an example of how terrorists often take advantage of the venality of petty crime. Rather than create their own facility for making false visas, the local support cells of terrorist organizations simply search out the local criminal traffic in such forgeries. Those who supply the visas neither know nor very often care that they are supplying the essentials of international travel to terrorists. Such, not incidentally, was the case with some in the United States who unwittingly supplied documents to September 11, 2001, conspirators. Thus, a successful terrorist plot can be woven of many threads, some of which appear in isolation to be innocent, or at worst, merely "petty crime." Mohammed Hammoud has offered several different versions of how much the fake visas cost—ranging from "I don't know" and $200 to as much as $1,500. It didn't really matter, because the visas did not have to be very good.

Hammoud and his cousins flew to New York on different flights landing within minutes of each other. Curiously, Mohammed Hammoud claims that they ended up on separate flights by accident. He even offered—under oath—the wild implausibility that he had inadvertently wandered onto the plane on which he arrived, not even sure of its destination. In any case, the three young men knew that they had virtually nothing to fear from the American immigration authorities. Terror groups like Hezbollah have long studied the details of American immigration and internal security, hunting for and easily finding its many weak points. In fact, several of Hammoud's family members had already tested and breached the system, preceding him to America. They found that getting through America's border controls and disappearing into its massive landscape was far easier than gaining entry into Iran, Syria, or Lebanon and disappearing—at least, that is, disappearing alive.

Each young man had a fake nonimmigrant visa, ostensibly permitting the holder into the United States as a tourist. None of the three expected their forgeries to hold up under even the casual gaze of the overwhelmed Border Patrol agents at Kennedy International Airport. That was part of the plan. Torn between trying to keep the lines moving and weeding out improperly documented aliens seeking to slip into the country, the agents were at best an irritant to sophisticated terrorist groups like Hezbollah. Once the fraud was detected, as it surely would be, it was simple enough to recite a well-rehearsed claim to be seeking political asylum.

So Mohammed Hammoud was only mildly flustered when the agent asked him to step into a small interview room. He expected it. He knew precisely what was coming and exactly what to say. His most pressing problem was resisting the impulse to laugh out loud.

He was, he claimed, caught in a life-and-death struggle between two terrorist organizations, neither of which he wished to have any part of. On the one hand, he said, Hezbollah was terrifying not only its enemies, but also all of the eligible youth in the poor slums from which he was only seeking to escape. On the other hand, there was the South Lebanon Army, sponsored by the Israelis. Months before, Hammoud said he was kidnapped by that group, held for days, and closely interrogated. He had nothing to tell them and after some serious manhandling, he was dumped back onto the mean streets of south Beirut. Now Hezbollah suspected him of the worst offense possible: collaboration with the hated Israelis. Already his family had been warned and he had scrambled to find some way, any way, to escape. A relative told him American visas could be bought easily in Venezuela. His family scraped together travel funds and here he was.

The agent listened, glanced at the long lines outside, and decided America faced worse threats than a frightened teenager. Besides, it would be up to an experienced examiner to decide whether Hammoud's fears were genuine or merely a ticket to ride on the American economic engine.

Mohammed Hammoud and his cousins were admitted and directed to appear before an immigration examiner, who would hear their claim for political asylum. Within hours Mohammed Hammoud and his cousins were out on the streets of New York, free to roam in the very belly of the Great Satan.

They quickly headed for a quiet town in the heart of the American South—Charlotte, North Carolina. Some years would pass before they met a brilliant and dogged federal prosecutor named Kenneth Bell, described by the local FBI chief as "the most courageous prosecutor I've ever met."

Ken Bell was born on July 22, 1958, in Bedford, Ohio. Bedford is five and a half square miles of classic Americana. Located about twelve miles southeast of downtown Cleveland, Bedford was incorporated as a town in 1837. It was the birthplace of Archibald M. Willard, who painted the charmingly patriotic American classic, *The Spirit of '76*. It is a comfortable, affluent suburb, remarkable for its proximity to Cuyahoga Valley National Park and the rushing waterfall at Tinker's Creek, which supplied the power for a gristmill and other industry as early as 1815.

Bell was born in the middle of America in the middle of the Eisenhower years, a time of measured tranquillity in America. But exactly one week earlier there was a faint portent of things to come—the U.S. Marines had landed in Lebanon. The Cold War defined America's view of the world. The boorishly belligerent Nikita Khrushchev had just become premier of the Soviet Union.

In 1957 President Eisenhower had persuaded Congress to pass a joint resolution endorsing the "Eisenhower Doctrine," which approved the use of U.S. force to "defend the territorial integrity and the political independence" of any Middle Eastern nation threatened by "communist armed aggression." Lebanon signed on to the doctrine.

Then as now, Lebanon rests on an uneasy division of political power among major confessional groups, including a large Arab-Christian population, unique in the Arab world. President Camille Chamoun, a Christian, packed the country's parliament with Christians in a by-election, part of a scheme to remain in power by amending a constitutional bar to his succeeding himself. Syria and Egypt had just joined in the short-lived United Arab Republic (UAR). Egged on by UAR President Gamal Abdel Nasser's call to pan-Arabism, Lebanon's armed Muslim opposition ignited a civil war. With the Lebanese army paralyzed on the sidelines, the conflict was essentially one between Christian and Muslim militias.

Chamoun appealed to the United States for help. Unsettled by troubling events elsewhere in the Middle East, Eisenhower invoked his new doctrine and sent the marines into Lebanon. They landed peacefully on Khalde Beach, four miles from Beirut and about 700 yards from Beirut International Airport, at 3:04 in the afternoon of July 15, 1958. The marines were greeted not by armed resistance, but by bathing beauties in bikinis, a road construction crew who immediately dropped their tools to gawk, excited villagers who quickly galloped up on horseback to watch the show, and soft-drink vendors who quickly grasped the commercial possibilities offered by a horde of thirsty marines.

The marine landing and a show of naval force stiffened the Lebanese army into restoring order. The soft-drink vendors did a booming business with the marines—one of whom remarked, "It's better than Korea, but what the hell is it?"—and the immediate crisis soon evaporated. United States forces were never engaged. But there were between 2,000 and 4,000 Lebanese casualties, mostly in the Muslim areas of Beirut and in Tripoli. In the end, General Fuad Shihab, then commander in chief of the Lebanese army, was chosen by the parliament to serve as president.

In spite of this brief Lebanese sideshow, Americans in 1958 were for the most part inwardly oriented, intent on enjoying the fruits of the country's material progress. The American consumer culture was hitting its stride, reinforced by the growing mass media culture exemplified by the movie *The Man in the Gray Flannel Suit*. The export of both cultural trends would soon impact the rest of the world, igniting dismay and reactionary anger among the sectarian hard core of more conservative cultures, nowhere more than among the Shiite Muslims of the Middle East.

Ken's father, Richard Bell, was a lawyer in general practice with his own father's law firm. In 1965 Richard Bell left Ohio and joined the faculty of the School of Law at Wake Forest University in Winston-Salem, North Carolina. Thus transplanted at the age of seven, Ken Bell today regards himself as thoroughly a North Carolinian. He calls Winston-Salem his hometown.

The town lies tranquilly in the piedmont, toward the center of the state. Quintessentially Southern, it is in every dimension of life as remote from the squalid tensions of Bourj al-Barajneh as the deepest part of Death Valley is from the far side of the moon. The smoky chain of the Blue Ridge Mountains rises about an hour's drive to the west of the town. Charlotte is no more than a few hours to the southwest, the Virginia state line a bit less to the north. Winston-Salem lies squarely within the famed Bible Belt, a region traditionally conservative in its social and political life, for decades the staunch voting base of a string of influential Republican senators like the irascibly powerful Jesse Helms.

Wake Forest University is the crown jewel of Winston-Salem. Founded by Baptists in 1834, Wake Forest had the overtly sectarian mission of turning out Baptist preachers and men of equivalent probity. The college moved from the small eastern North Carolina hamlet of Wake Forest to Winston-Salem in 1956, and became a university in 1967. Its motto is "Pro Humanitate"—for the good of humanity.

Like much of the South, Wake Forest University has in recent decades moved away from its conservative roots toward an accommodation to liberal humanism, a development that a few remaining old-line faculty members suspiciously decry as mere pandering to fashionable trends. The university prides itself as one of the nation's most technologically advanced campuses—

every incoming freshman is given an IBM Think Pad, and can plug into the university's Net and the universe beyond almost anywhere on campus.

Wake Forest severed its formal ties with the North Carolina Baptist Convention in 1986. Nevertheless, the campus recalls its original mission in the clean lines of its redbrick and white-columned Colonial architecture, and the well-ordered layout of its campus. The tall, cleanly sharp spire of Wait Chapel rises high into the sky at the northwestern end of a spacious quadrangle (the Quad) that is the heart of the university grounds. Each side of the length of the grassy quadrangle is lined with a double row of leafy hardwood trees, cooling in summer and magnificent in autumn. The Quad is flanked by residence halls and anchored by the solid eminence of Reynolda Hall. An orderly array of other buildings and facilities fan out around the Quad.

Wait Chapel was the site of the university's first homosexual wedding in 2000. The university's decision to permit use of the chapel for the uniting of two lesbians must have had its founders spinning in their graves, and caused not a few Southern Baptists severe heartburn. In the same year, Wait Chapel was the site of a presidential campaign debate between George W. Bush and Al Gore.

Winston-Salem is North Carolina's fourth-largest city. Its sky-line is dominated by the half dozen or so obligatory junior sky-scrapers that mark progress in many such Southern towns. Built on the North Carolina staple of tobacco, Winston-Salem today es-chews its roots and tobacco and emphasizes its value as a center for high-tech companies and advanced medical facilities. If one wished to cast a typically small-town–America movie set, com-plete with local college, Winston-Salem and Wake Forest Univer-sity would serve well.

When the Bell family arrived in 1965, however, both the town and the college were closer to their traditional roots. Ken, his brother, and his sister grew up on the idyllic grounds of the Wake Forest campus.

"Winston-Salem was a great place to grow up," Ken Bell re-calls. "And Wake Forest University was one big playground for us faculty brats. It was safe, comfortable, and familiar."

Bell is tall—six feet, two inches—and speaks with a quiet diffidence that belies his proven skill as a dogged prosecutor and consummate trial lawyer. His gaze never leaves the eyes of the person with whom he is speaking. He has a marked tendency to understatement, especially when talking about himself.

"I could just hop on my bike and ride over to the gym anytime," he says. "We practically lived in the gym."

Ken Bell's life followed an unerringly all-American hometown-boy path. He attended Spea Elementary School and Mount Tabor and R. J. Reynolds high schools. He was a member of the state high school championship tennis team. After high school, he elected to stay in Winston-Salem and went to Wake Forest University for both his undergraduate schooling and his law degree. In 1983—the same year Hezbollah bombed the United States embassy and the marine barracks in Beirut—Ken Bell graduated from Wake Forest School of Law.

A calling came to Ken Bell during law school. Ken's father taught commercial law, the sturdy details that regulate business contracts and dealings between principals and their agents. It is the staple of Middle-American law practice. But Ken Bell turned away from that well-trodden path. Although he had never before shown much interest in public speaking or intramural debate, there was something about trial practice, the contest between two opponents in the courtroom, that captivated him during his law study. Ken Bell emphatically decided that he wanted to get into the courtroom and try cases before juries.

"I don't know what it was," he recalls, "but something in law school got into my blood. I decided I wanted to do jury trials."

Whatever that indefinable something was, it led Bell to apply for a job with several United States attorneys, the presidentially appointed chief litigators in the nation's federal judicial districts. It was, he recalls, an act of naïveté: the 93 U.S. attorneys rarely hire young lawyers straight out of law school, preferring candidates with a bit of seasoning and a proven track record. But Ken Bell—and many who know him would say America—got lucky. The local U.S. attorney, responsible for the Western District of North Carolina, happened also to be an alumnus of Wake Forest School of Law. He took a chance, hired Bell straight out of law school, and assigned him to work in the district's Asheville office.

One month later, 25-year-old Ken Bell tried his first case on behalf of the United States of America. A more senior assistant U.S. attorney was dispatched to the trial to watch young Bell's prosecution of a counterfeiter. Bell won his first conviction handily. The senior observer reported back to the boss with the laconic observation "He'll be all right."

Ken Bell did a little more than "all right" over the next two decades. He lost only three out of scores of jury trials. Two of the losses he chalks up resignedly to the fact that virtually all of the witnesses, including the victims, were drunk at the time of the offenses on a Cherokee Indian reservation subject to federal criminal jurisdiction.

"It was hard for anyone to tell at the end of those trials who was in the wrong," he says.

The third trial involved the prosecution of a young man who was employed by a local drug dealer. The case promised to be a slam dunk for Bell: The prosecution's witnesses included not only two federal agents but the defendant's drug-dealing boss. The defense offered only a character witness—the defendant's grandmother.

When that grandmother took the stand, she looked straight at the jury and pronounced unflinchingly, "I need him at home."

It was enough for that homespun jury. Exercising what jurists call "jury nullification," they set aside the obvious facts and law and sent the young man home, free to help his grandmother.

That case, however, was a fluke. Word soon got out among defendants and prosecutors alike that Ken Bell was the new hot hand with the cool demeanor. By the time he was 27, Bell was the lead attorney on drug prosecutions in the Western District, working closely with the government's Organized Crime and Drug Enforcement Task Force.

Life was not all about putting criminals behind bars. Two months after he started as an assistant U.S. attorney in Asheville, Bell happened to be visiting friends in Winston-Salem. While there he met a young woman in a restaurant. She also just happened to be in town visiting friends. Her name was Gayle, and she was an English teacher in the small town of Tryon, North Carolina, about 30 minutes southeast of Asheville. It was close enough for the two to date. Romance blossomed, and three years later, on June 21, 1986, Gayle and Ken married.

In 1988 Bell left the federal prosecutor's office. He joined a law firm in Winston-Salem and two years later ran for Congress. He won a hotly contested Republican primary but lost the general election. The day after the 1990 election, the U.S. attorney called Ken Bell and invited him back to his old job. Bell returned and picked up his career where he had left off, except that the office had by now moved to Charlotte.

Bell resumed his focus on organized crime and drug trafficking, top-of-the-list concerns of the nation at large. Few in the United States, and even fewer in Charlotte, gave more than passing notice on March 17, 1992, when a Hezbollah car bomb leveled the Israeli embassy in Buenos Aires. The suicide attack destroyed the embassy, a Catholic church, and a nearby school. Although several Israelis died, most of the victims were Argentine civilians, many of them children. Later the same year, on June 6, 1992, Mohammed Hammoud and his cousin slipped anonymously into Charlotte. And on November 3, William Jefferson Clinton was elected president of the United States.

As is the usual practice, Clinton appointed his own cadre of United States attorneys. It is a measure both of the nonpartisan atmosphere of the Charlotte office and of Ken Bell's competence that in 1993 Clinton's new U.S. attorney promoted Bell—erstwhile Republican congressional candidate—to the rank of first assistant U.S. attorney for the Charlotte office. At 34 he was the youngest first assistant in the country. His career on a solid track, Ken Bell concentrated on raising his two sons and hitting home runs in the steady stream of cases that passed through the office. As first assistant U.S. attorney, Bell had his eye on all the cases. He could pick the ones he felt were so important that he should personally handle them.

The caseload that crossed Ken Bell's desk reflected the underside of Middle America—heavy on drug prosecutions, organized-crime cases, the occasional bank robbery, and public corruption investigation. Among them was what seemed to be a more or less routine investigation by local authorities and the federal Bureau of Alcohol, Tobacco and Firearms (ATF) of a garden-variety cigarette smuggling ring. The smugglers were running truckloads of contraband cigarettes from North Carolina to Michigan. The differential between North Carolina's tax-free sales and Michigan's high cigarette taxes yielded thousands of dollars' profit on each truckload. It was a lucrative operation, but not one likely to appeal to a jury in tobacco-friendly North Carolina. So in 1999—after the ring had been thoroughly investigated but before any arrests had been made—Bell was on the verge of approving a transfer of the case to Michigan for prosecution. Since Michigan taxpayers were the ones holding the bag in the scheme, the Charlotte prosecutors thought it more likely that a Michigan jury would be sympathetic to the federal case.

That decision, and Ken Bell's life, changed radically when his boss, the U.S. attorney, got an urgent call from the local office of the Federal Bureau of Investigation. Two local agents—Bob Clifford and Rick Schwein—wanted to come over and give the prosecution team a highly classified briefing in a secure room.

And they needed to do it immediately.

Rick Schwein grew up among men who seemed bigger than life itself. To begin with, there was his father, Richard Schwein. Like many FBI agents of an earlier era, the elder Schwein began his career in the lesser position of tour guide and night clerk at FBI headquarters. He went to school during the day and, when he won his degree—the first in his family to do so; his father was a telephone lineman—Richard Schwein applied to become an agent. He was accepted and went on to become a legend in the Bureau, noted for a record number of cases successfully closed by arrests, his integrity, dogged investigative skills, and personal bravery.

Rick's mother was also an FBI employee, a secretary at FBI headquarters. So, when the younger Richard Schwein arrived in 1961, he was born into a thoroughly FBI family. As the law touched Ken Bell and Islam touched Mohammed Hammoud, the traditions of the FBI touched Rick Schwein at his birth in Washington, D.C. Although those traditions shaped much of Rick Schwein's character, he did not at first seek out an FBI career; in fact, he resisted it.

Bell and Hammoud are essentially hometown boys. However

radically different Bourj al-Barajneh and Winston-Salem may be, both men grew to adulthood within the familiar embrace of locale, family, and long-term friends. In contrast, Rick Schwein's formative years were spent on the wander, the result of Rick's father being assigned to a succession of different FBI field offices. Rick's extended family were the FBI agents and their families who gathered in the Schwein home for social events. His extended neighborhood was living vicariously through their stories of the mean streets and the violence in which they operated.

Rick's father was assigned to the Birmingham, Alabama, field office when Rick was six years old. America was still struggling with racial violence—"Freedom Riders" seeking civil rights for all Americans had been arrested or savagely beaten in the South in the year Rick was born. In 1967 large-scale urban riots devastated Newark and Detroit. More and worse riots followed the murder of Dr. Martin Luther King Jr. in April of 1968. The nation was also increasingly divided over the Vietnam War. Boxer Muhammad Ali refused military service, and thousands of other young men sought to avoid the draft.

"It was a pretty charged time in our country," Rick Schwein says, looking back from the perspective of adulthood. "And the FBI was right in the middle of the civil rights struggle and the Vietnam War debate."

Schwein is a man whose boyish features belie a toughness warranted by his distinguished careers as an intelligence officer in the Army Rangers and a decorated agent in the FBI. More than one perpetrator—including members of Mohammed Hammoud's Charlotte cell—has found out too late the error of mistaking Schwein's amiability for softness or lack of attention to detail.

The Schwein family spent eighteen months in Birmingham. The elder Schwein was part of a team of agents who tracked down one of the guns of James Earl Ray, Dr. King's assassin. In the midst of that terrible time of struggle, young Rick began to perceive the first of several lessons that define his life.

"I used to go talk with an elderly black woman who lived nearby," he recalls. "I began to see that there is often an inherent unfairness in life, and the FBI that I knew as a child was there to help correct some of that unfairness."

He also saw the need for physical courage. "I remember my father coming home pretty badly beaten up by a Marine Corps deserter he had tracked down."

When Rick was in the second grade, his father was transferred to Philadelphia. For the next nine years, Rick grew into his teens in the suburbs of Camden County, New Jersey, across the Delaware River from Philadelphia. Although his life had the surface normality of any other kid's—the elder Schwein coached Rick's Little League baseball team—there was no getting around the fact that everyone quickly figured out that Rick's dad was an FBI agent. As a consequence, the family home was burglarized by a couple of youthful delinquents who figured (wrongly) that an FBI agent's house would be a good place to pick up guns.

The Bureau had a more tangible and longer-lasting impact on Rick's life in these years. His father worked first on the bank robbery squad, and later became supervisor of the truck squad. The men of the bank robbery squad and their families were especially close. When they gathered for squad parties or New Year's Eve, young Rick Schwein, and occasionally his friends, would sit enchanted as the men regaled one another with true-life war stories of the FBI. Among them was the tale of a one-eyed bank-robbing fugitive named Bruce who swam the Schuylkill River in an attempt to escape the FBI. The episode prompted the coining of a humorous all-purpose phrase among the agents, who thereafter exclaimed at any tense or lighthearted moment they deemed appropriate, "One-Eyed Bruce is on the loose!"

"It was classic good versus evil," Rick Schwein recalls of those informal sagas. "And the good guys always won."

He returns to the theme of fairness often when describing those days. "Growing up around the Bureau, I had a feeling of always seeking fairness. You need to be fair with people, even the bad guys."

"There were some real characters" among those men, and they loomed as giants in the young boy's life. His father, he says, "was very gregarious, but family-wise, he was very German. That means that he was not very demonstrative around his family, and he held us to high standards. There were two things he had no tolerance for—lying and talking back." Pursuit of his father's sparsely awarded approval was another of the molding influences of Rick Schwein's life.

In 1977 Richard Schwein was vetted to a midlevel management job at FBI headquarters. Rick finished his teen years in the northern Virginia suburbs, where he was by his own description an average student who played soccer, worked as a lifeguard at Wakefield Park, a regional recreational center, and got into the ordinary range of "mischievous things." In 1979 he enrolled in Radford University, a small state school on the cusp of the Blue Ridge Mountains in southwestern Virginia, founded in 1910 as the State Normal and Industrial School for Women.

Schwein chose Radford, he says, for three reasons. The first was financial. He wanted to put himself through college, and as a Virginia state school, Radford offered lower tuition to Virginia residents than some other schools he might have chosen. The second was that the school was known to have one of the better criminal justice academic programs in the area. And the third was personal.

"There were about six women to every guy"—he smiles—"because it had been a women's college until 1972."

Located in the small town of Radford, about fifty miles north of Winston-Salem, the university campus shares some of the red-brick, broad-lawn, leafy charm of Wake Forest. The school's athletic teams call themselves the Highlanders, celebrating the heritage of Scottish immigrants who settled southwestern Virginia in the eighteenth century. The university describes these early Scots as people characterized by "firmness of decision, resourcefulness, ardor in friendship, love of country, and a generous enthusiasm," traits that are writ large in Rick Schwein's life.

Schwein's father talked him out of majoring in criminal justice on the grounds that it was too narrow a focus to be of value later in life. It wasn't a hard sell. At that point in his life, Rick had no plans to follow in his father's footsteps. "I resisted the idea of joining the FBI," he says. He enrolled as a political science major.

Fortuitously, another door was opened by the resident U.S. Army major commanding the school's Reserve Officer Training Corps (ROTC) unit. Major Bob Applehans took Schwein aside one day.

"Have you ever considered making the military a career?" he asked.

The idea was greatly enhanced for Rick, who was burning candles at both ends, when he learned that enlistment in the ROTC brought with it a scholarship. He applied for the program and won a three-year scholarship. The kicker was a four-year commitment to service in the army.

"Originally, I thought I would just take a reserve commission and go to law school," he says. "But after going to advanced camp at the end of my junior year, I just felt like I had some natural ability for the military life. I am not one of those natural athletes; I have to work at things. But I loved the leadership aspects, the demands of a team working toward a common goal, and being outdoors a lot. Someone in the army must have agreed, because I won a regular army commission."

In 1983 Schwein was named the Distinguished Military Graduate of the Radford class, and commissioned a second lieutenant in the regular army. Again following the advice of his father, he chose the intelligence branch over the infantry, and a few months later reported to the army intelligence school at Fort Huachuca, Arizona.

"I immediately contracted food poisoning." Schwein grimaces. "I met the guy who was going to be grading me from a hospital bed. He immediately appointed me class leader."

Within days, another pivotal event occurred. An army ranger-qualified officer strolled in and asked if any of the class wanted to go to ranger school. The prospect took Schwein immediately. He found himself drawn toward something more than a little scary and exceedingly awesome.

"Ranger school is the toughest physical, emotional, and intellectual challenge an officer can face," he says. "I wanted that challenge."

To be a ranger is to be a singular man among singular men. It is accepted army wisdom that the career of an infantry officer who doesn't wear the coveted black-and-gold ranger shoulder tab is distinctly disadvantaged. But getting into the U.S. Army Ranger school is hard. Successfully finishing requires reaching deep inside and finding physical and emotional strength and depth of character that only a few men—even of those who enroll—possess.

For Schwein, the challenge of getting in was complicated by

the fact that most of the slots were reserved for infantry officers. Only a few were available for the military intelligence branch. Two of his classmates at Fort Huachuca helped him prepare for the physical and military skills testing he needed to ace in order to win a slot.

Lieutenant Schwein won his slot. There were four phases to the U.S. Army Ranger school then—a city phase at Fort Benning, Georgia; a low-level mountaineering phase at Dahlonega, Georgia; a desert phase at Fort Bliss, Texas; and a jungle phase at Eglin Air Force Base, Florida. In addition to physically gutting out the demanding course to the end, candidates were required to win a passing grade as leader of at least one patrol in each and every phase.

"It was," Schwein says, "a ballbuster. It was the toughest thing I have ever done."

There was a better than 70 percent washout rate. Of 180 men who started the course, 48 graduated. A few others were "recycled"—given a second chance because their failure to complete was not judged terminal. Schwein recalls two dark moments that could have left him on the wrong end of those statistics.

"The first was early in the training, when the ranger instructors were weeding out students who weren't in shape or who weren't committed to being there." During a long run, a student in front of Schwein stumbled and fell. Schwein and several others were tripped up, and Schwein suffered a bloody knee injury. He and the others were ordered to the "worm pit," a particularly unpleasant obstacle course whose length was filled with four to six inches of water. It was February, and the water was icy. Schwein endured the worm pit, but was then ordered to have the medics look at his badly swollen knee.

"The doc wanted to drop me from the course for medical reasons," he remembers. "But after working so hard to get there, I just wasn't willing or ready to take the easy way out and take a medical drop." He convinced the doctor to let him continue.

The second dark moment came near the end, during the jungle phase. Schwein had won a passing grade on five patrols in the other three phases. But he was suddenly leading the last patrol in the final phase, and he had not yet won a passing grade.

"I was about spent physically, mentally, and emotionally, and made some mistakes on my first two graded patrols, which I failed," he says. "We were at the last graded exercise. Talk about pressure!"

Each candidate has a "ranger buddy," and Schwein's understood the situation.

"He looked at me and said, 'Don't worry, we won't let you fail.' They didn't let me fail. I passed because of the efforts of the men to my left and to my right, and from that point on it became my goal to never let my colleagues down."

Schwein's recollections of the ups and downs, the importance of help from one's colleagues, and the leadership lessons learned are echoed time and again in the memoirs of others who have won the ranger tab.

"It was one of the benchmark experiences of my life," Schwein says with a mixture of pride and thoughtful self-contemplation. "It was one of the things that helped define who I am. It goes back to the kind of people I wanted to serve with, like the men my dad worked with when I was a young kid. In a way, it's the same thing. It taught me about myself—don't quit, no matter how much adversity you face; there is always something more there, you just have to find it."

He pauses and sums up.

"The measure of a man's character is what he does with adversity and what he does when nobody is looking."

One doesn't have to listen very hard to hear the voice of Schwein's father in that summation. Graduating ranger school marked Rick Schwein's life in another singular way.

"My dad told me he was proud of me on only three occasions. One of them was when I graduated from ranger school."

Finishing ranger school marked the opening of another phase in Schwein's military career. He was assigned to the 101st Airborne Division as an intelligence officer, and took the opportunity to go to jump school. After a few years in a variety of staff and troop-leading jobs, Schwein was approached by a more senior officer with a background in special operations.

"I've got a job I think you might be interested in," he said. "But you'll have to try out for it. Task Force 160 wants an intelligence officer. I think you'd be good for the job."

Task Force 160 is one of those special units in the U.S. military that are well known in general but highly secret in detail. It was formed in the wake of the disastrously failed attempt in April 1980 to rescue American hostages held in Tehran. One of the causes of that failure was the lack of an aviation unit specifically trained and equipped for such demanding special operations. Task Force 160 was formed from among the best of the army's aviators and given the best aviation equipment to perform such a special role.

"It is a high-speed, low-drag operation," Schwein says. He was accepted for the post of intelligence officer and spent several years with the 160th. He emphasizes that he was not an "operator"—one who goes directly into harm's way as a shooter in special operations—but provided "security and intelligence support" for the section.

Although he will not talk directly about any operations he was involved in, public sources indicate that in the mid-1980s he spent a substantial amount of time in the Middle East and acquired first-hand knowledge of the many intricacies of the Arab-Muslim world. He was probably in Cyprus more than once, and was at least in a position to observe the intense efforts the United States was engaged in at the time to find and rescue Americans kidnapped and held hostage by Hezbollah in Lebanon.

Rick Schwein might have made the army a career had he not met a pretty young majorette from Florida State University in 1986. Their meeting was the result of a series of boisterous events. Schwein clearly enjoys relating them as mementos of his wilder days.

It began in Panama City, Florida, where he and another ranger-qualified army buddy had come down from Fort Campbell, Kentucky, to listen to a sales pitch for a time-share condominium. They weren't that interested, but being willing to listen to the pitch won them four days' lodging. Near the end of the four days, they observed three young ladies on the beach behind them. Announcing himself the "beach social director," Schwein invited them to share a wine cooler. One thing led to another, and the last thing then-Lieutenant Schwein remembered was sitting in a hot tub singing the old Righteous Brothers hit song "You've Lost That Loving Feeling."

None of the three young women was destined to be Mrs. Schwein, but they invited the two officers to visit them at the Chi Omega sorority house on the Florida State University campus in Tallahassee. "My roommate won't mind," one of them said. Schwein took up the offer. The roommate answered the door, and in short order she and Rick married.

Schwein knew that his future wife—who holds an MBA and is a CPA—had her own career aspirations and would have been frustrated by the life of a military officer's wife. "I made a conscious decision. I wanted to marry this woman, and the military would have been hard for her."

In addition, he wasn't sure that he would be comfortable over the long haul as an officer in the garrison army. A longtime FBI buddy of his father had taken Rick aside at the wedding. He had been in a similar position to Rick's early in life. "The Bureau," he said, "is real every day." Schwein found himself at a decision point—the army offered him command of a military intelligence company, unusual because he had not yet completed the prerequisite of advanced schooling. But he was now drawn increasingly to civilian life. Still torn, he began applying to "anything with initials," meaning the FBI, CIA, DIA, and others.

In May 1988 Lt. Rick Schwein resigned his regular commission. The next month, he entered Class 8810 of the FBI Academy at Quantico, Virginia. Four months later, he graduated. His father presented him with his credentials, handing over the senior Schwein's badge to his son. And for the second time in his life, Rick Schwein heard his father say, "I'm proud of you."

His first assignment was to the Charlotte, North Carolina, field office.

"FOR THE VIOLENCE DONE IN LEBANON . . ."

For the violence done to Lebanon will overwhelm you;
The destruction of the animals will terrify you—
Because of human bloodshed and violence to the earth,
To cities and all who live in them.
                                        —Habakkuk 2:17

Call it fate, lady luck, chance, or divine providence. Whatever it was, on the morning of October 29, 1983, it favored a handful of young American servicemen away from their barracks. Then it unleashed the furies of Hell on the rest of the men of the 24th Marine Amphibious Unit (MAU)—marines, sailors, and soldiers serving as the American contingent of a multinational peacekeeping force in war-battered Lebanon.

The core of the MAU—the 1st Battalion, 8th Marine Regiment—was stationed at the Beirut International Airport. Its perimeter outposts nestled just southwest of Bourj al-Barajneh. The marines called the festering warren "Hooterville," but within days of their landing they were sharing rations with the Shiite slum kids who came scrambling down to their outlying positions. Mohammed Hammoud was ten years old—bright-eyed, alert, and impressionable. Ken Bell was in the first months of his career as a federal prosecutor in Asheville, North Carolina. Rick Schwein was a newly commissioned second lieutenant attending the U.S. Army's intelligence officer's school at Fort Huachuca, Arizona.

A multinational force had originally been formed in August 1982 to oversee the evacuation from Beirut of the Palestine Liberation Organization (PLO), which had been crushed by an invading Israeli army. That first multinational force was withdrawn within three weeks. A few days after the American marines departed, Lebanese president-elect Bashir Gemayel was assassinated by a bomb hidden in his headquarters. In retaliation, a splinter group of furious Christian militiamen rampaged through the Sabra and Shatila refugee camps for four days, slaughtering hundreds of un-armed Palestinian refugees. No one knows for sure how many died in that abattoir. The International Red Cross stopped count-ing when it had buried more than 300 victims. An Israeli commis-sion investigating the potential responsibility of its own forces estimated that between 700 and 800 died. Palestinians claim more than 1,000 were killed. All agree that most of the victims were women, children, and the elderly. The massacre prompted the for-mation of a second multinational force, of which the American marines were a part.

French, Italian, and British units had responsibility for other areas around the city. The French had the downtown area. The Italians, between the French and the Americans, were assigned the Sabra and Shatila camps. The Italian commander was noted for his special efforts to educate his men about the substance of Lebanon's agony and the history of its sectarian violence. Italian troops were given classes in Arabic. The American marines lifted weights, staged a boxing match, and watched movies flown in from the offshore fleet. *Rambo* and *Rocky II* were favorites.

On any given day, the U.S. force had a strength of about 1,250 men—59 marine officers, 1,143 enlisted marines, three navy offi-cers, 52 navy enlisted personnel, three army officers, and 28 army enlisted men. The unit chose a four-story building that had once been the offices of the Lebanese Aviation Administration Bureau for the headquarters of its nucleus, called the Battalion Landing Team (BLT). The building had been occupied first by the PLO, then the Syrian army, and finally the Israeli army. Its chipped, charred façade and blown-out windows showed the ravages of war. But it was judged to be ideal for the needs of the American peacekeeping force, whose mission was not to fight but, by its armed presence, to help tamp down relentless fighting among two occupying for-eign armies and several dozen renegade armed militias.

The building was centrally located within the American zone

of operations. It was well built of reinforced concrete, able to survive fire from most weapons known to be used in Lebanon. Its roof offered a good place to mount a radio antennae for communication with the American fleet lying off to the west, and for observation posts to watch the commanding heights to the east. On any given day, an average of about 350 men worked and slept in the BLT building. (The headquarters of the overall MAU were in an old firefighting school, a two-story building just north of the BLT headquarters.)

The city of Beirut lay to the north, at the far end of a four-lane airport access road. But the city, its bars, and the other pleasures that it managed to continue offering in the midst of its unrelentingly violent destruction were off-limits to the American grunts. A USO band had entertained the troops at the airport the day before. Weekend passes could be had, but only to be enjoyed elsewhere in the Middle Eastern cauldron. Thus, several score of the battalion's men happened to be in Egypt that morning, savoring the waning hours of a weekend liberty. Petty Officer 1st Class Steven I. Thompson, a navy communications specialist, was home on emergency leave in Grants Pass, Oregon. He had been granted compassionate leave after receiving a classic "Dear John" letter from his wife announcing that she wanted a divorce. But most of the battalion was in Beirut that morning.

The sun rose at 5:24 A.M. to a clear day. A few men were up and about. Col. Timothy Geraghty, the unit commander, was in the MAU headquarters building, just to the north, reading morning reports. Some of his men, among them Lance Cpls. Eddie A. DiFranco and Henry P. Linkila, were at guard posts around the perimeter of the main building. Cooks were preparing breakfast. A scattering of other men were otherwise attending to the orderly and infinitely routine business of military life. Lance Cpl. Adam Webb was standing guard duty on the roof as the sun crested the mountains to the east. Most of the men, however, were enjoying the privilege of sleeping in on a Sunday that promised fine weather. Reveille was set for 6:30 A.M. Brunch was scheduled to be served at 8:00 A.M. It would likely be followed by a round of pickup sports, and in the afternoon an all-American barbecue of hamburgers and hot dogs. The temperature was already 77 degrees.

The destiny of these several hundred sleeping men now lay in the hands of Ismalal Ascari, an Iranian operative of the nascent Hezbollah organization. His hands were at that moment clutched firmly around the steering wheel of a 19-ton Mercedes-Benz stake truck, coming down out of the heights to the east. The truck was packed with pentaerythritol tetranitrate (PETN), a commercially manufactured explosive used mostly by military organizations. Cylinders of propane gas were arrayed around the PETN to enhance the fury of the explosion.

Ascari's first destination was the marine barracks. Then Paradise.

By 1983 all the strands of Middle Eastern strife had been woven into a pitiless scourge lashed across the back of Lebanon, a country about the size of Connecticut. The land lies on the eastern shore of the Mediterranean, surrounded to the north and east by Syria, and to the south by Israel. Its people are an uneasy and shifting balance of Christians and Muslims, two competing vines sprung from the same soil and bound together by fourteen centuries of history.

Lebanon is roughly 110 miles long from north to south and 30 miles wide from east to west. Site of some of the oldest civilizations in history, the country is divided into four distinct geographical and climatic zones. All the major cities—Tripoli, Beirut, Sidon, Tyre—lie along a narrow coastal plain, which has a typically Mediterranean climate of cool, rainy winters and hot, humid summers. In addition to the renowned commercial tradition of the cities, the coastal plain produces fruits and vegetables.

The plain is broken in places by stony fingers thrusting down from the rugged Lebanon Mountains—also called collectively "Mount Lebanon"—that rise steeply from the coast and extend down the length of the country. Al Qurnat as Sawda, the highest peak, soars to 9,840 feet. The name Lebanon springs from the snows that top the crests of these magnificent mountains in winter. It derives from the ancient Semitic words *laban* (white) and *labnan* (to be white). The mountains, enjoying an Alpine climate, were the source of the fabled cedars of Lebanon of biblical times. For thousands of years, rulers from Egypt to Assyria prized the fragrant, durable cedarwood as a prime building material for palaces and temples. The hardy, long-lasting cedar trees are mentioned 70 times in the Jewish Bible, often given attributes of magnificence. In the tenth century B.C.E., ten thousand men sent by King Solomon felled an uncounted number of cedars for the construction of the First Temple in Jerusalem. The logs were floated down the Mediterranean to what is now the port of Haifa, Israel. The great cedar forests of antiquity have long been depleted, reduced now to a few scattered groves. Even so, many varieties of pine flourish in Lebanon. It is the most heavily forested of Middle Eastern countries, and the only one without a desert.

To the east of the Lebanon Mountains lies the Bekaa Valley, a central highland that extends the length of the country. The Bekaa is part of the Great Rift Valley, a geological fault that extends from northern Syria to central Mozambique. The valley's name derives from the Arabic word for "a place with stagnant water." It has hot, dry summers and cold, dry winters, sometimes slashed with snow and fierce winds. The Litani and Orontes rivers rise in the Bekaa. The Litani, the only river entirely within Lebanon, flows southward and empties into the Mediterranean north of Tyre. For decades Lebanese Muslims have darkly suspected Israel of having secret designs on the Litani's waters, a precious resource in a region of water scarcity. The Orontes flows due north, passes through Syria into Turkey, then doubles back to the southwest and empties into the Mediterranean. The Bekaa was known as the breadbasket of the ancient Roman province of Syria, and it is still Lebanon's primary agricultural area, producing wine, beets, and potatoes.

Other less-benign crops are also grown in the valley. They include poppies, which are the raw material of heroin, and marijuana. Cocaine has been produced there, made from cocaine base imported from Latin America. Trafficking in such narcotic drugs, and the printing of virtually undetectable counterfeit European and American currency—called "supernotes"—in the Bekaa have been mainstays of financing for Hezbollah, in partnership with corrupt Lebanese officials and the Syrian government, with which Hezbollah shares control of the valley. The U.S. Department of State has maintained officially for several years that Lebanon is no longer a "major illicit drug-producing or drug-transit country." Many Western intelligence officials, counterterrorism experts, and Lebanese émigrés dismiss this conclusion as the wishful thinking of diplomatic fantasists in pin-striped suits.

The Anti-Lebanon mountain range, roughly the length and height of the Lebanon Mountains, rises to the east of the Bekaa, forming a natural border with Syria. Although once renowned for its forest, the range is now stony and barren.

Until the late twentieth century, there was no such country as Lebanon. The area known today as Lebanon first entered recorded history at about 3000 B.C.E. It was called Phoenicia by the Greeks, who interacted with traders from the coastal settlements. Historical references to The Lebanon or Mount Lebanon refer for the most part to the western mountain region, which from antiquity was a rugged and inaccessible refuge for dissident religious and tribal groups. Two of these maverick groups shaped Lebanon's history and continue to have important impacts in modern Lebanon: the Christian Maronites and the Muslim Druze.

The earliest history of the Christian sect that became the Maronites is clouded by conflicting assertions of secular and sectarian historians. It is fairly clear, however, that the sect arose sometime during the fifth century, a period during which the Christian church was still sorting out its dogma, defining heretics, and winkling them out of its folds. By the end of the seventh century, the sect was either cut off or cut itself off from church authority. It appointed its own patriarch, John Maron, and repaired to a stronghold in the northern mountains of Lebanon. The first great wave of Islamic conquest erupted out of Arabia during roughly the same period and soon swept over the area now known as Syria and Lebanon. For the next fourteen centuries the Maronites and the lowland Muslim sea lapping around them engaged in a tidal cycle of conflict, occasional alliance, and long periods of uneasy truce. By the twentieth century, however, the Maronite Christians dominated the life and economy of Mount Lebanon, just as Sunni Muslims dominated the cities and controlled the lowlands.

The Druze religion originated in Egypt in the eleventh century, during the reign of the Caliph al Hakim, who among other things proclaimed himself an incarnation of God. After the collapse of the al Hakim caliphate, some of his followers emigrated to the southern end of the Lebanon Mountains, called the Chouf. The beliefs and rituals of the Druze are kept strictly secret, even from many of their own number. The religion was closed to converts shortly after its founding.

The Caliph al Hakim had another long-term impact on Lebanon. His oppression of Christians and the occupation and desecration of Christian holy places in Jerusalem inspired the Crusades, which began in the eleventh century. The physical remnants of the Crusaders' conquest of Lebanon can be seen today in the ruins of castles, strongholds, and churches dotted along the coast of Lebanon and in its mountain fastnesses. The more important legacy of the Crusades is intangible—the reintroduction of the isolated Maronite Christians to the broader world of the Church and their exposure to European culture. The French, heavily represented among the Crusaders, took a particular and long-lasting interest in the Maronites, who eventually resumed ties with the Vatican but kept their own rites and internal chain of command.

When the Ottoman Empire arose during the thirteenth century in what is today Turkey, and took control of the region in the sixteenth century, it was for the most part tolerant of minorities within its borders. The Empire ruled locally through a system of relatively autonomous, tax-paying feudal overlords—Maronite in the northern mountains, Druze in the southern mountains, and Muslim in the coastal cities and elsewhere.

By the mid-nineteenth century, the Druze and Maronites were at each other's throats in a series of bloody clashes. The sectarian conflict was thoroughly Lebanese in character, a forecast of things to come. There was a massacre in 1860 of perhaps 10,000 Maronites and other Christians by the Druze—the numbers are disputed. The Great Powers meddled, each promoting its own particular regional interest through the fighting surrogates—the French backed the Maronites and the British supported the Druze. The declining Ottoman Empire was unable or unwilling to restore order, perhaps hoping that its unruly subjects would exhaust themselves into docility. The French threatened to intervene following the massacre, which finally led to Ottoman action, and broke the power of the Druze. The result was Maronite supremacy firmly established in Mount Lebanon. The Druze repaired to their stronghold in the Chouf.

Another French action in 1920 marked the creation of the political entity that eventually became the country of Lebanon. The seed France planted bore the bitter fruit of Lebanon's implosion half a century later. The conception grew out of the collapse of the Ottoman Empire in 1909 and the succeeding Turkish government's choice of the wrong horse in the First World War. Turkey, the "Sick Man of Europe," at first wavered when The Great War broke out. But it eventually, and opportunistically, sided with the Central Powers—Germany and Austro-Hungary, the "axis of evil" of the day—when momentum seemed to be on their side.

The Allied defeat of the Central Powers in 1918 threw the vast holdings of the defunct Ottoman Empire, including the area of Syria and Lebanon, onto the carving block. Working under the imprimatur of the League of Nations, France and Great Britain sharpened their diplomatic knives and went to work. The two erstwhile allies maneuvered warily around each other, carving up the vast and prostrate Islamic empire to suit their respective and very competitive interests. Entire nations were created by simply drawing lines on maps and drafting words on paper. People who formerly thought of themselves simply as Muslims or Arab tribesmen now were to become Syrian, Iraqi, and Lebanese. In the process, the men who would be kings—tribal leaders aspiring to power in the new states—were crossed, double-crossed, and crossed yet again. The skeletal fingers of this dismal exercise in self-serving colonial arrogance still clutch at the West's throat throughout the Middle East.

In April 1920 the League of Nations awarded France a mandate over the region that includes modern Syria and Lebanon. The French were immediately faced with choosing between the competing plans of Muslim and Maronite. The Maronite plan was to create an entity known as Greater Lebanon, subsuming the Sunni cities and in effect extending Christian Maronite rule over the land from the Mediterranean to the Anti-Lebanon mountains. The Muslims recoiled at the prospect of Christian rule. They favored the creation of Greater Syria, subordinating all of Lebanon, including the Maronite mountains, to Muslim rule from Damascus. On

September 1, 1920, Gen. Henri Gouraud, the French administrator, announced the fateful decision. He proclaimed the creation of Greater Lebanon, effecting the Christian Maronite plan. The boundaries of the new entity were those of the present country, and Beirut was its capital.

In 1926 a constitution transformed the state into the Republic of Lebanon, modeled after the Third French Republic—a popularly elected unicameral chamber of deputies apportioned according to the religious or "confessional" population, a one-term president elected by the chamber of deputies, and a cabinet of ministers. On November 22, 1943, independence was declared or, rather, wrested from a reluctant France hobbled by the multiple embarrassments visited upon it by the Second World War. Christian and Sunni leaders devised an unwritten formula, known as the National Pact, that divided power along confessional lines. Originally intended as a transitional arrangement leading to a nonsectarian state, the pact instead fossilized—the president was to be a Maronite Christian, the prime minister a Sunni Muslim, and the speaker of the chamber of deputies a Shiite. Confessional proportions in the chamber were based on the 1932 census, which gave Christians a roughly six-to-five majority.

Thus were Lebanese Christians and Muslims left standing at opposite ends of a shaky teeter-totter. If either made a move—as, for example, when President Camille Chamoun sought to extend his power by changing the constitution in 1958—the action and re-action quickly destabilized the entire arrangement. It was for that reason that no census was taken after 1932, even though it became evident that the population ratio had changed in favor of the Muslims. No one had the strength to overcome the system's inertial force. Nor did anyone have the will to arouse Lebanon's dark angel, the threat of renewed sectarian violence that always hovered over the country. Pressure for change was also tamped down by a traditional system of local bosses who acted as power brokers. These bosses deliberately limited the power of the central government—the army, the judiciary, and the bureaucracy—each insisting that he get credit for even the slightest service extended to his particular constituency. When the bosses locked horns, government machinery froze until things smoothed over.

Despite its precarious government, Lebanon seemed to pros-
per and was to become known as the Switzerland of the Middle
East. Sophisticated Beirut was compared to Paris, its beaches to
the Riviera. But these were superficial attributes. The baling wire
of the National Pact and the patchwork of the bosses could not
stop the reality of mounting demographic and economic pressures, a runaway boiler ready to explode deep within the nation.

Nowhere was trouble brewing more than among the Shiites, a
repressed religious minority who had been virtually ignored by
the movers and shakers who created the country of Lebanon—the
French, the Christian Maronites, and the Sunni cosmopolitans of
the cities and overlords of the plains. For generations, Shiite families like Mohammed Hammoud's had silently borne their feudal
servility without complaint, lost in passive dreams of a better
world to come for the pious poor of this world. But new winds
were blowing from the east, from the heart of Shiite Islam. These
fierce winds would blast centuries of dust from men's souls.

The Shiite wing of the greater body of Islam emerged from a classic struggle of succession after the death of Mohammed the
Prophet in 632 C.E. Leaders of the movement gathered to decide
who would be the caliph (from the Arabic *khalifa,* meaning "successor" or "representative"), and what would be his function. One
group favored Mohammed's son-in-law and cousin, Ali ibn Abu
Talib. They called themselves the *shiat Ali*—the "party" or "supporters" of Ali. This faction's preference was more than political.
They believed that Mohammed himself had appointed Ali as his
successor, a singular manifestation of Divine Will. Some asserted
that secret knowledge was passed along this line and only this line
of legitimate succession. Thus, the rightful successor was a person
invested with much more than the merely temporal authority of a
secular caliph. He was an infallible spiritual leader called the
Imam. These matters of faith soon grew into dogma. Those who
followed it became the Shia or Shiites.

However, a rival group—those favoring Mohammed's father-
in-law, Abu Bakr—won the first three rounds of this epic (one
wishes to say "biblical") struggle for succession. The Shiites con-

tinued to press their claim with varying degrees of vigor, inspiring
two civil wars in the latter years of the seventh century. Ali was
eventually installed as the fourth caliph in 658 C.E., the first Imam,
according to Shiite doctrine. He was assassinated in 661 C.E. by a
member of yet another faction, the Kharijites, a violently fanatical
group who believed, among other things, that Islam should be imposed on the world by force—jihad was one of the pillars of their
faith. Angry that Ali had agreed to submit the question of the le-
gitimacy of his caliphate to arbitration following a challenge from
Muawiyah, the governor of Syria, the Kharijites insisted that the
matter had already been decided by God, and Ali was wrong to
submit his authority to earthly judgment.

Muawiyah seized the caliphate upon Ali's assassination,
moved its seat to Damascus, made it hereditary, and thus began
the Ummayad caliphate, the first of a series of Islamic dynasties.
The question of legitimate succession simmered along until supporters of Ali's son and the Prophet's grandson, Hussein, asserted
his claim. The ruling Ummayads promptly massacred Hussein
and most of his family in 680 C.E. at the town of Karbala, Iraq. The
dead were decapitated and their heads paraded on spears. This
slaughter and decapitation, set in the context of Ali's own violent
death, became a passionate touchstone of the Shiite faction.

Shiites fervently memorialize the date of Hussein's martyrdom, the tenth day of Muharram, the first month of the Muslim
calendar. It is one of the holiest and most emotional dates of their
religious calendar. The day, called Ashura, is marked by fasting,
passion plays, and public acts of penitence. Mass processions of
chest-beating men and wailing women are accompanied by gory
ranks of flagellants who strike themselves with lengths of chain
and cut themselves on the forehead with swords and razors, then
smack the wound with their palms to cause a drenching flow of
blood. "It is a volatile faith, one that requires outlets for the passion it encourages."[2] In Lebanon, male Shiite children like Mohammed Hammoud are introduced to the ritual, called *maatam*,
while barely of school age—some only two years old. In a photograph taken in southern Lebanon as recently as 2003, a proud father may be seen firmly holding a terrified child of perhaps three
years while the child's first cut is made with a straight razor. In an-

other, a mother looks on, beaming her approval, as her preteen son strikes his already-bleeding forehead with a sword.

In America and most of the Western world, this would be called child abuse. The parents would be arrested and prosecuted, and the children turned over to a protective authority. But in Lebanon, as elsewhere in the Shiite world, these acts are a blood bond to a faith in which passion borne of the remembrance of the violent martyrdom of Ali and Hussein is central. "This lost blood has meaning," said a Lebanese university student in 2001. "It symbolizes our readiness to sacrifice ourselves for our country and our religion, the way Hussein did."[3] Hezbollah's spiritual guide, Sheik Fadlallah, evoked that readiness in a fiery sermon delivered on Ashura in 1985 at a south Beirut mosque not far from Mohammed Hammoud's home: "Do you want to suffer with al-Hussein? The arena is ready. It is the Karbala of the South. There you're able to wound and get wounded, kill and be killed."[4] It is not a great step from this worldview to the martyrdom of suicide bombers.

The majority Sunni Muslims, by contrast, mark the fast day of Ashura as a commemoration of the day Noah left the ark. Some scholars see in Ashura an evocation of Yom Kippur, the Jewish Day of Atonement, a fast day blandly anemic by comparison to Shiite practice.

In recent years the leaders of Hezbollah, their antennae ever alert to world opinion, have discouraged the *maatam*. They seek to substitute blood drives, militant paramilitary displays, and incendiary rhetoric for the bloody mutilation they fear will be "misunderstood" as backward by outsiders. For example, Sheik Hassan Naserallah, Hezbollah's secretary-general, took the occasion in 2003 to denounce in virulent terms the pending American invasion of Iraq.

After Karbala, the ruling caliphates of the Sunni majority recognized Shiite aspirations as a serious threat and responded with often violent suppression. The Shiites themselves withdrew into a sort of mystical resignation. They eschewed the worldly strife that had gone so badly against them, and developed the concept of "occultation," which taught that the twelfth and last true Imam had gone into hiding from this world in the ninth century. He is invisible to human perception, but will return as the Mahdi and rule over a perfect—naturally, Islamic—world. It was a sin for fallible human beings to meddle in government affairs, proscribed as an act of disbelief in the certain coming of the Mahdi. (Some extremely fundamentalist Jews make the same argument against the creation of the State of Israel, arguing that any such state will be created at the time of the coming of the true Messiah.) From time to time, distinguished human leaders are given great spiritual and temporal authority and may be called Imam, as was the Ayatollah Ruhollah Khomeini. Unlike the Sunni majority, the Shiites are given to veneration of saints and pilgrimages to the holy sites associated with them. They are extraordinarily deferential to the religious leaders of their communities, whereas Sunnis generally hold that all are equal before Allah.

Living as a minority among an often violently hostile Sunni majority prompted the Shiites, as early as the eighth century, to practice sanctioned dissimulation, or *taqiyya*, as a survival technique. When there is a danger of loss of life or property, *taqiyya* allows Shiites to disguise their true beliefs and adapt to the mode of the dominant society, while mentally reserving their true beliefs. They also developed certain legal theories that differ from those of the majority Sunnis. Among them—particularly relevant to Mohammed Hammoud's story—is the practice of allowing temporary marriage, called *mut'a*. Such legal unions of man and woman fall somewhere between conventional marriage and adultery. The union is for a fixed time, as short as a matter of hours, and for a predetermined financial arrangement. The convention is considered to be a concession to the power of the human sex drive that does not rise to the level of sin specified in the Koran.

The Shiites were historically concentrated in an arc from southern Lebanon, across Iraq, and into Iran. The two holiest sites of the Shiites are located in Iraq: the tomb of Ali in Najaf, and that of Hussein in Karbala. Quite predictably, the two cities became hotly and emotionally contested focal points of unrest during the American occupation of Iraq. When the Safavid dynasty arose in Persia, now Iran, in the sixteenth century, it made Shiism the official state religion. The contest for power between the Shiite Safavids of Iran and the Sunni Ottomans of Turkey left the Shiites who lived between the warring empires in the difficult position of

ants when elephants dance. The Shiites of Lebanon in particular
were hammered into feudal servility. There they stoically endured
their serfdom, patiently waiting for the millennial day when the
mighty would be brought low and the lowly raised up.

The first winds of earthshaking change arrived from Iran in
1959, riding the cloak of Musa al Sadr, who came to be called
Imam by the Lebanese Shiites.

A common Shiite slogan is "Every day is Ashura, every land is
Karbala." For centuries, the message was one of resignation and
submission. Keep your head down and your mouth shut. Remember what happened to Hussein at Karbala. Wait for the return of
the Imam, the Mahdi, to even the score. Imam Musa al Sadr turned
the meaning on its head.

The Shiites of Lebanon were as far down the social and economic scale as could be gotten when Musa al Sadr arrived from
the city of Qum in Iran in 1959. Americans in that year were entering a period of vast socioeconomic reform—a federal judge ordered the integration of public schools in Little Rock, Arkansas,
rebuffing Orval Faubus, the state's die-hard segregationist governor. The Cold War was in a bizarre period of amiable hostility. Soviet ruler Nikita Khrushchev debated Vice President Richard
Nixon in Moscow, and visited the United States later in the year.
Cuban strongman Fulgencio Batista fled the island nation. Fidel
Castro entered Havana in triumph.

Savagely oppressed by the Sunni Ottomans, isolated in an un-
forgiving area of southern land called the Jabal Amil (mountain of
Amil), the Shiites of Lebanon scraped out a grim agricultural living. Those whom the pressure of a rapidly expanding population
sent to the cities were mere squatters. They fit in where they could
find a crack in the wall of Sunni and Christian dominance, cast in
the lowliest of urban roles—sweepers, porters, and suchlike—and
deferential to all. When they died, their corpses were shipped back
to the south. There was no Shiite cemetery in Beirut. A few of the
younger ones had migrated to the call of the political left, toying
with various Middle Eastern transmutations of Marxism's level-
ing promise: communism, Baathism, pan-Arabism. The secularity

of these movements, however, could not ignite the embers of religious zeal smoldering deep within the souls of the Shiites.

Musa al Sadr spoke Arabic with the Farsi accent of the Iranians. But his family roots were planted in the soil of Jabal Amil. His ancestors fled from Ottoman oppression in Lebanon to Najaf in Iraq. Later generations migrated to Qum, for centuries a center of Shiite learning, built around the tomb of Fatima, sister of the eighth Shiite Imam. His father was a distinguished academic who founded a religious university in Qum, and some of his living relatives were noted clerics in Lebanon. Musa al Sadr had taken a law degree in Tehran, then completed his religious education in Najaf—the same place where Ruhollah Khomeini had studied. He came to Lebanon, reversing the typical direction of migration, at the invitation of the mufti, or religious judge, of Tyre.

At six feet, six inches, Musa al Sadr was an imposing figure, meticulously elegant in dress, eloquent in speech. His biographer, Fouad Ajami, describes him as "a casting director's dream of a cult figure."[5] Radiating the confidence of a scion of a distinguished family raised in a culture where his religion was the majority, Musa al Sadr was the precise opposite of the typically unkempt and hapless Lebanese Shiite clergy of the day. He had a revolutionary message. Karbala was not about futility and submission. It was about courage—the courage to make a choice and take a stand against oppression. Musa al Sadr thrust the steel of centuries-old Shiite tradition into the flame of Shiite passion and hammered it into the sharp point of the solidarity of the oppressed in revolt against the oppressors.

His division of the world into the oppressed and the oppressors resonated in Lebanon, even across sectarian lines. Confrontation with the state or with the Maronites was not a part of Musa al Sadr's program. On the contrary, he actively promoted the view that rejuvenated Shiites could work within the system to gain their rightful share, and won government recognition for an entity called the Higher Shiite Islamic Council. He gave a well-received ecumenical Lenten sermon at a Catholic church in 1975. He began to draw adoring crowds—first tens, then hundreds, then thousands—to eloquent discourses in which he wove and rewove the Shiite nightmare into an inspiring dream. He established a grass-

roots group, the Movement of the Disinherited, to push for realization of the dream. But while he was wakening converts to his
new vision, violent events outside of Lebanon were forcing a sinister migration that would propel Musa al Sadr to new heights of
popularity while paradoxically eroding his power base. The same
migration would destroy Lebanon's fragile confessional balance
and set in train a series of events that would culminate in the creation of Hezbollah.

In the so-called Six-Day War of June 1967 the Israeli army dealt
a stunning blow to the Arab armies of Syria, Jordan, and Egypt,
which had massed in preparation for a coordinated attack on the
Jewish state. Rolling over those armies in a brilliant preemptive
counterstroke, Israel unified Jerusalem and occupied territories
from which terrorist raids and harassing artillery attacks against
civilians had been mounted for years, among them the West Bank
of Jordan and the Golan Heights of Syria. The war humiliated the
Arab armies and convinced organized Palestinian revanchists that
they could not rely on conventional force. They turned instead to
intensified guerrilla war and terrorist strikes. Among their leaders
was a then-unknown young man named Yasser Arafat, who
headed a group called Fatah. Arafat's Fatah mounted many of the
Palestinian attacks from within the borders of Jordan, which lies
along Israel's eastern border.

The rising toll of civilian casualties from these terrorist attacks
convinced the Israeli government in 1968 to storm Fatah headquarters in the Jordanian border village of Karameh. Although
more than 100 Palestinians were killed, the Israeli army in turn got
an unexpected nose bloodying—28 soldiers were killed and 80
were wounded. Arafat escaped with four tanks, and became a
popular hero overnight. He was lionized among the Palestinians
and throughout much of the Arab world as the man who had re-
stored dignity to the common cause. Young Palestinian men
scrambled to enlist in Fatah, money and arms from Arab states
poured in, and Arafat was elevated to head the umbrella PLO.

These developments may have been exhilarating for the Palestinians, and superficially good news for the Arab world. But they
presented a serious problem to Jordan's King Hussein. Arafat's organization acted as if it were a state within a state. His heavily

armed men and those of other Palestinian groups strutted arrogantly about, acting not only like princes of the refugee camps, but as if they were masters of the Jordanian cities as well. They refused to pay taxes or to put Jordanian license plates on their cars. They even set up checkpoints on royal Jordanian roads. Their disdainful acts would have been an affront to any sovereign state. But given the huge number of Palestinians living within Jordan's borders, they were ominous tremors, warnings of a real potential for armed overthrow of the Hashemite Kingdom, itself a precarious by-product of the Anglo-French division of the Ottoman Empire a half century earlier. That was in fact precisely what the more radical left of the Palestinian movement wanted. For his part, the wily Arafat characteristically played both ends against the middle. Pushing and shoving between the monarchy and Palestinian groups intensified, all under the watchful eye of other Arab states, who urged King Hussein to exercise restraint.

Events were brought to a head on September 1, 1970. There was a failed attempt on the king's life, Palestinians hijacked three Western airliners, bringing two of them to Jordan, and within days declared a "liberated zone" in the kingdom. Enough was enough. On September 17, King Hussein's forces struck against the headquarters of the Palestinian organizations, including in the capital Amman itself. The fighting was fierce and hundreds of Palestinian militants died, inspiring among the survivors the sobriquet Black September to commemorate the date, and the formation of an eponymous terror wing to honor it. Two years later the Black September terror organization kidnapped and held hostage eleven Israeli athletes at the Munich Olympics before murdering them.

A series of failed truces ensued, but by the end of 1971 the Palestinian state within a state had been crushed and its arrogant forces driven from Jordan. The evicted Palestinians fled to Lebanon, which, unlike Syria, was too weak to keep them out. History repeated itself. Arafat and his PLO promptly set about erecting another ersatz state, and launched terror attacks across the Lebanese border into Israel. For the delicately balanced Lebanese system, a schoolyard bully suddenly had jumped onto the teeter-totter and began recklessly rocking back and forth. Within five years the old and now murderously well-armed confessional front lines had been emphatically redrawn into two bristling camps, each further subdivided into pugnacious internal bands. Militias, essentially private armies, sprang up by the score among Christian, Druze, and Muslim factions and clans. The Maronites hunkered down within their territory and edgily faced off the Palestinians and their Lebanese Muslim supporters.

On April 13, 1975, the spark landed and the powder keg at last blew up. Unidentified gunmen opened fire on a church in east Beirut and killed four Christians, who promptly retaliated, shooting up a busload of Palestinians, killing 26. There were no neutrals in the bloody civil war that ensued. The state was fractured, the army effectively neutralized. Beirut became a rubble-strewn war zone, torn in half—the Christian east and the Muslim west—separated by the so-called "Green Line," named after the grass that grew in the no-man's land between the two. Americans might be forgiven if Lebanon seemed too far away to care about. Two weeks after the Lebanese civil war began, the city of Saigon fell in Vietnam. Americans watched on the nightly news disturbing images of the frenzied evacuation of U.S. personnel and South Vietnamese refugees from the rooftop of the American embassy.

The Palestinian presence was for Lebanese Muslims like an overly long visit from a dangerously violent blood relative. It inspired mixed emotions, at best. While Lebanese Muslims were sympathetic to the Palestinian plight as fellow Arabs, the sudden presence of yet another well-armed and assertive element into the delicate mix grated on proud sensibilities, especially those of the traditional leadership structure. For the Shiites, it was unmitigated disaster. The Sunni Palestinians not only took over the traditional Shiite land, but by their terrorist cross-border attacks provoked retaliatory raids from the Israelis. Tens of thousands of Shiites fled to the cities, where they were caught in the meat grinder of the civil war. In 1976, in an act that would have more than one unintended consequence, the Maronites consolidated their area and forced more than 100,000 Shiite squatters from an old Armenian-Shiite neighborhood northeast of Beirut. Among those expelled at gunpoint was another émigré Shiite cleric. He was less well known then than Musa al Sadr. But he would soon thunder over the land as the voice of Hezbollah.

Musa al Sadr equivocated on what to do about the Palestinians, torn in conflicting directions by his Shiite soul, his Arab sensibilities, and his ecumenical vision. "While he felt the pull of solidarity, he dreaded the inclusion of the Shiites in the ring of suffering that surrounded the Palestinians."[6]

Oddly enough, his division of the world into the oppressed and the oppressors appealed to Lebanese of all factions, since they all had a complaint about some bigger entity—the local bureaucrat, the bigger Lebanese state, each other, the West, the indifferent Arab states, the world at large, and so on up the food chain. Musa al Sadr came to be called by the honored title of Imam. On the other hand, his public appearances became armed rallies, with emotional firing into the air. He secretly formed a militia, led by a lawyer named Nabih Berri, breaking ground for the hitherto feckless Shiites. The existence of the militia came to light after 27 young men died in a training camp, killed when antitank explosives accidentally went off. The incident affected too many Shiite families across Lebanon to be covered up. Musa al Sadr made the best of it and hastily gave his militia the name "Amal," Arabic for "hope" and an acronym of the words *Afwaj al Muqawamah al Lubnanya*, the units or battalions of the Lebanese Resistance. But Musa al Sadr was no military leader. He could commit neither himself nor his Amal militia to enthusiastically fight for overthrow of the Lebanese state, as was proposed by the PLO and its allies, or the savaging of the Maronites, on the agenda of the Druze. He was among those who encouraged the Syrian government to intervene, which it did in May 1976, sending its army in to ensure that the state would not collapse.* But Musa al Sadr was no fan of the secular state favored by the revolutionary left and the pan-Arabist elite. He wanted the state preserved as a means of stability, to allow his dream of a resurgent Shiism to grow. The left and the pan-Arabists came to see him as the enemy of their progressive agenda.

In March 1978—the same year the Camp David peace agree-

---

* Musa al Sadr and the Syrian leader Haffaz al Assad were close. Sadr had provided Assad with a vital fatwa, or ruling of religious law, that Assad's minority Alawite sect was indeed authentically Muslim.

ment between Egypt and Israel was signed—the Israelis launched "Operation Litani," a limited crossing into Lebanon to force the PLO away from the border. A by-product of the incursion was an alliance between Israel and a surrogate force, the South Lebanon Army (SLA). The SLA, a militia founded by Saad Haddad, a Greek Catholic army officer, was manned by Christians and some Shiites disaffected by PLO abuses in the south.

On August 31, 1978, Musa al Sadr vanished. He was last seen leaving his hotel en route to a visit with strongman Muammar Qaddafi in Libya. His mysterious disappearance has never been resolved. The incredible official Libyan story is that he and his companions safely left Libya for Italy. There is no independent evidence that this was truly the case. It is generally assumed that he was the victim of foul play within Libya. How and by whom is not clear. The evocation of the occultation of the twelfth Shiite Imam implicit in Imam Musa al Sadr's disappearance was powerful. It ensured his remembrance as a heroic spiritual figure in annual memorial events throughout Shiite Lebanon. His Shiite followers adorned the walls of their slums with posters of his likeness. In 1982, a fateful spasm of violence erupted around just such a memorial posting. It would drag the American marines into the Lebanese maelstrom.

Musa al Sadr laid the foundation for the arousal of the Lebanese Shiites. His Amal militia was led by middle-class lawyer Nabih Berri and a secular elite away from its religious roots. It became yet another violent player oriented from the political left. Within a decade, Musa al Sadr would be eclipsed by another cleric from another land east of Lebanon—Sayyid Mohammed Hussein Fadlallah.

If Musa al Sadr was a freshening wind for the Shiite soul, Mohammed Hussein Fadlallah was a hurricane of fundamentalist inspiration.

Mohammed Hussein Fadlallah was born in 1935 in the Shiite holy city of Najaf in Iraq, site of the Imam Ali's tomb and several renowned Shiite seminaries. His father, a religious teacher, had left the south of Lebanon in 1928 to study in Najaf. The younger Fadlallah was a brilliant and extraordinarily literate student, quicker than his peers. He made periodic visits as a young man to his family in Beirut and southern Lebanon, and made a name for himself on the Lebanese Shiite social and literary scene. In 1966 he moved to Beirut and settled in an Armenian-Shiite shantytown northeast of Beirut.

In the United States, the first black American ever was appointed to a cabinet position by President Lyndon Johnson in 1966. The Senate rejected a fair-housing bill. In a very hot July, riots broke out in the ghettos of Brooklyn, Atlanta, Omaha, and San Francisco.

The circumstances of Fadlallah's move to Lebanon are not clear. According to a biographical essay by scholar Martin Kramer, Fadlallah may have been inspired to return to his roots by the example of Musa al Sadr's success. Or he may have been recruited as a promising competitor by a powerful landed Shiite clan unhappy with Musa al Sadr's stirring up of the serfs and anxious to dim his star.[7] Whatever the case, he labored in comparative obscurity throughout the 1960s and most of the 1970s. But, as he ministered to the downtrodden Shiites in the wretched neighborhood, he sharpened his message and his mode of delivery.

Unlike the equivocating Musa al Sadr, Fadlallah had a clear and sharp answer to the Palestinian question, which he saw as merely part of a wider conflict between Islam and the West. "The conflict to the south was not a problem between Jews and Arabs in Palestine, but between two blocs contending for the world. The Shiites . . . could not opt out of this conflict, for they too were slated for victimization."[8] He developed a style of speaking that began with a cool discourse that laid out the academic foundations of his message, and ended in a fiery sermon that roused his audience's passion. Here was a man who could scourge the Great Satan and the Little Satan with great effect.

In 1976 the Christians drove Mohammed Hussein Fadlallah and 100,000 others from the shantytown in which he lived. The area fell behind the hardening sectarian lines separating Christian from Muslim. Aside from the radicalizing influence of the armed eviction, it led to the first of two events that sent Fadlallah's stock soaring. The first came with the intervention of a wealthy Shiite émigré, who contributed funds to Fadlallah for the renovation of the Imam al-Rida mosque in southern Beirut. It was an impressive modern structure that became the cleric's base. The second was the disappearance of Imam Musa al Sadr. Fadlallah now had an impressive pulpit and a clear channel for his revolutionary rhetoric.

The Shah of Iran fell in 1979. The dour Ayatollah Ruhollah Khomeini became the living embodiment of the reversed reading of Karbala for which Musa al Sadr had argued: Instead of keeping its head meekly down, avoiding the futility of involvement in worldly affairs, Shiism would now impose a stern religious authority on the Iranian state. Fadlallah had no qualms about grasping and articulating the meaning for the Shiites of Lebanon in the ascendence of a Shiite state committed to the export of the Islamic revolution. He promptly reached out to the mullahs of the Iranian theocracy. A society of mutual admiration and benefit was quickly woven between them. Fadlallah provided an authentic Lebanese clerical base. The Iranians provided money and other support. By the 1980s, cassette tapes of Fadlallah's incendiary speeches were among the hottest items in the markets of Beirut. The prospect of quickly spawning another state of the Shiite Islamic Revolution had the Iranians on the hook.

At the same time, the new leaders from Iran were not happy with the secular direction in which the Shiite militia, Amal, had wandered. They began to provoke the formation of a radical and thoroughly sectarian alternative. Their purpose was to draw away from Amal the fervently religious Shiite young men, who were already becoming disenchanted with its direction. There lacked only the element of some grand event to electrify the process, galvanize the youth, and speed the creation of an armed religious force in Lebanon worthy of the Islamic Revolution. On the morning of June 6, 1982, the tanks, jet aircraft, and soldiers of the Israeli Defense Force provided that grand event. Israel invaded Lebanon, determined to eliminate once and for all the threat from Yasser Arafat and his PLO terror machine.

The Shiites of the south originally sat out the Israeli invasion, which swiftly drove the PLO farther south, into Beirut. Some were even friendly. The Israelis had done for them what they could not do for themselves. They had rid their land of the swaggering PLO. The amity was to be short-lived.

As it happened, the leading Shiite clerics of Lebanon were attending a conclave in Tehran at the very moment of the Israeli invasion. The Iranians were overjoyed and offered their religious confreres immediate aid. It was accepted. The switch was closed, the circuit completed. The high voltage of the Islamic Revolution flowed into Lebanon in the form of money and—perhaps more important—more than 1,000 members of the Iranian elite security and military unit, the Islamic Revolutionary Guard (IRG), or Pasdaran, sometimes incorrectly called the Iranian Revolutionary Guard Corps. The Iranians set up their headquarters in the town of Baalbek in the Bekaa Valley, safely out of reach of the Israelis. The fledgling Iranian Ministry of Intelligence and Security (MOIS), successor to and grafted on the Shah of Iran's feared secret service, respected as the best in the Middle East after that of the Israelis, supported and underwrote it all. In 1983 alone Iran spent between $50 million and $150 million on terrorism activities, much of it funneled to what would become Hezbollah.

A joyfully frantic traffic ensued. The Lebanese clerics and their affiliated organizers traveled clandestinely to Baalbek and to the Iranian embassy in Damascus to confer with their more experienced Persian brothers. Syria allowed the bustling trade to continue, adopting a pattern of intervening forcefully only when it felt that it must to protect its own interests. Otherwise, it remained a silently approving partner.

Among the Lebanese clerics was Hassan Naserallah, who was prominent among those who had left Amal, unhappy with the secular direction in which it had been taken by Nabih Berri. In 1992 he would become the secretary-general and secular head of Hezbollah. The budding alliance between the Iranians and the hard-line Lebanese Shiites had two main objectives. The first was to train inexperienced young Shiite men in the dark arts of terror, unleash them against the invaders, and support their operations through the Iranian diplomatic and security services. The steel-eyed men of the Revolutionary Guard took care of the training. They set up camps in the Bekaa. Scores of young men were taught how to blow things up and kill people. They would soon set about applying their lessons, supported by the Iranian diplomatic service and the MOIS.

The second objective was to reverse the tolerant, if not friendly, reception the Shiites were extending to the Israelis. This was primarily the task of clerics like Fadlallah, who delivered blistering sermons denouncing the Israelis and excoriating those who were not actively opposed to them. This was no new message for Fadlallah. He had preached his own apocalyptic view long before Khomeini's revolution, nurtured from the same intellectual soil in Najaf. Even so, it was an uphill pull at first. But on October 16, 1983, the Israelis themselves loaded the Shiite propaganda gun with high-powered ammunition in an act of appalling insensitivity.

The Iranians could not have staged a more effective incident. That day was Ashura. Tens of thousands of Lebanese Shiites were marching in the memorial procession in the town of Nabatiyeh. An Israeli military convoy chose the moment to assert its authority and drive through the crowd. A riot ensued; the Israeli soldiers called in help. Two Shiites were killed and fifteen injured. Although the final act of a whipped-dog withdrawal from Lebanon would take several more years to unfold, the Israeli fate was sealed on that day.

It is not clear exactly when Hezbollah became a discrete entity, but by 1985 the nascent organization that would become Hezbollah began carrying out a range of acts of terror under a variety of names, among them, Islamic Jihad, Right Against Wrong, and the Revolutionary Justice Organization. The invisible strings controlling all of these mysterious organizations all led back to the center of the web in Baalbek, and thence to Tehran. Western intelligence officials were aware that something new was going on. But they failed to penetrate the Shiite terror mechanism and could not put their finger on exactly what it was or who was responsible.

Their interest turned to frenzy verging on panic at 1:05 P.M. on the afternoon of April 18, 1983, when a smiling driver crashed into the main entrance of the American embassy in Beirut and set off hundreds of pounds of explosives packed into his vehicle. The force of the explosion—the first large-scale attack against a U.S. embassy anywhere in the world—was enormous. Seven floors of the crescent-shaped building collapsed. Seventeen Americans were killed, as were 46 citizens of other nationalities, and more than 100 were injured. The carnage was appalling. Republican Senator Barry Goldwater said it was "high time we bring our marines back." The Reagan administration dismissed his suggestion.

Special damage was done to the United States that day. Robert Ames, the CIA's top Middle East terrorism analyst, was visiting Beirut. He and six other CIA officers, including the station chief and his deputy, were meeting at the embassy. All of them were killed, dealing a profound blow that would have telling consequences in the days to follow in Beirut. The loss of Ames destroyed another closely held American initiative. He was the secret U.S. contact with the PLO. He had met clandestinely not only with Arafat, but with Ali Hassan Salameh—the mastermind of the Black September assault on the Munich Olympics. (Salameh had been killed by a car bomb in 1979.) Ames had helped arrange the terms of the PLO's evacuation and had enlisted the PLO's cooperation in ensuring the safety of American diplomats in Lebanon.

The loss of the best the CIA had to offer in Lebanon crippled initial American efforts to fix responsibility for the devastation. Perhaps it was a Soviet-sponsored attack, Secretary of Defense Caspar Weinberger hinted darkly: "The Soviets love to fish in troubled waters." Or maybe it was indeed a new group, Islamic Jihad, which had claimed credit for the blast. Within a month, however, Weinberger and others were confidently pointing a finger at Iranian involvement and suggesting Syrian complicity. They did not reveal the source of their confidence. They were relying on Iranian diplomatic communications, intercepted by the supersecret National Security Agency but decoded and translated only weeks after the events.

More and worse was to come. The concept of the suicide bomber was the ultimate contribution of Ayatollah Khomeini and his Iranian regime to the protégé Hezbollah. Bombs were nothing new as a tool of terrorism. Since at least the nineteenth century the bomb and the gun have been the favorite tools of the terrorist. In fact, bombs of various sorts—sometimes in cars, sometimes planted in buildings, and so on—were already being left and set off with some regularity around Beirut. Likewise, men and women throughout history have proven themselves willing to die for a variety of causes. Suicide missions like those of the Japanese kamikaze pilots who crashed into American warships in the final days of the Second World War are but one example of the many occasions in history when human beings have found some cause greater than the value of their own life. Martyrdom was honored in the Shiite tradition, but it had always been the martyrdom of standing on one's feet against superior force. The religious fanatics of the Iranian Islamic regime extended the concept to the suicide bomber, sending waves of children against Iraqi lines in their war with Iraq. Ayatollah Khomeini formally blessed the idea of "self-martyring" by suicide bomb, which the majority Sunni had rejected.

Now Hezbollah refined the concept of the self-martyring human bomb. There were no waves of children to exploit in fixed battles in Lebanon. But a relative handful of human beings could be turned into precisely controlled weapons as devastating as the best cruise missile money could buy. And coordinated attacks of more than one bomber striking different locations could shake the confidence of even a superpower like America. The most spectacular of these new human missiles was to land on the sleeping men of the 1st Battalion, 8th Marine Regiment.

On September 26, 1983, a secret message was transmitted from Tehran to the nominal Iranian ambassador in Damascus, Ali-Akbar Mohtashemi. In truth, "Ambassador" Mohtashemi performed no actual diplomatic functions. His real job was originating and supervising Iranian terrorist operations in the region. Mohtashemi already had overseen the transfer of more than a million dollars to the Iranian embassy in Beirut to pay for the American embassy bombing, among other things. Specialized Iranian personnel had also been sent into Beirut before the bombing and then withdrawn immediately after the explosion and returned to Tehran, stopping in Damascus for a congratulatory hug from the "ambassador" en route. Now a new enterprise was in the offing.

The September message instructed Mohtashemi to contact the leader of Islamic Amal, a Shiite splinter group that had broken off from Nabih Berri's Amal and was to become subsumed under the new Hezbollah. Mohtashemi was to tell Islamic Amal "to take a spectacular action against the United States Marines." This instruction was cleared not only by the MOIS, but by Khomeini himself.

At this point, the bloom was off the rose of the American force in Beirut, largely because of the legacy of the Imam Musa al Sadr. On another Sunday, August 28, 1983, several Shiite youth putting up posters to commemorate the Imam's disappearance were killed in a drive-by shooting. The Shiites went to arms and the most fierce fighting erupted since the civil war began. The Druze and Amal joined in, pounding the Christian militia, suspected of the shooting. Within weeks the Christians found themselves pushed out of much of their mountain turf by the Druze and very nearly overrun. Desperate, they turned to the Americans for help. Against the wishes of Colonel Geraghty, the marine commander, American warships shelled the Druze. It was all the Shiite radicals needed to demonstrate that the Americans were not really neutral, but were in Lebanon as a clever conquering force.

Shortly after the Iranian instruction was sent to Mohtashemi, a meeting was held in Baalbek. Those attending included the chief of the Revolutionary Guard force in Lebanon—an Iranian named Kanani—and three Lebanese clerics who were, in succession, later to serve as secretaries-general of Hezbollah: Subhi Tufayli, Abbas Musawi, and Hassan Naserallah. The order for the attack on the marine barracks was given at that meeting. Plans were developed to carry out that order, and to mount a simultaneous attack against the French barracks. A third attack on the Italians was considered and rejected—they were not conveniently concentrated in a single barracks building. A man named Imad Mugniyah—from the slums of south Beirut and a former member of Arafat's elite PLO Force 17 security service—was put in charge of the attack. Of him, more later. Suffice it to note here that the elusive Mugniyah, at the top of America's Most Wanted list for this and other terrorist acts, has skillfully eluded the best-laid plans for his capture for over two decades.

After the Baalbek meeting the conspirators set their plan in motion. A nineteen-ton stake truck similar to one that routinely delivered water and other supplies to the marine barracks was modified in a garage to carry a vast amount of explosives. Drivers were brought in—one Iranian and one Lebanese. Early in the morning of October 23, members of Hezbollah lay in wait for the real truck, out of sight of the barracks. Another operative waited on a hilltop, where he could observe both the barracks and the truck hijacking. After the regular truck was hijacked, the Iranian, Ismalal Ascari, took his place behind the wheel and set out for the airport, the sleeping marines, and martyrdom. Today would be his Ashura and the Beirut International Airport his Karbala.

It was not as if no one had considered the possibility of a terrorist bombing. In fact, there had been dozens of vague intelligence reports of threatened bombings for weeks. The marines had even been warned to be on the lookout for odd behavior. One alert cautioned against dogs bearing bombs. One marine quipped that the neighborhood had been cleansed of its wandering feral dog population by nervous marine sharpshooters. It had also been noticed that marine patrols in Hooterville had increasingly been the subject of angry abuse. But there was no specific, hard intelligence. And the possibility of a human missile driving a nineteen-ton truck had never been discussed. Seen retrospectively through the lens of September 11, 2001, it is an eerie reminder that Islamic terrorists are not stupid—they skillfully plan for each succeeding blow to fall in a unique time, place, or manner that cannot be precisely predicted by the patchwork of information we call intelligence.

Lance Cpl. Eddie A. DiFranco was standing duty at guard post six in front of the building. At about 5:00 A.M. he saw the truck enter and circle a parking lot south of his post, then leave. A little more than an hour later, the truck returned. It circled the lot once again, gathered speed, and then, as if hurled from a slingshot, sliced through a concertina barbed-wire barrier, swerved around several pipe obstacles, flattened a sandbagged guard booth, and crashed into the lobby of the building.

Another Marine guard, Lance Cpl. Henry P. Linkila, saw the truck coming. However, his M-16 rifle was empty, in accordance with the strict rules of engagement imposed on the marines. The rules were intended to keep the peacekeeping force as benign as possible. A federal judge later observed that, because of these rules, the marines in Lebanon "were more restricted in their use of force than an ordinary U.S. citizen walking down a street in Washington, D.C."[9] Linkila inserted a magazine and chambered a round. By then it was too late.

The truck exploded with a force that has been described as the greatest nonnuclear explosion since the Second World War, pulverizing much of the building and collapsing all of the floors. The concussion woke sleepers all over Beirut, including young Mohammed Hammoud and his family. The cloud that boiled into the sky from the explosion looked exactly like a smaller version of the familiar nuclear mushroom. FBI experts concluded that, even if the truck had been stopped in the main roadway, 100 yards from the building, the explosion of the equivalent of 12,000 to 20,000 pounds of dynamite would have caused significant casualties.

As it was, the blast took the lives of 241 men and horribly wounded scores of others. Lance Cpl. Adam Webb, the marine on guard duty on the roof, remembers "riding" the roof down as it collapsed. Then he and the other survivors looked around in stunned disbelief. Bleeding men, pinned and mutilated by concrete slabs, cried out for help. Others had been vaporized. The reinforced concrete building was simply gone.

And within months, the American force was also gone, sailing away from Lebanon across the wine-dark seas of the Mediterranean. Hezbollah had won a great victory within months of its birth. It had humbled the Great Satan. The lesson resounded throughout the world of radical Islam.

"I KNEW WHAT HE WAS THINKING. . . ."

I knew what he was thinking. He knew what I was thinking.
                                    —*Angela (Angie) Tsioumas*

Charlotte, North Carolina, was just the kind of place that Imad Fayez Mugniyah was looking for to send Hezbollah's best and brightest—smart and fanatically dedicated people like young Mohammed Hammoud. Mugniyah knows Hammoud's type well. He grew up in a south Beirut slum very much like Bourj al-Barajneh. Like many other master killers in political warfare, the diminutive Mugniyah pulled himself up from squalor with a pathological ruthlessness. He rose swiftly to become the head of Hezbollah's international terror apparatus, sometimes described as the foreign department, the security service, or the operations branch. Hidden behind impenetrable clouds of deliberate obscurity, he directs Hezbollah's network of cells in the Western Hemisphere. These embers of Shiite fanaticism are sprinkled from the South American pampas to the Canadian plains, waiting for a word from the East to ignite into the flame of jihad—Holy War.

The United States has a $5 million bounty on Mugniyah's head. A secret federal indictment of the world's most mysterious terrorist has been pending since 1985. He is charged with leading the hijacking that year of TWA Flight 847 and the brutal murder of a U.S. Navy diver on board. But the indictment is the tip of an iceberg of American blood. Imad Mugniyah has planned and directed an infamous chain of Hezbollah terrorist attacks around the world. Until Osama bin Laden's attacks of September 11, 2001, Mugniyah held the terrorist record for killing Americans. He was thought by experts to be the most dangerous terrorist in the world. Some think he is still more dangerous than bin Laden. "Bin Laden is a schoolboy in comparison with Mugniyah," an Israeli intelligence official observed recently.

Yet Mugniyah has skillfully eluded repeated American attempts to snatch him up and bring him to justice. Two of America's putative allies in the war against terror helped him escape from American attempts to arrest him. Only one or two photographs of Mugniyah exist in Western files, and these are decades old. He is short and baby-faced, deceptively ordinary in appearance, devoid of any remarkable features. Some reports say that he has had several rounds of plastic surgery to alter even that bland visage.

Mugniyah was born the eldest of four children on July 12, 1962, in Tayr Dibba, a tiny village in the mountains above Tyre in the far south of Lebanon. The movie *Lawrence of Arabia*—a vastly romanticized version of Great Britain's manipulation of Arab tribal chieftains against the Turks during the First World War—was a big hit in the United States that year. The Beatles released their first recording ("Love Me Do") in Britain. Marilyn Monroe committed suicide. The world miraculously stumbled through the toe-to-toe nuclear confrontation of the Cuban missile crisis without blowing itself up. Future President Richard M. Nixon lost the California governor's race and told the news media "you won't have Dick Nixon to kick around anymore." A relatively small number of United States military advisers were in Vietnam.

Imad Mugniyah's father was a Shiite religious judge of some note. Much of the rest of Mugniyah's life is obscure, the public record smudged or erased, probably by his own hand. But he is believed to have grown up in Ayn al Dilbah, a squalid slough of despair south of Beirut. The slum sits close to the airport, very near where the marine barracks later were bombed under Mugniyah's direction. He was eight years old when the PLO fled to Lebanon from Jordan, and barely into his teens when the Lebanese civil war broke out. Drawn to the violent action, he quit high school when he was about fourteen years old and joined Force 17, Yasser Arafat's elite personal security organization. In addition to fighting in gun battles against Christian militias, Mugniyah became adept in the dark art of making and setting off explosives.

American and other Western intelligence experts who have studied Mugniyah's career describe him as a sick man, pathologically drawn to killing, sometimes for personal rather than ideological reasons. He appears to be a dedicated Shiite, and was for a time the personal bodyguard of Hezbollah's firebrand preacher, Sheik Mohammed Hussein Fadlallah. He was quite naturally among the hard-line religious activists who were attracted to the nascent Hezbollah when it began to coalesce in the early 1980s. Mugniyah was soon marked as a person of special potential by the Iranian Islamic Revolutionary Guard cadre that was stirring things up in the Bekaa Valley. It is logical to assume that he got a boost from Fadlallah, who had been chummy with the Iranian radicals since the 1979 Islamic Revolution. In any event, Mugniyah made his mark convincingly by orchestrating the 1983 bombings of the U.S. embassy and the Marine Corps barracks.

The Iranians lavished special attention on Imad Mugniyah after that tour de force. They have given him not only the unqualified support of the Iranian diplomatic and security apparatus, but command of his own special subunit of the Iranian Al Quds ("Jerusalem" in Arabic) Force. The Al Quds Force is the most elite of five units of the Revolutionary Guard. It consists of about a thousand handpicked members, who receive training in all aspects of terrorism and guerrilla fighting, including explosives, assassination, and ambush techniques. The Al Quds Force was responsible for the assassination of anti-Khomeini Iranian exiles during the early 1990s, including the bold stabbing murder of former Iranian prime minister Shapour Bakhtiar in a Paris suburb. The Force was implicated in the shooting of the Norwegian publisher of Salman Rushdie's novel *The Satanic Verses*, and in attacks on Japanese and Italian translators of the work, which Islamic fundamentalists consider to be blasphemous. The Al Quds Force has trained a score of foreign terrorist groups. Its cadres operate with Palestinian terrorist groups. They have most recently infiltrated

Iraq, bringing with them weapons and other materials useful to the Shiite resistance battling the American armed forces. Former members of the Islamic Revolutionary Guard are known to have entered the United States from various points. They are in a support role here, but they have had experience with Hezbollah. They keep up sympathetic contact with Hezbollah abroad.

Mugniyah has a personal unit of about 100 to 150 men at his disposal called the Islamic Jihad Organization (IJO). "They are salted around in many places, but have a home base in Beirut," according to a former U.S. intelligence official. The IJO operates covertly. It picks its own men by spotting the best candidates, then quietly subjects them to a rigorous vetting process before tapping them for admission to the elite unit.

Mugniyah is so closely aligned with the Iranians through his Al Quds connection that some have described him as a sort of consulting expert who, in addition to overseeing Hezbollah's terrorist operations arm, also engages in ad hoc projects on behalf of the Iranians among the floating coalition of interest groups that is the hallmark of today's Islamic terrorism. He is said to have been directly involved in finding safe haven in Lebanon for senior al Qaeda members fleeing the American strikes in Afghanistan.

The blood debt Mugniyah owes to America did not end with the 1983 bombings in Lebanon. In March 1984 he supervised the kidnapping and brutal torture of William Buckley, the CIA station chief sent to Lebanon after the 1983 embassy bombing wiped out the CIA's resident staff. Buckley's identity may have been compromised when the Iranian revolutionaries painstakingly pasted together shredded documents they retrieved from the American embassy in Tehran after they seized it in 1979. Mugniyah is said to have personally tortured Buckley to death. He was also involved in the kidnapping of scores of Western hostages in Lebanon during the 1980s, including the kidnapping and torture murder of U.S. Marine Corps Lt. Col. William Higgins, who was assigned to a United Nations peacekeeping force in Lebanon.

Imad Mugniyah directed a team of Hezbollah terrorists who hijacked TWA Flight 847 from Athens to Beirut on June 14, 1985, and later boarded the plane himself. The terrorists singled out U.S. Navy diver Robert Stethem for special treatment. Stethem was savagely beaten for hours. The terrorists jumped so viciously on his chest, using it like a trampoline, that it collapsed. They then shot him in the temple and dumped his lifeless body onto the tarmac. This hijacking is the offense for which Mugniyah was indicted by the United States, based in part on his fingerprints having been found in the plane's lavatory.

Mugniyah and Osama bin Laden are known publicly to have had at least one meeting. Ali Mohamed, a naturalized Egyptian-American citizen and former U.S. Army Green Beret turned al Qaeda operative, testified in federal court to having arranged security for the 1994 meeting in Sudan. Mohamed told the federal court in New York that the premise underlying al Qaeda's terror campaign was that Hezbollah had shown by driving American forces out of Lebanon that the Americans could be forcibly ousted from the entire Middle East. As a result of the meeting, Hezbollah provided explosives and training to bin Laden's al Qaeda and the affiliate with which it later merged, Egyptian Islamic Jihad. Mugniyah is also said to have tutored bin Laden in the operational principles of the well-tested Hezbollah trademark attack—closely synchronized multiple bombings causing mass casualties. These principles were manifested in the near-simultaneous bombings of the American embassies in Tanzania and Kenya in 1998, and most dramatically as of this writing in the attacks of September 11, 2001. The Iranian Ministry of Information and Security held a terrorist summit in Tehran in 1996, during which Mugniyah conferred with one of bin Laden's senior deputies.

Other reported contacts between Hezbollah and al Qaeda include a March 2002 meeting in Lebanon among Hamas, Hezbollah, and al Qaeda figures, and a June 2002 terrorist "summit" in Tehran, attended by delegations from 23 countries, including 160 representatives of groups listed in the U.S. State Department's annual report on global terrorism. The organizer of the meeting was the former Iranian figurehead ambassador to Syria, Ali-Akbar Mohtashemi. Known as "Hezbollah's godfather," Mohtashemi was actually Iran's regional terror coordinator and the go-between for the marine barracks and U.S. embassy bombings. Mugniyah and his spiritual mentor, Fadlallah, reportedly attended a small closed-door session with a more limited group. The meeting focused on evading countermeasures against suicide attacks.

The 9/11 Commission Report describes a series of contacts

with some of the hijackers by Hezbollah officials. This includes travel on the same plane that took a group of the future hijackers from Beirut to Iran by "an associate of a senior Hezbollah operative." The report does not identify the senior operative, but it is reasonable to believe that it may have been Mugniyah. In any case, the report notes, "The travel of this group was important enough to merit the attention of senior figures in Hezbollah."

These meetings and continuing contacts are sobering evidence of cooperation among the world's most ruthless terrorists. They rebut optimistic analysts who claim that Sunni and Shiite terrorists do not cooperate because of their religious differences—a Pollyannaish view pithily dismissed by a retired Israeli military intelligence general with one word: "Bullshit." In fact, although Shiites and Sunnis may never be the warmest of friends, the Shiite Hezbollah have shown time and again that they will cooperate with al Qaeda and other Sunnis when it is in their interest, and vice versa.

Mugniyah has been linked to the June 1996 bombing of the U.S. military barracks at Khobar Towers in Saudi Arabia. He was indicted by Argentina for his role in the March 1992 car bombing of the Israeli embassy in Buenos Aires. In 1997 a Mugniyah spectacular of historic proportions was accidentally averted. A Lebanese Shiite Hezbollah operative entered Israel with the intention of setting off a bomb while aboard an El Al flight, which would have been a dramatic first. Instead, he blew the lower half of his body off while assembling the infernal device in an East Jerusalem hotel room. He survived and told authorities that the operation was to have been a "special gift" to Israel from Imad Mugniyah.

Mugniyah is driven in part by the deaths of his two brothers, which he blames on Israel and the United States. One brother, Jihad Mugniyah, was killed when a massive car bomb exploded outside Sheik Fadlallah's Beirut home on March 8, 1985. News reports later linked that bombing to a secret Lebanese force said to have been trained by the CIA. The CIA and the Reagan White House emphatically denied that the United States had authorized or condoned the bombing. Mugniyah's other brother, Fuad, was killed on December 21, 1994, when another car bomb exploded near Fadlallah's Beirut mosque. The bomb was placed in front of a market owned by Fuad. Hezbollah blamed the Israelis for that attack, which has been speculated to have been in retaliation for the Hezbollah bombing of the Jewish Community Center in Buenos Aires earlier in the year.

Mugniyah was never a public figure, but he was eventually driven deep underground in Iran, in part by the deaths of his brothers but more likely because of apprehension raised by a lightning Israeli dawn raid in May 1994. During the seven minutes of that operation, helicopter-borne commandos snatched a senior Hezbollah official, Mustafa al-Dirani, from his home in Lebanon. Iran sent Hezbollah a number of armored Mercedes cars after the raid, for the greater protection of its officials. But Mugniyah has since made himself more than ever exceedingly scarce. Ask any three Western intelligence officials where he is at any given moment and one gets four different answers. The consensus, however, is that he operates out of Tehran. He occasionally travels to Syria and Lebanon under the strictest secrecy, never announcing his visits in advance. He refuses to transit the Beirut International Airport because he is convinced that American operatives are waiting there to arrest him.

The United States has indeed come close to nabbing Mugniyah at least three times. The first was in December 1985 when he spent several days in Paris.* The purpose of Mugniyah's visit is not clear. By one account, he was fleeing Soviet retaliation for the September 1985 kidnapping of four Soviet diplomats in Beirut.† Another more likely reason was negotiation with the Socialist French government, which was facing legislative elections in March 1986 and was desperately seeking the release of four of its citizens held as

---

* Two French newspapers, *Le Figaro* and *France-Soir*, reported this episode several months later, in February 1986. Their reports were picked up by American news wires. As a result, the year of Mugniyah's travel to France is often reported as having been in 1986.

† The reported resolution of the September 1985 kidnapping of the four Soviet diplomats (one of whom was killed, his body dumped near a stadium) has become folk wisdom in the counterterrorism community. The KGB, playing by its own rules, kidnapped a dozen Shiites, including the brother of a prominent leader, whom they castrated and shot. The severed organs were then sent to Hezbollah with a warning that other relatives would be dealt with similarly if the three were not released. They were freed within one month, well before Mugniyah's visit to Paris.

hostages in Beirut—two diplomats, a journalist, and a political researcher—before the elections. The United States learned of Mugniyah's planned travel to France in November 1985 and asked the French to hold him when he arrived at Charles de Gaulle Airport. The CIA gave the French a copy of the passport Mugniyah was using, and French agents spotted him in Paris. Nonetheless, then-president François Mitterrand refused permission to arrest Mugniyah, an act that clearly would have blown up the hostage negotiations. French officials told the United States that Mugniyah had never arrived.

The second known attempt was in 1995, when a flight Mugniyah was on was scheduled to make a stop at Jeddah in Saudi Arabia. American officials asked the Saudis to detain Mugniyah, and a team of FBI agents flew to Jeddah to arrest him. But the Saudi government refused the FBI plane permission to land, and the terror master again eluded capture.

Finally, on July 23, 1996—a month after the bombing of the American barracks at Khobar Towers in Dhahran—Mugniyah was reported to be traveling on a ship, the *Ibn Tufail,* in the Gulf of Arabia. A Navy SEAL operation was laid on to snatch him from the vessel off the coast of Qatar. A squadron of navy ships began shadowing the *Ibn Tufail* while 60 Navy SEALs and supporting marines practiced the details of the planned operation, using blueprints of the vessel that had been obtained overnight. Within 24 hours, on July 24, the operation was primed and ready to go. The Clinton administration, however, called off the mission at the last moment, claiming that the intelligence was inadequate to confirm for sure that Mugniyah was aboard the ship. The SEALs and their commanders, stunned and angry, were ordered to stand down. Mugniyah sailed on, free to create more lethal mischief. Some sources believe that he visited South America briefly after his stay in Qatar.

By 1992 Mugniyah and the leaders of Hezbollah had made a deliberate decision to plant support cells in the American hinterland for two reasons. Fund-raising to finance terror is an important one. Resident support cells can tap into the Great Satan's wealth by quietly soliciting contributions from sympathetic émigrés, and by diverting some of the loot from criminal enterprises to the terror group's coffers in Lebanon. Giving money or providing any other form of "material support" to a group like Hezbollah that the United States has officially designated as a foreign terrorist organization is a serious federal crime. The 1996 federal law banning material support has become the cornerstone of the prosecutions of Hezbollah and other terrorist support cells uncovered in the United States. Fund-raising for terror now must be done on the sly and under threat of serious punishment. The law is controversial among civil libertarians. It survived its first full-dress legal ordeal in the Charlotte case.

The other reason for establishing cells in America is more directly threatening. A relatively quiet support cell, sometimes called a "sleeper cell," can remain benign for years. Yet its key hard-core members stand always ready to be activated to provide local logistics—reconnaissance, identification documents, housing, transportation, other direct support, and sometimes participating personnel—for violent terror attacks. As we shall see, this is exactly what Hezbollah did in Argentina under Mugniyah's direction. Observers of radical Islamic terrorism worldwide have seen a trend of support cells mutating into attack cells since the American response to September 11, 2001. A confidential informant who infiltrated the Charlotte Hezbollah cell and observed it firsthand for several years told the FBI that Mohammed Hammoud was prepared to carry out any such orders he might get from Lebanon.

"Hezbollah has the capacity to strike against American interests anywhere at any time of its choosing," according to a senior FBI official who monitored the terrorist group's U.S. operations for years. The open question is when and if Iran or Hezbollah will decide it is in their interest to take the risk of executing an attack within America's borders. The consequences of their getting caught doing so would be enormous, at least in theory. Because Hezbollah and Iran operate from specific geographic territory, both would be vulnerable to direct and devastating military retaliation from the United States, à la Afghanistan. Syria would also be at some risk. Its relationship with Hezbollah has been described as a "bad marriage"—it allows Hezbollah to continue its operations and tolerates the flow of support to Hezbollah through its territory. However, it has from time to time reined in Hezbollah, especially when it fears strong Israeli retaliation. If, however, the American public sufficiently wearies of wars in far-off lands like Afghanistan and Iraq, the threat of retaliation will become less credible. Hezbollah's leaders themselves must certainly remember that President Ronald Reagan promised retaliation for the 1983 bombings that took such a terrible toll of American life, yet in the end never allowed to be carried out the punitive strikes that were planned by Special Forces operatives. How likely is it that America would tolerate, say, an invasion of Iran, Syria, or Lebanon? Other troubling scenarios are possible, including, for example, a "false flag" operation in which Hezbollah would provide expertise and carefully concealed support for an attack within the United States actually carried out by some other terrorist group, which itself may not even know of Hezbollah's covert role. That other group would take credit for the attack and—wittingly or not—insulate Hezbollah from blame for the operation.

In any event, Hezbollah was looking for American cities where the focus of law enforcement was far removed from terrorism, new operatives could infiltrate a legitimate expatriate Lebanese community, and opportunities existed to engage in middling but profitable criminal schemes. These criminal operations, often built on the mercantile traditions of the Lebanese diaspora, would "fly between the radars." They would be nonviolent, so they would not attract the attention of local police. And each individual scheme would be on a scale small enough not to draw the interest of federal law enforcement agencies.

Charlotte, North Carolina, fit the bill perfectly—as have at least a dozen other cities to be surveyed in a later chapter. The city was enduring problems in 1992 very different from those Hammoud had left behind in Beirut. One was described by a local business observer as a "bloodbath" in the commercial real estate market. The downtown was overbuilt, largely because of the construction of the 60-story NationsBank headquarters building. Irreverently called the "Taj McColl"—a reference to NationsBank chief executive officer Hugh L. McColl—the Cesar Pelli–designed skyscraper was taller than any building south of New York and east of Chicago. It still dominates Charlotte's skyline. Prime office space went begging for tenants. And, like the rest of America, Charlotte had been hard hit by the economic downturn that followed the booming 1980s. The slump helped turn President George H. W. Bush out of office that November in favor of Arkansas governor William Jefferson Clinton. Just a year earlier President Bush was enjoying the triumph of America's armed forces over Saddam Hussein's hapless army in Operation Desert Storm, a stinging defeat for Saddam but a humiliation for Arab pride.

Another more literal bloodbath was in progress on Charlotte's streets. The American drug wars were in full fury. Criminal gangs were shooting it out in turf battles connected with the lucrative cocaine market. There were a record 115 murders in 1991, many of them associated with the drug trade.

Some law enforcement officials who relate the story of the Charlotte Hezbollah cell conjure up images of Mayberry, the sleepy North Carolina hamlet that was the fictional setting of the 1960s hit television series on CBS, *The Andy Griffith Show.* The implicit inference is "If it can happen in Mayberry, RFD, it can happen anywhere." The inference is sound. It *can* happen anywhere. The comparison is not. Mayberry was modeled after Griffith's birthplace, Mount Airy, North Carolina, a bucolic village that lies off Interstate 77 about 100 miles north of Charlotte. But Charlotte, "The Queen City of the Piedmont," is no rustic Mount Airy. It is an aggressively pro-business city, and in 1992 it was enjoying the fruits of a decade of hard work through which it had decisively outpaced other promising competitor cities in the New South. It was emerging as a world-class financial and marketing center. The third- or fourth-ranking center of American finance in 1992, it is today the second, behind only New York.

Charlotte's way of doing business was strikingly like that of Lebanon in at least one way—it had its own system of bosses to whom the local government was decidedly subordinate. Known around town simply as "The Group," this semisecret alliance of banking magnates, corporate executives, and the publisher of the local newspaper, *The Charlotte Observer,* had a firm grip on the city's helm. Their vision was the all-American dream of growth, progress, and prosperity. They made sure that the city lived up to its billing by *Fortune* magazine as number one in America in "pro-business attitude." Civic projects they blessed got going. Those they disapproved withered. "If consensus is not reached, the issue probably doesn't progress," the president of the Charlotte Chamber of Commerce explained at the time. A local economist remarked about the Chamber of Commerce, "They sell Charlotte like Honda sells Hondas."

The local government's subordination was to some observers symbolized by the location of a clutch of bank headquarters, including Taj McColl, on a ridge that dominates the city, an area known locally as "uptown." Government offices are located downhill of the ridge. Corporate newcomers were quietly advised to get on board The Group's program. "If a corporation moves here and doesn't get involved, a delegation goes and tells them that's not how we operate here and gets them involved," one of the corporate movers and shakers from Duke Power said in 1992.

The Group had excellent raw material from which to mold its push for growth in the 1980s. To begin with, North Carolina was attractive to business because of its moderate climate, low labor costs, and law against closed union shops. The city itself had a long commercial tradition. Europeans came to the area now known as Charlotte in the middle of the eighteenth century, settling at the southern end of a trading path between Virginia and the by-then decimated local Native Americans. Charlotte was incorporated in 1768. Gold was discovered in the area in 1799. Charlotte became the gold-mining center of the United States during the first half of the nineteenth century, and the site of a federal government mint for three-quarters of a century. The gold eventually was mined out, and with the arrival of the railroad Charlotte became a trade hub.

Today it sits at the junction of two major interstate highways, I-85 and I-77. By the 1980s it had become a major service and distribution center for manufacturing plants in outlying areas, and the home of several large banks. When federal banking law was eased in the 1980s to allow regional banking, Charlotte's banks leaped at the chance to grow. The USAir hub at Charlotte's international airport helped the city's explosion during the 1980s. In

1991 the airport handled 500 flights a day and a total of 8.4 million passengers, with direct flights to London and Frankfurt. Not counting Hezbollah, Charlotte saw the arrival of 69 new foreign-based enterprises between 1989 and 1992, many from Germany, Japan, and Britain.

In sum, Charlotte was a global city in 1992, catching its breath after a marathon of growth during the 1980s. It was getting used to the presence of foreigners in its midst. North Carolina's population of foreign-born Muslims—as opposed to American-born, primarily black converts or adherents to American-based splinter movements—was still relatively small. But there were enough living in and around Charlotte to inspire the occasional newspaper lifestyle piece on food, religious holidays, and ritual observances. The presence of a quiet, well-groomed, attractive young Lebanese like Mohammed Hammoud was not going to turn heads or prompt calls to the local constabulary—as it might have in the mythical world of Mayberry, RFD.

Nevertheless, Charlotte had cracks in its well-planned pavement. One was that the rural-dominated state legislature choked off metropolitan road-building money, spiting what some representatives of the farm constituencies called "the independent state of Mecklenburg," the county in which Charlotte resides. That left the city's traffic tied in a continual knot. The other was that Charlotte was a pretty violent place to live. In addition to its record of 115 murders in 1991, it had an overall rate of 2,176 violent crimes per 100,000 residents, not far behind New York City's rate of 2,318 per 100,000.

State, local, and federal law enforcement officials were determined to contain the violence in Charlotte and shut down the drug traffic. Federal prosecutor Ken Bell and FBI agent Rick Schwein were up to their elbows in the alligators of that swamp when Mohammed Hammoud quietly came to town.

Both of them were independently involved in a major investigation of the local federal Organized Crime Drug Enforcement Task Force called "Operation Clean Sweep." It was aimed at members of the infamous Colombian Medellín cartel, which had set up operations in Charlotte, supplying cocaine to a ring of local drug dealers. The ring set up front businesses, some of which were staffed with local jail inmates let out on daytime "work release" programs. The "work" the inmates were engaged in was selling drugs. The investigation and prosecution was successful—57 hardened bad guys were sent to prison, sentenced by a tough federal district court judge named Graham C. Mullen. Rick Schwein was gaining experience in complicated investigations involving organized crime. Ken Bell was honing his skills in difficult prosecutions. And Judge Mullen was handing down record federal prison sentences. On a future day of reckoning, Mohammed Hammoud would be at the focal point of the attention of all three. In the meantime, however, the FBI squad nominally charged with keeping tabs on terrorism was patronizingly called "the white elephant squad" within the Charlotte field office. The action was in putting handcuffs on drug lords and other homegrown bad boys. No one in Charlotte was staying up nights looking for international terrorists.

Hammoud met two people in 1992 who eventually would have a dramatic affect on his life. One was a cute, vivacious, and very smart nineteen-year-old Greek-American woman named Angela Georgia Tsioumas, known as Angie. The other was another émigré from Bourj al-Barajneh, a slick operator with a puckish smile named Said Harb, considerably less religiously observant than his peers. Neither would play an immediately important role in Hammoud's life. But within a few years Angie Tsioumas, barely out of her teens, would prove to be the best thing that happened to Hammoud in America. Said Harb would be the worst. In the meantime, Hammoud went carefully about the business of settling into America and tapping into the Great Satan's wealth on behalf of Hezbollah.

Mohammed Hammoud did not arrive with an expense account and an encrypted book of instructions. Quite to the contrary, cash was expected to flow to, not from, Lebanon. Hezbollah cast Hammoud onto America's shore like the seed of a hardy parasitic vine. He was expected to be clever enough to take root and resourceful enough to thrive without detection. He was not entirely alone. In addition to the cousins with whom he traveled in 1992, two brothers preceded him to the United States. On the way in they tested the notorious elasticity of America's flimsy border security, well known to terrorist organizations worldwide. A cluster of other Lebanese of varying backgrounds and immigration status, many from the same Bourj al-Barajneh neighborhood, also lived in Charlotte. Hammoud's task was to nestle in and organize Hezbollah sympathizers into a functioning support cell. Some of the Lebanese would become enthusiastic members of Hammoud's cell. Others would have quite the opposite reaction.

There are rumors among senior U.S. officials that the Mossad, the Israeli intelligence organization, began monitoring Hammoud's group at some point around 2000, using Lebanese émigrés who were former members of the South Lebanon Army (SLA). A Lebanese who was involved in some of Hammoud's criminal activity and ultimately cooperated with the FBI did indeed name one former SLA member who lived in Charlotte. He said several more whose names he did not know had moved into the area. Hammoud and his circle were worried about the presence of these men, their bitter enemies. It was a faint echo in North Carolina of Lebanon's bloody wars.

If it is true that these former SLA members were operating on behalf of Israeli intelligence, it might help to explain a curious reluctance later on the part of the Israelis to help the United States prosecute the Charlotte Hezbollah cell, operatives of one of Israel's most dedicated and violent enemies. One senior federal prosecutor was so angry at the Israelis that he coined the phrase "Because of you, for you . . . fuck you!" to sum up his feelings toward them. Some survivors of a 1994 bombing in Argentina also accused the Israelis of not sufficiently cooperating to bring Hezbollah to justice there. It must also be said, however, that senior U.S. Justice Department officials do not share the prosecutor's view.

Mohammed Hammoud rose to his challenge exceedingly well. The federal intelligence and law enforcement officials who eventually became his worst nightmare characterize him as smart and personable, but very careful, methodical, and in control of himself. One intelligence officer said Hammoud had "excellent tradecraft." He explained that—unlike at least one other important member of what became the Charlotte Hezbollah cell—Hammoud never took reckless steps, always kept within the character or "legend" that he established for himself, and took care not to draw attention but rather to blend into his surroundings.

Hammoud's overriding concern during the first years was getting immigration status as a permanent resident alien. It was, he said, "always in my mind I want to fix my status here. I want to get my green card. I want to be able to go home and come back." Hammoud's goal is, of course, shared by many otherwise benign would-be immigrants who want to stay in the United States but who have entered illegally or overstayed a legal entry.

It is not very difficult for the determined terrorist to get into the United States, as Hammoud's bold entry shows. All 19 of the September 11, 2001, hijackers entered the United States legally, as do about 330 million legitimate foreign visitors and about 400,000 immigrants every year. About 200 selected State Department consular offices process 10 million visitor applications and 500,000 immigration applications every year. There are more than 50 categories of visitors' visas, but the most common are tourist, student, and business. Mohammed Hammoud's older brother, Chawki, came into the United States legally on a temporary exchange visa issued by the U.S. embassy in Damascus.

For those who, like Mohammed Hammoud, cannot win a legitimate visa, there is the two-step process of a forged entry visa followed by an instant asylum claim. As a last resort, there is always the bold illegal crossing of America's enormous land borders, the only choice available for millions of Latin Americans. A Hezbollah operative now awaiting trial on federal charges in Detroit rode into the country from Mexico concealed in the trunk of a car.

Once in, many foreign visitors simply walk away from the visa restrictions and hunker down to the good life, hoping they won't get caught. It's a pretty good gamble, and some three to four million visa-jumpers are estimated to be living in the United States. In spite of reforms since 2001 and reorganization under the new Department of Homeland Security, U.S. officials charged with border security are still overwhelmed by the endless, colossal tide. They have only primitive means of keeping track of visa-jumpers, much less the uncounted number of aliens who sneak into the United

States without any papers at all. Even so, it is difficult for illegal aliens to move about freely, and certainly to engage in criminal behavior, without being hampered by a real fear of apprehension, even if only by chance. Most important, it is impossible for them to leave the country and be sure of getting back in.

These are not satisfactory conditions for a long-term terror operative. It is the very ability to move about openly, to come and go across international borders without hindrance, that is precisely the highest priority of terror operatives. The nature of international terrorism, sometimes described as "asymmetric warfare," dictates that priority. Military forces like those of the United States use jet fighters and bombers, tanks and other armored vehicles, tons of high-explosive ordnance cleverly designed to wreak maximum havoc, high-technology weaponry, hundreds of thousands of troops, and vast air and naval transportation fleets to project an armed force that is capable of precisely visiting apocalyptic violence on virtually any spot anywhere in the world. Terrorists do not have such forces at their disposal. Their principal weapons are clever, dedicated, individual human beings who use stealth and the most conventional and available weapons—including hijacked jetliners—to attack by surprise, against civilians, and without regard to the rules of formal warfare.* Even though the ultimate trigger-puller or fuse-lighter may be a local operative, the instructors, technicians, and professional organizers of terrorism must move across international borders to make things go bang. This is especially so for those who wish to take their war to the American mainland. Al Qaeda did not send stealth bombers to the United States. It sent fanatical men willing to die.

Terrorists sometimes use stolen or forged documents for travel or other purposes. For example, a passport stolen in 1998 from an

---

* There are many definitions of terrorism. The U.S. intelligence community is guided by the definition of terrorism contained in Title 22 of the U.S. Code, Section 2656f(d):

—The term "terrorism" means premeditated, politically motivated violence perpetrated against noncombatant targets by subnational groups or clandestine agents, usually intended to influence an audience.

—The term "international terrorism" means terrorism involving the territory or the citizens of more than one country.

—The term "terrorist group" means any group that practices, or has significant subgroups that practice, international terrorism.

American medical student traveling in Barcelona ended up in Hamburg, where it was used by Ramzi Binalshibh, the alleged co-ordinator of the September 11, 2001, attacks on the United States. Interpol, the international police organization, says over a million travel documents, including passports, have been reported lost or stolen in recent years, including 80,000 blank passports stolen from various countries, including some major European states. The U.S. Department of State was preparing in 2004 to hand over to Interpol details about 400,000 lost or stolen U.S. passports. A booming traffic in false and stolen identification documents thrives in the American criminal underground and is available to terrorists. An émigré from Singapore, for example, was arrested and successfully prosecuted in Florida after fellow habitués of a strip club became suspicious of his behavior and alerted local police. Although subsequent investigation did not uncover any direct links to terrorism, police found in his car trunk 67 stolen driver's licenses, 8 stolen U.S. passports, 27 certified copies of birth certificates from various states, and 11 driver's licenses in his name.

The gold standard of terrorist travel documents is the American passport, which is why Osama bin Laden made recruiting American citizens an al Qaeda priority. Egyptian-born Ali A. Mo-hamed—the naturalized U.S. citizen and former Army Green Beret sergeant who set up security for the meeting between bin Laden and Mugniyah—joined al Qaeda in the early 1990s. He used his U.S. passport to travel abroad frequently, training al Qaeda terrorists and conducting surveillance of targets, including the American embassies in Africa that were bombed in 1998. One of his close associates, another naturalized Egyptian American, Khalid Abu al-Dahab, told an Egyptian court that bin Laden personally congratulated him for recruiting ten U.S. citizens into al Qaeda. Khalid Abu al-Dahab and Ali A. Mohamed arranged a secret 1995 fund-raising visit to the United States for Ayman al-Zawahiri, the number two man in al Qaeda.

The next best thing to a U.S. passport for a terrorist operating in the United States is the so-called "green card," an alien registration document issued to foreigners who have been granted permanent residence as immigrants. A green card is the first step toward citizenship and the golden ring of the U.S. passport. Its holder can move about the country freely, and can travel out of the United States for long periods of time without needing special permission to reenter. But how does a person like Mohammed Hammoud go about getting a green card?

Hammoud first stalled the system by going through the motions of applying for asylum. Putting aside the question of his fraudulent story—a lie that legally invalidated the whole process—Hammoud was able by gaming the asylum process to keep the appearance of being legally in the country. In November of 1992 he filed a sworn written application, repeating the fiction of his having been caught between the rock of Hezbollah and the hard place of the South Lebanon Army. A special corps of asylum examiners heard almost 68,000 claims for asylum in 2001, of which slightly more than 20,000 were granted. A bit more than half of those granted were from two countries, Colombia and China. Had Hammoud been granted asylum, he would have enjoyed most of the privileges of the green-card holder, but he still would have been short of lawful permanent residence. Significantly, he would have needed advance permission to return from any trips abroad. Given the basis of his pitch for asylum, trips to Lebanon would have been awkward, to say the least. The benefit of asylum can also be revoked if the basic conditions in the home country change for the better. In any event, an immigration judge saw through Hammoud's story and denied the asylum application a little more than one year later. The dauntless young man promptly filed a notice of appeal. While that appeal was creeping along in the bowels of the former Immigration and Naturalization Service (INS), Hammoud jumped onto a faster track to the coveted green card: a merry-go-round of phony marriages.

The impediments of matrimony itself aside, marrying a U.S. citizen is one of the easiest ways for an alien to win permanent resident status and the coveted green card. "It is," said an INS official, "the path of least resistance."

The privilege is not automatic—the act of marriage does not in and of itself confer the status, but it sets up a fast track to permanent residence. The American spouse must file a visa petition with immigration authorities, informing them of the marriage and requesting a visa be issued to the foreign-born spouse. At the same time, the alien files a request for an "adjustment in status," asking to be granted a green card. The applications are reviewed, an interview is scheduled, and if all goes well, bingo, the alien spouse is in. The examiner, of course, must be convinced that the marriage is for real. An Arab-American news service provided tips in 2003 about the kinds of evidence that support an application—joint bank records, joint tax returns, pictures with family and friends, birth certificates of children—and things that "look fishy," such as different addresses on driver's licenses and separate credit applications.

This method is so popular that do-it-yourself kits are sold over the Internet, which is cluttered with immigration lawyers' websites offering to grease the skids. The potential for fraud is obvious. The old INS—now the Bureau of Citizenship and Immigration Services (CIS) under the new Department of Homeland Security—investigated about 3,000 phony marriages a year. But the congressional watchdog General Accounting Office reported in 2002 that hundreds of cases ripe for investigation were backed up without action in regional offices all over the country—and these were just the cases INS knew about.

The mechanics of marriage fraud and its vicissitudes were portrayed in the popular 1991 film *Green Card*, in which an American spinster (Andie MacDowell) and a French cad (Gérard Depardieu) engage in a fake marriage to keep Depardieu from being deported. The two fall in love and, after working through personal and bureaucratic peril, eventually survive the examination process. Of course, in the fantasy of the silver screen, it's all charming and funny, with a heartwarming happy ending. In real life, it's sordid and dangerous, exploiting the poor, exactly the kind of low-level crime that terrorists use to advance their vicious ends. Americans who engage in fraudulent marriages with aliens may rationalize their acts as merely petty crime. But a fraudulent marriage could be an important cog in a violent terrorist plot, as serious as giving a gun or a bomb to a terrorist.

The American spouses, usually women, are typically paid a modest sum in cash, goods, or a service such as car repair. They aren't required to live with the alien spouse and usually they just fill out the forms and show up for the interview. The scam is on all over America. A Harlem welfare mother pleaded guilty in 2003 to 27 phony marriages to men from five Latin American countries, India, and Pakistan. The same year 221 people were charged in a South Carolina operation that netted 107 sham marriages. The women were given between $1,000 and $1,500 to marry men from Tunisia and Pakistan. One accepted $500 worth of baby clothes instead of cash. Marriage fraud rings were broken up between 2002 and 2004 in such unlikely places as Albuquerque, Kansas City, Milwaukee, and Cedar Rapids, among others. In most such cases, the American "spouse" is either not prosecuted or allowed to take a plea involving only probation, in exchange for cooperating in the prosecution and deportation of the alien.

Mohammed Hammoud and his Charlotte confederates turned marriage into a three-ring circus. Seven aliens connected to the Charlotte Hezbollah cell were involved in twelve phony marriages. Two of the "wives" were actually a lesbian couple who lived together rather than with their supposed Lebanese male spouses. Hammoud, his brother Chawki, and his cousin Ali Fayez Darwiche burned through several wives each before hitting a winning combination to get through the immigration screen. The INS, meanwhile, was so wrapped up in its own bureaucratic red tape that it never noticed their repeat trips to the well.

Because Hammoud is an intensely religious man, one might wonder how he could justify his marital misconduct—especially since he and his family in Lebanon continued diligently working to line up a suitable Muslim wife for him. One answer certainly lies in the Shiite traditions of temporary marriage (*mut'a*) and dissimulation (*taqiyya*), disguising one's true religious beliefs and fitting in with the dominant culture. Hammoud was also still in contact with Sheik Fadlallah and relied on him for advice about how to thread the needle of his conduct in the decadent West. "I think Fadlallah now is the best among them," he said of Shiite clerics. "Especially for someone who is here in the West, he has a lot of knowledge about the West culture."

Hammoud allegedly married an American named Sabina Lucas Edwards in December 1994, while his asylum appeal was pending. He would later claim at his criminal trial that he never heard of her, that the whole thing had been cooked up sight un-seen for a suitable fee through a corrupt New York lawyer. Be that as it may, marriage loophole paperwork purporting to be from Ed-wards and Hammoud was submitted to the INS. That agency opened an entirely new file on Hammoud. It completely over-looked the existing file that contained the details of his original suspicious entry and the denial of his asylum request. In August 1996 an INS examiner ruled that the Hammoud-Edwards mar-riage was fraudulent. Hammoud was ordered to leave the country within a month. Of course, he had no intention of doing so. In-stead, he started looking for another perfect bride.

He thought he found her in a woman named Jessica Eileen Ed-wards, who worked in a Domino's Pizza store managed by Mo-hammed's brother, Chawki. Mohammed's proposal fell short of the romantic ideal. "I told her I need her," he said. "I knew that she was the kind of person, seems to be like, who can do something like this. I told her, look, I need to fix my papers and the only way I can do it is by marriage. So I pay you money. And you can do it for me. She said no problem."

It turned out there was a problem. Hammoud concluded that "Jessica was not a good person." Her alleged drinking and drug use would make her an unreliable marital witness under INS scrutiny. By now Hammoud had a serious problem of his own. He had been in the United States illegally for five years, skating by on a bogus asylum claim and an overwhelmed INS file system. He had pulled a core of Charlotte-area Lebanese Shiites together into a functioning Hezbollah support cell. Members of the cell were in-volved in a variety of criminal activities, some of them in common, some of them merely overlapping. But he was going nowhere on getting his immigration status adjusted.

Then Angie Tsioumas, the vivacious young woman he first met in 1992, stepped back into the picture. Not only did the smart-as-a-whip Angie solve Hammoud's immigration problem, but her considerable business skills turned his criminal enterprises into major moneymakers.

Mohammed Hammoud's first two years in America were—immigration fraud aside—relatively unremarkable. He enrolled in an English language course at Central Piedmont Community College. He told people he had come to America to get an education, like his older brother, Chawki. And he went to work at an American icon, Domino's Pizza. Hammoud's "legend" matched that of millions of other young immigrants, starting at the bottom rung and reaching high to pull themselves up the ladder through hard work and education.

Domino's Pizza was something of a town square for the Charlotte Hezbollah cell. Angie Tsioumas and Chawki Hammoud worked together in one store for a while, which is how Mohammed Hammoud first met Angie, then became managers of different stores. Mohammed and a number of others worked as Domino's deliverymen. But starting in 1997 Angie Tsioumas noticed that many of her more reliable drivers had become less reliable, drifting away from pizza delivery to something that was more lucrative. It took some time for Angie to figure out what was going on. But once she found out, she immediately wanted to be cut in on the deal. The deliverymen were being drawn to a new criminal scheme that, with the help of Angie's enthusiastic expertise, would end up making millions of dollars for Mohammed Hammoud's Hezbollah cell.

Hezbollah's criminal windfall was the unintended consequence of a taxpayer revolt in a quiet corner of rural northwest Michigan. In 1993 property owners in Kalkaska, a small factory town and retirement haven about 240 miles northwest of Detroit, voted down a proposed property tax increase. As in most other states the 3,286 public schools in Michigan were funded from local property taxes, among the highest in the nation. The property tax system annoys homeowners, who don't like being stuck with the bill for school administrators' ambitious tabs, and civil rights activists, who don't like the disparity between tax hauls from rich and poor neighborhoods that results in unequal spending on schools. In the same year, the U.S. Supreme Court declared that the school systems in four states—Alabama, Missouri, Tennessee, and Massachusetts—were operating unconstitutionally because of funding disparities. Civil rights groups had hauled more than half the states into court on charges of discriminatory school spending.

When the aging homeowners of Kalkaska, increasingly without school-age children, said "enough is enough," the local school system quickly ran out of money. The school board laid off teachers, cut bus service, charged athletes $50 per sport, and sent the kids home for summer vacation at the end of March, with snow still on the ground. Parents set up a tutoring system in a church basement and held a beef stew supper to raise money for band uniforms. It was a news media dream story. Kalkaska became the embarrassing poster child for America's school financing mess. Squeezing enough money out of irate taxpayers to pay for equalizing school system spending became a Gordian knot.

At the urging of Michigan's Republican governor, the state legislature abruptly cut through the knot with a radical change in the state's tax system. It cut allowable property tax rates, raised the general sales tax rate from 4 percent to 6 percent, and tripled the tax on cigarettes to 75 cents a pack, at the time the highest in the nation. Increasing taxes on cigarettes not only increased revenue, it advanced the cause of antismoking public health advocates. Michigan voters overwhelmingly approved the new plan in a March 1994 referendum, ignoring the grumblers who warned that Michigan's smokers would turn to out-of-state sources to feed the monkey on their backs. The Michigan plan became the model for some other states.

The grumblers were soon proven to be right. Cigarette sales in Michigan plummeted by 41 percent while they soared in stores along the borders of neighboring states. Although the tax enforcement unit of the Michigan State Police promised to crack down on bootleggers, angry merchants dismissed the promise as "crap" and accurately predicted that professional smugglers would soon be drawn to the bait. It is an age-old phenomenon that when governments limit access to a popular commodity, whether by prohibition or taxes that consumers perceive as excessive, the smugglers are not far behind. The difficulty of stopping cigarette smuggling is graphically illustrated by the fact that it is rampant throughout America's prisons, among the most controlled environments in the world.

The worldwide phenomenon of cigarette smuggling takes two forms: running contraband from low-tax areas to high-tax areas, and bringing in cheap, low-grade foreign products (often Chinese) fraudulently labeled as popular domestic brands. Terrorists are increasingly piggybacking on these and other organized crime operations to raise funds for their activities. Cigarette smuggling has long been a major source of revenue for the Irish Republican Army (IRA). It is popular with organized crime and terrorists alike because, although it yields high revenues, the penalties are typically minor. In the United States, for example, authorities often simply confiscate contraband tobacco without bothering to prosecute the smugglers. When smugglers are prosecuted, more often than not they get the wrist slap of probation. The cost-benefit ratio therefore is much more favorable to criminals and terrorists than trafficking in drugs, an offense that carries long mandatory federal prison terms.

Hezbollah's leaders constantly scan the horizon for just such criminal opportunities, and it wasn't hard for them to find this one. The Detroit area is heavily populated with Shiite Lebanese, among them Hezbollah operatives. When enterprising convenience store and gas station owners looked south to low-tax tobacco-producing states like North Carolina for cheap, low-tax contraband cigarettes, Hezbollah was not far behind. It was a classic fly-under-the-radar scheme—nonviolent, and not regarded by federal officials as worth a lot of enforcement resources.

The North Carolina-Michigan pipeline was favorable to a smuggling scheme. The tax in North Carolina was only five cents per pack, and in January 1994 the state abandoned its requirements for tax stamps. It was a curiously convenient coincidence of timing that only just preceded the pending referendum on the triple hike in Michigan cigarette taxes, by then a winner in the polls. Michigan, too, had no tax stamp requirement. Tax stamps, either preprinted on every package or applied like postage stamps, are tangible proof that taxes have been paid. Although, like any other official document, they can be counterfeited, the absence of a tax stamp requirement greatly simplifies the smuggler's job. Without tax stamps in Michigan and North Carolina, it was impossible to tell whether or where taxes had been paid on any given package or carton of cigarettes. Low-taxed North Carolina cigarettes could easily be dispensed in Michigan outlets, evading the high Michigan tax. It's not clear who, but some enterprising Lebanese in Detroit hooked up with a fellow countryman in North Carolina and organized trafficking began.

Mohammed Hammoud soon heard about the scheme.

"The Lebanese community in Charlotte, it's like a small town," he said. "If somebody does something, second day everybody knows, regardless, good or bad. Everybody tells everybody."

Hammoud and several of his associates had by then accumulated a web of false identities. Mohammed, for example, took over wholesale the identity of his friend Ali Abouselah when the University of North Carolina student returned to Saudi Arabia. He acquired a driver's license, obtained credit cards, and set up bank accounts in Abouselah's name. Others in the ring engaged in even more elaborate identity fraud as part of other criminal scams. At the southern end of his cigarette-smuggling pipeline, Hammoud opened a fraudulent cigarette wholesaler trading account at the JR Tobacco Warehouse in Statesville, North Carolina, a 20-minute drive north from Charlotte on I-77.

The JR outlet in Statesville is one of three that the New Jersey-based national discount tobacco empire has established in North Carolina, each one at a strategic location along Interstates 77, 85, and 95, the main north–south routes through the state. Travelers who smoke can't miss at least one opportunity to stock up on cheap weed when driving through the Tar Heel State. Hammoud falsely represented to the Statesville JR outlet that he had registered as a wholesaler with North Carolina authorities. JR accepted the paperwork and never independently followed up with state officials. Wholesalers and state regulatory authorities share a relaxed attitude toward the cigarette trade in North Carolina. It is still a major crop in the state's agricultural base. What's good for tobacco sales is good for North Carolina.

The Statesville JR outlet is a triumph of tacky American clichés. The building is a rectangular vastness of cinder block, painted in garish red, white, and blue, mutilated with signage in giant letters intended to be visible from the highway. It squats defiantly at one end of a dismal, asphalt-paved mall nestled under the armpit of an interstate interchange. A collection of gas stations, grimly functional fast-food outlets, and instantly forgettable retail stores hang around the perimeter like abandoned children.

The entrance is a pair of glass doors, similar to those of the typical suburban grocery store. Inside, the space devoted to the sale of tobacco products is a surprisingly small part of the public floor. As one enters, to the far left is a small cigar store enclosed in glass, in effect a big humidor. Cigarettes are sold retail and wholesale alike from a plain counter along the right-hand side of the rear wall. The rest of the vast floor space is devoted to an eclectic mélange of rural oddities, such as cured hams, bizarre chotchkes, miscellaneous discount clothing, and odds and ends impossible to classify rationally. A bank of checkout registers completes the circuit. Uniformed, off-duty Iredell County sheriff's deputies provide moonlighting security.

The vigilant curiosity of one of those deputies, Bob Fromme, would later play a major role in Mohammed Hammoud's undoing. In the meantime, Hammoud, his brothers, and his other friends and relations went enthusiastically into the cigarette-smuggling business. They loaded rented vans and trucks with thousands of cartons of cigarettes bought primarily at discount from the JR outlet, then drove them up I-77 to a collection of regular customers. The buyers were fellow Lebanese, proprietors of gas stations and convenience stores, called "party shops," in the Dearborn area of Detroit.

Each load contained from 1,000 to 1,500 cartons of cigarettes, and the smugglers made a net profit of from $1 to $2 per carton, depending on the brand and the original discount price. Over the entire time of the smuggling operation, the organization is known to have bought 497,149 cartons of North Carolina cigarettes for a total of $7,457,239. Michigan taxpayers were cheated out of $3,728,619. Hammoud regularly sent money back to Hezbollah. But because a great deal of it was in the form of cash or cashier's checks couriered in envelopes simply stuck into the pockets of trusted travelers to Lebanon, or otherwise transmitted in untraceable form, no one knows for sure just how much cash that should have gone to Michigan's schoolkids went instead to buy AK-47s, explosives, ammunition, and sophisticated military gear for Hezbollah terrorists around the world. But it was more than enough to break the federal law against giving material support to designated terrorist organizations.

The drivers were originally Lebanese, some siphoned off from Domino's delivery work. But when a few of the drivers were stopped and busted by highway patrols in West Virginia, Kentucky, and other states en route to Detroit—their loads confiscated and the drivers usually released without charge—the syndicate "outsourced" the risk and recruited American drivers. Among them was pretty little Angie Tsioumas, the Domino's Pizza manager who had been at the fringes of the Hammoud circle since 1992.

Angie Tsioumas, a perky 5-foot-7-inch dynamo with an engaging smile, has been in a hurry to make money all her life. She was born in Charlotte on May 25, 1973, the first of three children. She has two younger brothers. Her parents, Jimmy and Georgia, emigrated from Greece in the late 1960s and in due course became naturalized citizens. They live in a modest house in one of Charlotte's many suburban cul-de-sacs. Angie speaks proudly of her Greek heritage. She supplemented her public education by attending an after-hours Greek school for six years.

Angie was blessed from an early age with a quick grasp of finance and a nimble mind. "From the time I was twelve, I would pay the bills and balance the checkbook for my father when he was out of the country," she recalled.

Many of Angie's extended family members are in the restaurant business, and she got the bug early to join the tradition.

"My first job was at Domino's when I was fifteen," she said. "When I was sixteen I had my own checking account." She attended Harding University High School, a magnet school with a college preparatory curriculum. But Angie Tsioumas was in too much of a hurry to waste time at Harding Rams homecoming dances or twiddling her thumbs in class. "I was very money-hungry." She quit high school in the twelfth grade to work full-time at Domino's, where she had become a manager. But even that jump off the usual track didn't satisfy Angie's special itch. She wanted her own business. "I knew I wanted to work for myself, to be my own boss."

All of the investigators and prosecutors who came to know Angie agree with one summing-up. "She was the smart one," they say, or, "She was the brains of the operation." Managing things came naturally to Angie, even in her family life. "I am the one who everyone in the family comes to if they need something, like the 'go-to' person."

Careful observers are struck by a gradual insight when talking to Angie about the Hezbollah cell—the conversation is more than an ordinary two-way exchange of question and answer. Instead, she seems to be processing the questions at lightning speed behind a careful mask of quick smiles and a façade of perkiness worthy of a television network morning anchor. The insight arrives the same way a photo print slowly emerges from the developer chemical bath. The picture is suddenly there, and one realizes that she is adjusting her responses on the fly, screening the information she gives, and subtly "spinning" not just the answers but the entire conversation in a favorable direction. It is a disquieting phenomenon, more than slightly scary, that only slowly grows on the participant. It may be a glimpse into the tragic flaw in a character that otherwise had all the basic ingredients to become a great American businesswoman or corporate whiz kid. A mind like that of Angie Tsioumas can simultaneously seize larcenous opportunity and weave a protective web of justification and personal rationalization.

When the opportunity for criminal lucre knocked, Angie was ready. She had already noticed the episodic disappearance of her Domino's drivers. "I became aware when a lot of my employees were out days at a time or weeks at a time or just months at a time." Angie finally learned what was going on from Medhat Karout, an associate of Mohammed Hammoud's and one of her drivers. He asked her if she wanted to drive. She agreed and first got her toes wet as a driver, making a few trips to Detroit for $500 a pop. "I would just get into a car or a van and just drive them up to Michigan, drop them off, collect the money and drive back down to Charlotte."

It seemed too easy to believe. A month or two later, she quit her job at Domino's Pizza and plunged into the smuggling operation up to her neck.

"It was a challenge, and I liked a challenge—I can do this!" It wasn't only the money that attracted her to the smuggling operation. "I had plenty of money before I started doing it," she says now. This is a bit of bravado, since she was soon raking in more illicit cash from moving contraband cigarettes than she could have earned in years as a Domino's manager pushing pizzas. But, money aside, Angie grasped quickly that here was her chance to run the show, to be her own boss. She proved to be very good at it, bringing to bear her considerable business skills.

At about the same time, Angie and Mohammed Hammoud hopped hand in hand onto the marriage-go-round. They married on September 12, 1997. Both ignored the slight legal technicality that they were each still married to someone else, and thus could not legally marry each other. Hammoud hadn't bothered to divorce his last bride, Jessica Eileen Edwards. Angie had married a man named Timothy Guy in September 1996. They separated three weeks later. Her divorce from Guy would not become final until December 1997.

The day after their putative marriage, the pair filed papers with the INS for Hammoud's green card. The documents were filed with the INS office in Michigan, because it was known to be faster and easier than the Charlotte office. The newlyweds falsely claimed in the papers to be living in Dearborn. An associate at that end of the smuggling pipeline, gas station owner Hussein Sharour, gave the couple phony employment documents to help put the scam over on the INS.

The third marriage was a charm for Mohammed Hammoud. He won his coveted green card on July 8, 1998. Elsewhere on the domestic marital scene that day, the front pages of newspapers from *The Charlotte Observer* to *The New York Times* reported a federal appeals court ruling handed down in Washington: Three Secret Service agents would have to appear before a federal grand jury investigating the cover-up of President Clinton's extramarital sexual liaisons with former White House intern Monica Lewinsky. Less than one month later, on August 7, 1998, two nearly simultaneous truck bombs devastated the American embassies in Nairobi and Dar es Salaam. On August 20 the United States retaliated with fruitless cruise missile attacks on a chemical plant in Khartoum, Sudan, and Osama bin Laden's bases in Afghanistan. Muslim critics around the world scoffed that the missile strikes were an attempt by President Clinton to draw attention away from the Lewinsky scandal, itself further proof of American decadence.

An informant within the Charlotte cell told the FBI that in the interim Angie bragged she would marry any other Lebanese for cash as soon as Hammoud had his green card in hand. And Angie admitted in court that she was already married when she and Hammoud entered into their union. But she insists now that the romance, the courtship, and the marriage itself were for real and all about love, something ripped from the pages of *Modern Bride*.

"I was never in an arrangement with Mohammed," she says defiantly. It is either a masterful acting job or a sad example of self-denial, painful to observe. According to Angie, she and Mohammed had a casually cordial relationship between 1992 and 1997. "We weren't dating then," she says. "We would see each other from time to time and we'd just say, 'Hey, how are you doing?'" She met Hammoud's mother when she visited the United States. (Hammoud's brother Bassam, who lived in Dearborn, had boosted his naturalized citizenship into a green card for his mother. She could come and go freely from Lebanon to the United States.)

Then, one day—just coincidentally sandwiched in with everything else that was going on, like smuggling trips to Detroit—lightning struck. "I was somewhere one day and we had lunch. He asked me out to dinner and I thought, He's cute. Mohammed is definitely good-looking. We went out to Harper's that night. There was chemistry," she says. They talked a lot that night about their respective families. Angie says that, even though they were from different religions, they had a natural bond in their common Mediterranean background. "He is very attractive, very soft-spoken, very nice, very respectful with people."

The chemical bond grew, Angie says, into a "very loving" relationship. "He called me 'sweetie' and said he was crazy for me." Unlike the other phony couples in the Charlotte organization, Angie and Mohammed actually moved in together. They bought—in her name—a modest colonial in a well-kept suburban neighborhood. Mohammed's cousins, Ali Hussein Darwiche and Mohammed Atef Darwiche, moved in at the same time. Nevertheless, she claims, they settled down to a typical suburban routine. He played soccer every Sunday, sometimes basketball. They went bowling and bought a satellite dish.

What Angie doesn't like to talk about are the days when Mohammed went off with the guys to shoot AK-47s and crawl around in the woods. Or the trash bags full of illicit cash that had to be counted, bundled, and poured back into the smuggling business. Or, most of all, the Thursday night religious meetings when the shades were drawn and Mohammed showed Hezbollah propaganda videos to local Lebanese Shiites and made his pitch for donations to the terror organization.

Angie could see that the cigarette-smuggling business was going to be a problem in 1998, when Michigan decided to require cigarette tax stamps in order to stop its tax hemorrhage. Continuing in the smuggling racket would then require that they get into counterfeiting, and her intuition told her that was not something she wanted to get involved with. So she started directing a program of money laundering, gradually moving cash from the cigarette smuggling into legitimate businesses. By 2000 she and Mohammed were owners of a new service station at a good location on I-77, and part owners in Cedar Land, a Lebanese restaurant in a strip mall that still serves world-class Mediterranean dishes.

Life seemed good. Mohammed was able to return to Lebanon for a long visit and make the pilgrimage to Mecca that is obligatory for every Muslim. The laundered money was stacking up in accounts and business investments. What neither Angie nor Mohammed knew, however, was that their little security blanket had already begun to unravel. It began first from the inside, progressed through a series of foolish indiscretions by their associate Said Harb, and then fell under the keen eye of an unusual FBI agent named Bob Clifford.

"I BELIEVE IN THE SUN . . ."

*I believe in the sun, even if it doesn't shine, in love even when I
don't feel it, and in God, even if he remains silent.*
                                    —Inscription, Memorial to Victims of
                                            Buenos Aires Bombings

Insects buzzed in the clammy heat when agents from the FBI's
New York field office stepped out of the plane. They had taken
care to keep a low profile on their visit to the notorious Tri-Border
Region of South America. The steamy junction of Brazil, Argentina, and Paraguay is best known to tourists as the site of the
magnificent Iguaçú Falls and the home of beautiful orchids and
other exotic flora and fauna. To intelligence, counterterrorism, and
law enforcement officials, the area is infamous as a simmering
cauldron of international organized criminals and terrorists of
every stripe, from al Qaeda through the IRA to Colombian rebels.

There was no official welcoming party for the FBI agents. Only
the minimum advance notice had been given to the host country's
officials. This was to be a quiet surveillance of Hezbollah operations in the region, done with a level of discretion only one notch
above undercover work. Before the agents could complete the
short walk across the tarmac to the terminal building, however,
the chirping of their pagers joined the drone of the buzzing insects.
Someone in New York urgently needed to talk to them.

The news was sobering. A fax had just arrived at the New York field office. It contained only a picture of the agents—as they left the plane minutes before. The implicit message was clear: We know you're here. We're watching. It was a classic example of Hezbollah's superb counterintelligence, another reason why American officials consider the group to be so dangerous.

"Hezbollah has a very robust counterintelligence capability," says FBI agent Ken Piernik, until recently in charge of monitoring Hezbollah in the United States. "They know that everybody in the world is trying to penetrate them. Israel has even tried to use other Lebanese Shiites to get inside Hezbollah."

Counterintelligence can be thought of as the mirror image of intelligence, which is one group's efforts to learn another group's secrets, its hidden capabilities, intentions, strategic goals, and tactical plans. During the Cold War, for example, the United States and the Soviet Union tried many different means—from human spies to satellites scooping up electronic signals and photographic images from cold space—to discover each other's secrets. What new weapons were in hand or being developed? Under what circumstances would they be used? What were the leadership's most closely held strategic plans? Both sides used an assortment of military and civilian intelligence services. They and every other intelligence service in the world expended vast amounts of effort and resources seeking and sifting through as much secret detail as possible about the major and minor actors in the game of nuclear balance.

At the same time, each side fashioned a variety of safeguards against the other's intelligence services. These safeguards are collectively called counterintelligence. They can be defensive or offensive. Defensive counterintelligence is a bundle of security procedures designed to identify intelligence ferrets and keep them out. The bundle includes surveillance of known and potential adversaries to identify likely snoops, erecting fences and installing locks—physical and technological, setting down rules that limit who gets access to secrets, vetting personnel security clearances, and creating means of accounting to keep track of secrets and who has access to them. Offensive counterintelligence goes beyond merely keeping the other side out. It tries to actively penetrate the other's intelligence services, and to manipulate and deceive them.

Some Cold War penetrations are well known. For example, Soviet GRU officer Oleg Penkovsky and KGB officer Oleg Gordievsky exposed their respective intelligence services to the West.* Likewise, CIA officer Aldrich H. Ames and FBI agent Robert Hanssen revealed devastating information about American intelligence operations to the Russians. Other cases remain sealed in secret archives. Intelligence and counterintelligence are popularly thought of in such terms as nation pitted against nation. But they are also important attributes of modern terrorist groups. Al Qaeda manuals stress deception in operations, including floating false signals to confuse the enemy's intelligence services or send them down a fruitless trail. This might be done by issuing proclamations or taking credit for operations using a new and entirely different name, as Hezbollah did in its early days, obscuring accountability and requiring intelligence services to expend effort trying to gather information about the putatively new group. Detailed threats of attacks never intended to be carried out can also be disseminated by a variety of means including Internet websites and channels of communication known to be monitored. The Shiite practice of dissimulation (*taqiyya*) is a form of offensive counterintelligence. By blending into a hostile society, Shiite activists can not only protect themselves from discovery, but also more easily gather information about their targets. Hezbollah has extensive and sophisticated systems of defensive and offensive counterintelligence.

"Wherever they are in the world," according to Piernik, "Hezbollah's operatives try to get into any political group that has anything to do with Lebanon." Such penetrations yield information about what fellow Lebanese are doing at home and abroad. Since some Lebanese expatriates—primarily Maronites and former South Lebanon Army members—cooperate with Western intelligence and counterterrorism services, circulating within their circles may yield, by way of gossip or loose talk, information about government programs against Hezbollah.

---

* The KGB (*Komitet Gosudarstvennoi Bezopasnosti*), or Committee for State Security, was the principal Soviet intelligence and internal security organ. The GRU (*Glavnoye Razvedovatel'noye Upravlenie*), or Main Intelligence Administration, was the intelligence arm of the Soviet military. Both survived the fall of the Soviet Union and the transition to the Russian Federation in slightly modified form.

Penetrating Hezbollah is from the start an almost impossible challenge for the FBI and the CIA, given the hurdles that must be overcome. Lebanon is a tribal society and Hezbollah's day-to-day operations and governance cluster around clans and families whose members know each other well. No stranger can simply walk into a Shiite neighborhood in Lebanon or abroad and join the cause without intense scrutiny. Yet, amazingly, the FBI has successfully penetrated Hezbollah in more than one instance, both in Lebanon and in the Lebanese diaspora. These cases are so sensitive—literally matters of life and death—that the Bureau refuses to talk about them and the public will never know the details. The authors agreed not to write about one such dramatic case since even to hint at any particular aspect of the matter would certainly cost lives. The complex network of bonds among Lebanese makes the creation of a plausible "legend," or false personal history, for a so-called mole difficult. In addition, Hezbollah employs many techniques that legitimate governments use to sift out candidates for operational roles—interrogating intensively, wiretapping phone conversations, checking with known friends, and running broad background investigations. And the terror group uses other screening techniques that Western, certainly American, counterintelligence services would shy away from.

"A candidate might be asked to do an intolerable thing, such as getting a gun and shooting a politician, as a test," according to Piernik. "Hezbollah gives you lots of time to run on your leash in such a case. If you don't come through, then you are either deemed not reliable, or you are very closely controlled."

Hezbollah's counterintelligence program is backed up by the worldwide services of the Iranian diplomatic and intelligence services.* Iran's highly regarded intelligence service trains Hezbollah

---

* The United States was able to definitively pin the blame on Iran and the fledgling Hezbollah for the 1983 bombings of the U.S. embassy and marine barracks by breaking the Iranian diplomatic code and intercepting Iranian communications—unfortunately, not in time to prevent the attacks. If it is true that Iraqi pretender Ahmed Chalabi warned the Iranians in 2004 that America was reading Iranian cable traffic, as public accounts allege, the case would be a grave example of the rewards of counterintelligence. The Iranians, by developing Chalabi, who was close to the highest levels of the U.S. government, were able to foil a very strong card of American intelligence.

operatives to a level of skill rivaling that of professional Western intelligence organizations. Hezbollah's intelligence skill is often an important element of its contribution to its alliances with other terrorist organizations. Hezbollah also exploits common criminals and criminal organizations as extensions of its intelligence and counterintelligence operations. It provides drugs to narcotics traffickers in exchange for information that the dealers can pick up in areas that are difficult for Hezbollah itself to infiltrate. It has, for example, thoroughly inserted itself into the drug trade in Israel to subvert Israelis (including soldiers) to provide intelligence and allow infiltration of the border. In addition to finding the answers to specific questions, criminals and drug users have been used to gather public information like maps, phone books, and compilations of statistics, which Hezbollah integrates into its operations-planning database.

The Iranian intelligence and diplomatic backup was particularly useful when Hezbollah arrived in the jungles of South America in the mid-1980s, just as it had been central to the successful bombing of American targets in Lebanon in 1983. Eventually the Iranians and Hezbollah used sleeper cells to mount two of the most devastating international terrorist attacks ever in the Western Hemisphere (excepting, of course, those of September 11, 2001). The lesson of those attacks in Argentina is one for Americans to ponder.

On September 18, 1998, agents of the New York Joint Terrorism Task Force (JTTF) scrambled. They had just received word that the Paraguayan National Police in the Tri-Border city of Ciudad del Este had arrested Mohammed Gharib Makki, the former leader of the New York City Hezbollah cell and a fugitive since his 1995 indictment on federal charges of mail and wire fraud in Brooklyn.* Makki, a naturalized citizen, had surrendered his U.S. passport as a condition of his release on bond, then fled the country. He was known since to have been living in Lebanon, a senior Hezbollah

---

* The story of Mohammed Gharib Makki's New York indictment is told in more detail in Chapter Five.

lieutenant reporting directly to Secretary-General Hassan Naseral-lah. Two task force members, New York Police Department detective Wayne T. Parola and FBI agent John G. Sorge, quickly packed and grabbed the next flight to Asunción. Mohammed Makki was a big fish who got away and his capture would be a triumph for the JTTF. But Parola and Sorge were in for a puzzling surprise when they arrived in Paraguay the next day.

JTTFs are teams of federal, state, and local law enforcement agencies coordinated by the FBI. The first JTTF was created by the FBI in New York in 1980. That far-seeing move built on the successful experience of a joint FBI-NYPD bank robbery task force in 1979. The combination of federal and local law enforcement resources was credited with halting a record-setting run of bank robberies in the city during 1979. Robberies had soared to 126 in July and 140 in August, reaching a total of 642 by early September—more bank robberies than any previous entire year—when the bank robbery task force was created. The robberies dropped sharply to 75 in September, 58 in October, and 52 in November. Already seeing the threat of terrorism in the United States, the FBI decided to apply the concept to a standing counterterrorism task force. The growing danger led the FBI to gradually create more JTTFs in other cities. Today there are 66 JTTFs—double the number before September 11, 2001—including one in each of 56 FBI major field offices and ten in smaller offices. More than 2,300 law enforcement personnel work in the task forces. The FBI calls them a "force multiplier" that combines a range of expertise to collect intelligence on domestic and international terrorist organizations, prevent terrorist attacks, and identify and prosecute the perpetrators of such attacks.

Detective Parola has been a member of the New York JTTF since 1985 and worked on the case against Makki. He took Mohammed Makki's original U.S. passport with him to Paraguay in order to make a positive identification. When he and FBI agent Sorge stepped into the immigration office at the Silvio Pettirossie International Airport in Asunción, where their quarry was being held, Parola had one immediate observation.

"This is not Mohammed Makki," he said.

Although the man in custody insisted that he was Mohammed

Makki and even had a U.S. passport—number Z7189091—issued in Damascus, Syria, as a replacement passport in the name of Mohammed Makki, a check of his fingerprints confirmed that he was not the indicted man. Over the next several weeks an international investigation gradually lifted the veil from the mysterious impostor and revealed who he really was—a Hezbollah operative considered to be even more dangerous than Mohammed Makki. It also became clear from the man's background that what he was doing in the Tri-Border region could not be good for the United States.

The man who held U.S. passport Z7189091 left Lebanon on September 14, 1998, aboard an Air France flight to Asunción, the capital of Paraguay. After an overnight flight, he was met at the airport on September 15 by Hussein Ali Hmaied, a Lebanese resident of the Paraguayan city of Ciudad del Este and an aide to one of two factions of Hezbollah active in the Tri-Border area. Although they share an overall common purpose, the two factions have jousted for influence in the region. One is led by the Abdallah clan and identifies closely with Sheik Fadlallah, Hezbollah's spiritual leader. The other, led by the Barakat clan, aligns itself with Hezbollah's secretary-general, Hassan Naserallah. Hmaied was the right-hand man of the Barakat clan leader.

Immediately upon their meeting, the two went to the Brazilian consulate in Asunción, where the visitor represented himself to be Mohammed Gharib Makki, an American citizen on vacation, and applied for a tourist visa to Brazil. Several things about the application aroused the suspicion of the Brazilian officials. The fact that the man presented a replacement passport was one flag. Why was he in such a hurry for a tourist visa? He had obviously come straight from the airport upon arrival and seemed anxious to get the visa right away. Most significantly, the passport was not signed. Why not? When the consular official asked the man to sign the passport, he declined, took the passport back, said he would take care of the matter in Ciudad del Este, where he intended to journey, and left the consulate. The consular official picked up the telephone and called the United States embassy.

Believing the man to be a fugitive, American officials asked the Paraguayan National Police to assist them in apprehending him. At 8:30 the next morning, the Brazilian consul general in Asunción called the consul in Ciudad del Este to alert him to the matter. He was told that the man was already in the consulate, filling out paperwork for the visa. He meanwhile had signed the passport. When the man was asked for his travel itinerary, he sent his "taxi driver"—actually Hmaied—back to the hotel to get it. The consul was advised to delay matters. The man was told to return in two days.

Hmaied and his guest had already traveled across the border to Brazil and registered in a hotel, taking a room in Hmaied's name. They were also busy making visits to a number of Lebanese residents in the Tri-Border. These calls and their significance would be revealed later in the investigation.

On the morning of September 18, the man returned to the Brazilian consulate in Ciudad del Este, and was admitted promptly upon its opening. He became agitated and evidently suspicious when an American came into the office and began speaking in English to the woman who was handling his visa application. He demanded return of his passport and left the consul. When he stepped outside, he was arrested by agents of the Paraguayan National Police and flown to Asunción, where he was held in the immigration office until the arrival of Detective Parola and FBI agent Sorge.*

Confronted by those officers with the fact that neither his face nor his fingerprints matched those of the man known to be the real Mohammed Gharib Makki, and that the passport had obviously been altered by the substitution of his picture, the man changed his story. He was, he told them, really Hassan Mohammed Makki, a cousin of Mohammed Makki.

"I stole my cousin's passport because I wanted to come here to

---

* When Hmaied learned of the man's arrest, he returned to the hotel room, retrieved the traveler's suitcase, broke into it, and no doubt removed critical and incriminating documents. After waiting a day or so, he voluntarily appeared at a police station and made a self-serving and implausible statement in which he claimed that he knew nothing of the man other than that he was a Lebanese businessman who needed help from a countryman to find his way around the area.

start a business," he said. "I could not get a Paraguayan visa in Lebanon, but I knew Americans did not need a visa."

The man stuck to his story through several interrogations. He was arrested on U.S. passport misuse charges and flown to Miami. There he was arraigned under the name of Hassan Mohammed Makki, processed into the American justice system, and transferred to Washington, D.C., to stand trial. When the man appeared at a bond hearing, the federal prosecutor stood up and informed the judge that the man before the court was not Hassan Mohammed Makki either. The United States, however, now knew who he was—a Hezbollah terrorist convicted of plotting to bomb Americans in Germany.

Michael J. Hudspeth, an eighteen-year veteran of the U.S. Diplomatic Security Service, made a brave decision late in September 1998. Serving in Lebanon, he had been tasked with finding out who the "John Doe" representing himself first as Mohammed Gharib Makki and then as Hassan Mohammed Makki really was. Hudspeth had a long-term informant within the Hezbollah apparatus who would only meet with him one on one—away from the embassy and without the usual additional security that American agents traveled with in Lebanon. Based on trust he had developed over several years, Hudspeth decided to travel alone to a remote rural area, a dangerous decision, where he showed his informant a picture of the man.

"The recognition of the individual depicted in the photograph by the confidential informant was both immediate and obvious," Hudspeth wrote later in an affidavit. "The face of the confidential informant clearly registered the emotions of surprise, fear, and anger upon viewing the photograph."

The trembling informant identified the mystery man as Bassam Gharib Makki, the older brother of the fugitive Mohammed Gharib Makki. Moreover, the informant said, all three of the Makkis whose names had come up in the case—Mohammed, Bassam, and their cousin Hassan—were trusted senior lieutenants who reported directly to Hezbollah's secretary-general, Hassan Naserallah. Bassam Gharib Makki was involved in the physical, hands-on training of terrorists. The informant warned that any attempt at further investigation, even so much as inquiring into public files in Lebanon about any of the men, would be taken by Hezbollah as a direct attack on Naserallah. The inquirer would immediately be targeted for execution. The informant told Hudspeth that Bassam Gharib Makki had been expelled from Germany around 1990, but wasn't sure why.

This, said Hudspeth, was the first time he had seen his informant so frightened. He (or she), he wrote in the gender-neutral phrases agents use in discussing such informants publicly, "was visibly angered at me for exposing him/her to this risk." When Hudspeth inquired about Makki again at a later date, the informant refused to talk to him further and said "too much" had been revealed already.

Now that they had their man's real name, the investigators turned to Germany, where Bassam Gharib Makki first traveled sometime in the mid-1980s, shortly after Hezbollah was born as an organization. Fluent in German, he originally filed a claim for asylum, but upon learning that he could not attend university in such a status, he withdrew his claim and returned to Lebanon. With the help of an unidentified church group, he came back to Germany, and by 1988 was ostensibly studying physics at the Technical University in Darmstadt. The city lies in the southwestern quarter of Germany, just below Frankfurt. It is located right in the middle of a belt across southern Germany that is sprinkled with American army and air force bases. It was a convenient spot for Bassam Makki's real mission in Germany—preparing to bomb U.S., Israeli, and Jewish targets. Whatever actual studies he may have been engaged in, he spent a great deal of time reconnoitering targets, acting both on specific instructions from Hezbollah in Lebanon and on his own initiative.

On September 23, 1988, German authorities intercepted a package Bassam Makki sent to his contact in Lebanon. It contained an atlas of the Rhine-Main area, the site of several major American bases, and color photographs of more than a dozen Israeli targets. Later, the Germans intercepted a list of 20 American targets Makki sent to Lebanon, along with the information that he was ready to mount attacks as soon as he acquired the requisite weapons and explosives. The American targets included government buildings and military installations, along with bars and restaurants frequented by Americans. When German security agents arrested Bassam Makki on June 22, 1989, he was carrying a letter identifying all of the targets. When the agents searched his apartment they found codebooks hidden in a suitcase and behind a picture frame. Also hidden were instructions on the use of explosives.

Bassam Makki's codebooks were simple, but they quickly explained the seemingly innocent phrases in some of his communications. His targets were identified by automobile brand names—Israeli and Jewish targets were identified as BMW, American targets as Mercedes. "I have found a car in good condition" meant a good bombing target had been identified. Model numbers within the brands provided more detailed information. Reference to a "Mercedes 200" meant bombing damage could be done to American property. "Mercedes 220" meant human beings including Americans could be injured or killed by bombing, and "Mercedes 230.4" meant American human beings could be harmed without injuring Germans. Makki indicated in a letter that he was enthusiastically wanting to "buy" (bomb) several of the top-of-the-line Mercedes targets—bombings that would hurt or kill Americans but not Germans.

There were other phrases. "Your brother-in-law sends his greetings" meant "Leave the country, you are in danger." Reference to the "mark" meant a dynamite charge, while "franc" meant another form of explosives. "Your mother sends greetings" meant "Be careful, you are being watched."

On December 16, 1998, Bassam Gharib Makki pled guilty in Washington's federal district court to passport violations and served time under close watch in a federal prison. In December 1999 he was transferred to Miami, where he pled guilty to making false statements to federal agents about who he was in their several interviews with him and at his original arraignment. On March 7, 2000, he was deported from the United States and returned to Lebanon.

Additional investigation revealed that his younger brother,

Mohammed Makki, had easily obtained a replacement passport after he fled the United States. Even though his original passport was confiscated in New York, the State Department keeps no list of such passports. Accordingly, when Mohammed Makki went to the U.S. embassy in Damascus, Syria, and claimed that his passport had been lost, the State Department's records indicated that he was the legitimate holder of a U.S. passport, and a replacement was issued—number Z7189091, the passport used by his older brother.

It was also learned that, using the legal status of his father and brother, Bassam Gharib Makki had applied in 1989 for an American green card while he was in a German prison, claiming that he was residing in Lebanon. Because the INS was not aware of his true location, he was notified in 1991 that he had been approved for an immigrant visa and green card. However, in 1993, after he filed his application for the visa at the U.S. embassy in Damascus, the State Department checked his background and discovered his German criminal record. His application was denied.

Why was Bassam Gharib Makki in the Tri-Border and making such an effort to conceal his real identity? The U.S. government says on the official record that this "may never be known," but it is certain that he was up to no good. Bassam Gharib Makki is a well-trained terrorist, a seasoned operative, and a dedicated Hezbollah lieutenant who frankly told the court during his trial in Germany that he hated America and Americans. He is a man to be reckoned with.

Officials believe that there are several complementary explanations for his activity. First, Makki met with leaders of both factions of Hezbollah in the Tri-Border during his few days of activity before his arrest. He likely was attempting to get the two factions to put aside their rivalry in the interests of more effective operations against American, Israeli, and Jewish targets in Latin America. Second, Makki met with Hussein Alawieh, a business owner whom informants identify as the principal connection between Hezbollah in the Tri-Border and Hezbollah in Canada.* It is believed that Makki's long-term goal was to infiltrate the United

* Hezbollah's significant operations in Canada are described in Chapter Seven.

States—something he had been trying to do for almost ten years—by way of Canada, after he had concluded his business in the Tri-Border. Third, his experience in planning bombing attacks and in training terrorists indicates that he may also have been planning to conduct training, either for the long term or for a specific attack. In this regard it is worth noting that only three months after Makki was arrested, a police raid in Paraguay is reported to have broken up plans by Hezbollah and al Qaeda to make simultaneous bomb attacks on Jewish targets in Buenos Aires, Ciudad del Este, and Ottawa. Moreover, the Tri-Border had already been used in a similar manner to support two devastating attacks in Buenos Aires, against the Israeli embassy and a Jewish community center.

Whatever Makki's ultimate intentions, his case demonstrates the combination of factors that worry American counterterrorism officials about the Tri-Border, a region marked by lawlessness and heavy Hezbollah infiltration.

Anyone who has seen the 1986 Cannes Film Festival grand prize–winning movie *The Mission* recalls the haunting opening scene of an anonymous Jesuit missionary—crucified by Guarani Indians and thrown with his cross into a broad river—drifting downstream, to finally plunge over an enormous waterfall. That waterfall is called the Bozzetti. It is one of 275 cataracts that pour down from a horseshoe nearly two miles wide. Together they make up the great Iguaçú Falls straddling the border between Argentina and Brazil, the Tri-Border's greatest tourist attraction. In the rainy season many of the falls blend into one great thundering cascade. The panoramic drop of these collective falls is so impressive that Eleanor Roosevelt was said to have exclaimed on seeing them, "Poor Niagara."

The Tri-Border is an area where Paraguay, one of the most corrupt states in the world, butts up against two other nations with only marginally less corrupt histories, Brazil and Argentina. In 2003 the independent Berlin-based organization Transparency International—using opinion surveys of businesspeople and country analysts—ranked Paraguay in a tie with Myanmar (formerly Burma) as the fourth most corrupt country in the world. The organization defines *official corruption* as the abuse of public office for private gain. With a score of 1.6 on a scale of 10 (not at all corrupt, a score obtained by Finland, for example), Paraguay was rated only slightly less corrupt than Haiti (1.5), Nigeria (1.4), and Bangladesh (at 1.3 the most corrupt state in the world). Argentina (2.5) was about a quarter of the way up the ladder, sharing its ranking with countries like Albania, Pakistan, and the Philippines. Brazil, with a score of 3.9, tied for corruption with Bulgaria and the Czech Republic. (The United States was scored at 7.5, tied with Ireland as the eighteenth least corrupt state.)

This confluence of official corruption is a petri dish for the international criminal culture. Smuggling, counterfeiting, drug trafficking, gunrunning, money laundering, intellectual property and trademark theft, immigration fraud, and other schemes thrive in the Tri-Border, an ideal milieu for Hezbollah and other international terrorist groups. Because of this cat's cradle of official corruption and rampant criminality, Hezbollah was able not only to carry out two of its most horrific terror attacks, but also to escape punishment for them to this day.

The Tri-Border lies just below the Tropic of Capricorn on the 25th parallel of southern latitude, roughly the same distance from the equator as the Everglades of Florida. The subtropical climate is humid. The annual average temperature is 68 degrees Fahrenheit in the Brazilian city of Foz do Iguaçú. The region is at a junction where a thick finger of Argentina thrusts up between Brazil and Paraguay. The Iguaçú River, flowing to the west, defines the border between Argentina and Brazil along the northern tip of the finger. About fifteen miles below the falls, the Iguaçú joins the Paraná River, which flows southward and marks Paraguay's border with Brazil and Argentina. The Argentine city of Puerto Iguazu lies on the southeast point of this juncture, connected to Foz do Iguaçú, north across the Iguaçú river, by the Ponte Presidente Tancredo Nieves. That city is in turn connected by the International Friendship bridge to the Paraguayan city of Ciudad del Este, which lies across the Paraná River to the west.

In addition to the waterfalls, tourists enjoy an Eden of tropical flora and fauna in the surrounding national parks. More than 2,000 plant species, unnumbered insect families, 400 varieties of birds, and an ark of other animals thrive in the warm humidity of the subtropical habitat. They include ubiquitous orchids and butterflies, wildcats, tapirs, deer, snakes, monkeys, and an odd species of river rodents about the size of a large dog, called the capybara. Abandoned Jesuit missions molder throughout the area.

The region's "Wild West" of chaos and corruption can be traced directly to the guile of General Alfredo Stroessner, an old-fashioned Paraguayan dictator. Stroessner, son of a German Paraguayan family, served in the bloody Chaco War (1932–35) between Bolivia—which wanted a route to the sea after Chile took away its Pacific coastal zone in another war—and Paraguay, which lay inconveniently in the way to the Atlantic. More than 100,000 men lost their lives in the war, although most Americans have never heard of it. Stroessner became commander in chief of the Paraguayan army in 1951 and seized power in a 1954 coup. Keeping a firm grip on the army, Stroessner ruled through eight phony elections, until he was himself deposed in 1989 and fled to Brazil. Stroessner was known as *El Generalissimo.* He made Paraguay a safe haven for Nazi war criminals and turned the government into a personal preserve, doling out official posts and shady business deals, all with a string of kickbacks attached.

Paraguay was the archetypal "banana republic" during Stroessner's rapacious reign. "In our country the electoral process is more advanced than in the United States," went an old Paraguayan political joke. "In the United States, computers can know the results of an election just two hours after the polls close. In Paraguay we know the results two hours before the polls open."

After he seized office, *El Generalissimo*'s greedy eye quickly fell on the tariff differential between Paraguay and its neighbors, Brazil and Argentina. To protect their domestic industries, the two bigger and more richly endowed nations imposed high import duties on consumer goods and outright bans on import of some products, such as electronics. Stroessner made Paraguay's Tri-Border territory a unilateral and unofficial free trade zone. The Generalissimo renamed a hitherto sleepy fishing village on the Paraná River border "Puerto Presidente Stroessner." The village boomed as a center for criminal activity that was not merely overlooked by corrupt Paraguayan officials, but actively encouraged by Stroessner, who parceled out various crime franchises to his fellow kleptocrats. Of course the illicit trade *did* provide jobs for poor Paraguayans and helped to stifle unrest.

Since then, a cornucopia of consumer goods has poured into

Paraguay, including consumer electronics, watches, Scotch whisky, designer clothing, computers and computer software, toys, power tools, cameras, and pornographic videos. Some goods are stolen in large quantities in countries like the United States, transshipped through the Tri-Border, then passed on to markets in Central Europe and elsewhere, cleansed of their criminal origins by easily obtainable phony papers. Counterfeit knockoffs of real goods followed the real thing into the bustling free trade zone. These are cheap imitations of designer goods, sometimes merely ersatz designer labels sewn into mass-produced garb from the world's sweatshops.

Some of the goods are sold from scores of streetfront stalls in Paraguay directly to consumers from Brazil and Argentina, countries with large populations who want imported goods that are better than the shoddy products of their government-protected domestic manufacturers. Much greater quantities, however, are smuggled into the two neighboring countries. These goods move on the backs of human carriers called *hormigas* (ants), shuffling in anonymous lines over the International Friendship Bridge to Foz do Iguaçú, or are stuffed into vans, automobiles, trucks, boats, or even thrown off the bridge into the arms of coconspirators waiting below. The illicit trade has seduced many Brazilian and Argentinean customs and border officials, who nonchalantly overlook *hormigas* and bulging motor vehicles alike, so long as an appropriate bribe is pressed into their palms. Goods are also smuggled from Paraguay to be sold by street vendors and small retail shops from Rio de Janeiro to Buenos Aires.

In 1971 the Paraguayan legislature passed a law making official the international free trade zone at Puerto Presidente Stroessner. When Stroessner was booted out by another general in 1989, the city was promptly renamed Ciudad del Este, by which it is known today. Despite repeated claims of reform by a succession of Paraguayan strongmen, occasional efforts to clean up the mess by the leaders of Brazil and Argentina, and predictions that a regional trade agreement would dry up the smuggling, the Tri-Border remains mired in lawlessness. Desperately poor and getting poorer, Paraguay continues to suffer from political violence and instability, and relies on what the U.S. Department of State politely calls the "informal economy" to keep itself afloat.

Tobacco smuggling is an enormous business in Paraguay. Nearly 95 percent of the 45 billion cigarettes the country produced in 2002 were smuggled out of the country, through the Tri-Border and Bolivia to the north, to destinations throughout Latin America and the United States. The contraband weed is often marketed in the guise of popular legitimate brands. Marijuana is the major illicit export crop. There is also a vigorous traffic in stolen cars—even the former president of Paraguay, Luis González Macchi, and his wife have been accused of driving a BMW limousine and a Mercedes stolen in Brazil. Guidebooks caution tourists to take extraordinary measures to protect their vehicles from theft. Trade in stolen and counterfeit goods, from designer clothing to computer video games, flourishes. Automatic assault weapons are sold over the counter. Explosives are easily obtained, as are counterfeit documents to paper over criminal trade and lubricate international travel by criminals, terrorists, and illegal immigrants.

Although tariff reform may have caused a slight reduction in smuggling of consumer goods, drugs and firearms now flow through trails originally blazed by Stroessner's petty crooks. Drugs move from Colombia through Paraguay to destinations in Brazil, Argentina, Europe, and North America. Hezbollah and other terrorist groups piggyback the trade to raise funds for weapons and terrorist operations. Sophisticated, clandestine money-laundering systems, with links as far away as India and China and points between, are an entrenched part of the Tri-Border scene.

Émigré merchants from the Middle East and Asia have taken root in the area. Estimates of the number of Middle Easterners in the Tri-Border run as high as 30,000. No one knows exactly—the region's porous borders have always invited easy comings and goings. The majority of the Arabs are Lebanese, the bulk of them having fled Lebanon during the civil war. Most of the Arabs conduct business in Ciudad del Este, a city of remarkable squalor, but live in the nicer environs of well-kept Foz do Iguaçú.

There is much animosity toward America and sympathy for its Islamist enemies in the Islamic community here. Joyful public demonstrations broke out on news of the September 11, 2001, terror attacks. The date has been marked since by similar enthusiasms. To help fan the flames, propaganda tapes from Hezbollah's

Al-Manar television network are sold throughout the market warrens of Ciudad del Este.

Hezbollah's agents recruit sympathizers and raise funds through an informal, putatively voluntary, tax levied on Lebanese merchants, smuggling, the drug trade, gunrunning, trademark theft and counterfeiting, and the familiar spectrum of other criminal enterprises. Unlike the United States, Paraguay has no law forbidding fund-raising for terrorist organizations. Other Islamic terror groups, Hamas and al Qaeda, are also active in the Tri-Border. Organized paramilitary training goes on in the jungles and on remote plantations owned by sympathetic Arabs.

Just as in the United States, Hezbollah's cells in the Tri-Border might for the most part be described as mere support cells primarily intended to raise funds, recruit sympathizers, and acquire restricted dual-use military technology, rather than operational cells charged with conducting specific attacks. But in 1992, and again in 1994, local operatives in the Tri-Border "support" cells were activated to help mount brutal terrorist bombings in Buenos Aires, Argentina—the first against the embassy of Israel, the second against a Jewish community center. Those bombings—the largest peacetime loss of Jewish life since the Holocaust—illustrate the international reach of Hezbollah. American officials caution that the day may come when Iran's mullahs weigh the balance and decide that it is in their interest to strike a heavy blow inside America. On that day, Hezbollah cells like those in Argentina will lie waiting in the United States. And, as one U.S. official put it, "Hezbollah cells are always a bit operational."

The story of how the violence of the Middle East migrated to the New World in the form of Arab terrorists blowing Jewish children to bits in Buenos Aires begins with one of the oldest tales in the Bible and the Koran. These religious roots of Islamist anger are important to a thorough understanding of Hezbollah because, although such tales seem like ancient and faraway fables to most Westerners, the devout members of Hezbollah and its Islamist peers remember the stories as if they happened only yesterday.

Jews and Muslims claim descent from a common spiritual ancestor, Abraham (Ibrahim in Arabic), the first great voice of monotheism in the defining stories of both religions. Jews believe that thousands of years before the Common Era the first prophet wandered at God's direction out of an area that is now Iraq into the land that is now Israel, and that his descendants eventually became the Jewish people. Islam also recognizes Abraham as "a man of truth, a prophet" of God—along with other Judeo-Christian notables, including Jesus—but teaches that Jews and Christians strayed from the commands of God delivered through the prophets. According to Islam, God sent Mohammed in the seventh century C.E. as his final messenger to straighten out humanity once and for all, and Mohammed's message sealed prophecy for all time.

Told in slightly different ways, the story of Abraham's life unites Jews and Muslims, and the Arabs in particular among Muslims. Abraham's first son was born of Hagar, an Egyptian slave girl or concubine whom Abraham bedded on the suggestion of his until-then-barren wife, Sarah. That son is Ishmael "God hears" in Hebrew, Ismail in Arabic. Once Hagar was pregnant, she became insolent toward Sarah. The latter responded with such abuse that Hagar fled into the desert. An angel of the Lord persuaded Hagar to return and endure Sarah's wrath. The angel promised Hagar that she would give birth to a son called Ishmael, who would be "a wild ass of a man: his hand against everyone, and everyone's hand against him; and over all of his brothers shall he dwell."*

According to Jewish legend, Ishmael was a problem child who became estranged from Abraham and fathered the Ishmaelite people. By the time of the Middle Ages, Jewish tradition identified the Ishmaelites as Arabs. According to Islamic lore, however, Ibrahim and Ismail reconciled late in life and journeyed together to Mecca. There they rebuilt the Kaaba, a sacred shrine central to the ritual of the Islamic pilgrimage, originally constructed by the first man, Adam, but destroyed in the Great Flood. Ismail became a prophet, the father of all the Arabs, and a direct ancestor of Mohammed.

The Arab and Jewish cousins descended from the children of Abraham have contested their respective rights in the region

---

* Genesis 16:12.

known as Palestine ever since Islam erupted from the Arabian peninsula in the seventh century C.E. Both believe that God awarded them exclusive stewardship of the Holy Land. To today's Islamists, America is a nation of infidels and its presence in the region a profanation. In modern times, armed combat between Arab and Jew has ebbed and flowed in the Middle East since the first quarter of the twentieth century. The twists and turns of a century of events eventually brought this running war to Argentina, geographically and culturally remote from the scorpion's nest of the Middle East. The lesson for Americans is not that this is merely an extension of the tangled Middle East conflict, but that Hezbollah, allied with Iran, has the power to strike forcefully in the Western Hemisphere.

The early stories of the Arab and Jewish migrations to Argentina parallel each other in some ways. Drawn by the same magnet of Argentinean immigration policy, their migrations began at about the same time and for similar reasons—to escape oppression and find opportunity. Argentina's immigration policies and resulting patterns of immigration have been more similar to those of the United States than to those of any other Latin American country.

After Argentina won its independence from Spain on July 9, 1816, its leaders saw a pressing need to fill the land with settlers. Mass immigration was delayed for more than three decades, however, by a deeply ingrained animus toward non-Catholics and the bloody rule of the dictatorial *caudillo* Juan Manuel de Rosas, known as "the Caligula of the River Plate."* The Argentine Congress passed a liberalized immigration law in 1876, the same year that the introduction of refrigerated shipping methods set off a worldwide demand for Argentine beef. Agriculture and railroad development boomed, creating an urgent demand for labor. The new immigration law opened the country's gates to meet the demand, and by the turn of the century a flood of immigration re-

---

* Rosas was a ruthless tyrant who drove many of Argentina's best minds into exile. His brutal style of governing and a series of running disputes with France and England discouraged immigration to Argentina until after he was overthrown in 1852.

Bassam Hammoud *(left)*, brother of Mohammed Hammoud, and Mohammed Atef Darwiche, their cousin, counting cash from cigarette smuggling operation that netted cell millions of dollars. At the time the two were reporting income of about $12,000 a year as pizza deliverymen. *(Courtesy U.S. Department of Justice).*

Said Harb examines fake credit cards and forged driver's license during trip to Vancouver, B.C., in August 1999. Hezbollah used the fraudulent documents to finance "dual use" military equipment that was sent to Lebanon. Face of Hezbollah procurement official Mohammed Dbouk is obscured to Harb's left. *(Royal Canadian Mounted Police surveillance photo, courtesy U.S. Department of Justice).*

Teenager Mohammed Hammoud poses with AK-47 assault rifle at Hezbollah Center near his home in Bourj al-Barajneh, a suburb of Beirut. *(Courtesy U.S. Department of Justice)*.

Sheik Hassan Naserallah, secretary-general of Hezbollah. *(Courtesy U.S. Department of Justice)*.

Teenager Bassam Hammoud, Mohammed Hammoud's brother, posing with poster of Ayatollah Ruhollah Khomeini, leader of Iran's Islamic Revolution and spiritual father of Hezbollah. *(Courtesy U.S. Department of Justice).*

Mohammed Atef Darwiche *(left)*, cousin of Mohammed Hammoud, holding rocket-propelled grenade on rooftop with other Hezbollah militiamen in Lebanon. Prosecutor Ken Bell used a series of such photographs to demolish a defense witness who testified that he knew the Hammoud-Darwiche family and claimed they had nothing to do with Hezbollah.

Charlotte Hezbollah cell leader Mohammed Hammoud *(right)* and his cousin Mohammed Atef Darwiche at the White House, one of a number of similar tourist pictures seized by the FBI. Such ostensibly innocent photographs can double as surveillance pictures of terrorist targets. *(Courtesy U.S. Department of Justice).*

Mohammed Hammoud at a young age is embraced by Sheik Naserallah, with whom he had a close relationship. Hammoud was able to call Hezbollah's secretary-general direct from the United States, and have his call taken. *(Courtesy U.S. Department of Justice).*

Ken Bell fashioned innovative legal theories to use federal racketeering law and Canadian intelligence evidence. He successfully prosecuted the Charlotte Hezbollah cell, the first case to go to trial under the federal law banning providing material support to designated terrorist organizations. *(Photo by Tom Diaz).*

Iredell County Deputy Sheriff Bob Fromme was moonlighting as a security guard at JR's Tobacco Warehouse (in background). His curiosity about activities of the Hezbollah cell led to a massive investigation by the Federal Bureau of Alcohol, Tobacco and Firearms, and was central to the racketeering charges against the cell. Fromme now lectures all over the world on how local police can identify criminal activity by terrorists. *(Photo by Tom Diaz).*

Cell leader Mohammed Hammoud and Angie Tsioumas moved into this house in a middle class suburb of Charlotte after entering into a fake marriage to win Hammoud a green card. The Hezbollah cell held weekly meetings here. *(Photo by Tom Diaz)*.

The U.S. Small Business Administration helped Mohammed Hammoud and Angie Tsioumas build this gas station, part of their operation to launder cigarette smuggling money into legitimate enterprises. The couple also owned a share of a Middle Eastern restaurant and retail tobacco stores. *(Photo by Tom Diaz)*.

FBI agent Rick Schwein shows the official shield of his father, highly decorated retired agent Richard Schwein, which the younger Schwein now carries as his own. *(Photo by Tom Diaz).*

New FBI agent Rick Schwein *(right)* receives his official credentials from his father on graduation from the FBI Academy. *(FBI photo courtesy of Rick Schwein).*

Lt. Rick Schwein in uniform with coveted Ranger patch and airborne insignia. *(Photo courtesy Rick Schwein).*

Dynamic and cute, young Charlotte native Angela (Angie) Tsioumas was by all accounts the business brains behind the Charlotte cell's criminal operations. She insists her marriage to Mohammed Hammoud was genuine, even though they both were not yet divorced from other spouses at the time, and that she knew nothing of the Hezbollah connection. *(Photo by Tom Diaz).*

shaped Argentina. Between 1895 and 1914 Argentina's population grew from 3 million to 7.8 million. More than 100,000 immigrants arrived every year between 1904 and 1914. Large numbers of Jews and Arabs were among the wave.

It is estimated that at least 100,000 Middle Easterners, probably more, came to Argentina at this time. The great majority were men from the area now known as Lebanon. They left their native land for economic and social reasons—population growth, scarcity of land, demise of the silk industry, a worldwide infestation of vineyards, including those in Lebanon by the native American aphidlike insect phylloxera, and religious tensions. Most of this early wave were Christians. Many of the minority of Muslims who came in this wave married Argentinean women and converted to Catholicism. For the most part, this cohort of Arabs quickly assimilated into Argentine society.

These Lebanese immigrants eventually became established as Argentineans, and many of their families today count back to their ancestors' arrivals through five and six generations. The nature of Lebanese immigration changed over time, however, as conflict in the Middle East and eventually the Lebanese civil war prompted more and more Muslims to emigrate. By the last quarter of the twentieth century, the Tri-Border boom invited entrepreneurship, and many of the latest wave of immigrant Lebanese settled in the area. These later waves of Muslims differed from their antiquarian predecessors—much more strongly religious, they were not the least interested in converting, and were determined to preserve their religious and ethnic identity. They are the sea within which Hezbollah swims.

The Jewish community in Argentina is one of the largest in the world. It accounts for more than half of all the Jews in Latin America. The first Jews in Argentina were refugees from the Spanish expulsion of 1492. These early Jews kept their heads down and quickly assimilated into the Catholic population. Small numbers of Jews drifted into Argentina through the late nineteenth century, leaving wisps of their existence in public records. But there was no rush to the newly opened doors of Argentina until events in Russia convulsed the world of European Judaism. In March 1881 Russian revolutionaries assassinated Czar Alexander II and plunged the nation into chaos. The government found a scapegoat in the Jews of Russia, who at the time represented about half the Jews in the world. Government-inspired and supported pogroms— riotous looting, murder, and rape—broke out in 1881 and were re- peated for years, peaking in 1905, but continuing for decades. Jews were expelled from Moscow and repressive laws rescinded the small gains in civil rights that the Jews had won under Alexander II. From 1881 to 1914, more than 2,000,000 Jews fled Russia. The majority went to the United States, but others went to Palestine, Western and Central Europe, and wherever else they could find a foothold.

Just as this great migration of Jews was going on, the govern- ment of Argentina expanded its efforts to attract immigrants. It opened information offices in Europe and set up a program of transportation subsidies. A new destination was added to the list of places for Russian Jews to go. On August 14, 1889, the first large contingent of 820 Russian Jews arrived aboard the German vessel SS *Weser.* Before this group's arrival, there were some 1,500 Jews in all of Argentina. The *Weser* immigrants settled as farmers about 300 miles northwest of Buenos Aires in a community called Moi- ses Ville. Many more Jews soon followed. By 1909 there were about 70,000 Jews in Argentina, the majority of them living in the countryside.

In the 1930s emigration again became urgent for the Jews as they fled anti-Semitism in Europe and the realization of its ruth- less logic in the brutal Nazi regime of Hitler and the strutting fas- cism of its allies. At the same time, the Argentine government imposed restrictions on immigration, secretly limiting Jews in par- ticular. There, the national elite gradually turned away from its ad- miration of all things liberal and European to a narrower and more conservative nationalist orientation, sympathetic to the country's Catholic and Spanish heritage. The Argentine army learned the goose step from German military instructors and began to inter- vene openly in politics. A tinge of official sympathy for Hitlerism crept into the political, religious, and cultural leadership, finally personified in the rise of strongman Juan Perón in the 1940s. Perón instituted a kind of state populism, but openly admired the fas- cism of Benito Mussolini, and conspired to give safe haven to Nazi war criminals after the defeat of Hitler's Third Reich. That sympathetic heritage continues today, as neo-Nazi individuals and groups operate openly in Argentina. This deep vein of Jew hatred—much more blatant and deeply ingrained in the society and official institutions of Argentina than the comparatively weak neo-Nazi and anti-Semitic fringe in the United States—has complicated dealing with the actions of Hezbollah and other terror groups in Argentina.

Jewish emigration to Argentina virtually ceased with the creation of Israel after the Second World War. The Jewish population in Argentina peaked at about 300,000 in 1960 and has since slipped back to around 200,000. The great majority live in Buenos Aires, a city which—like Beirut—has been compared to Paris and its suburbs. The Jewish community in Buenos Aires is vibrant and supports many religious, cultural, educational, and communal organizations. Among them is the central Jewish community center, an organization known as AMIA—the Asociación Mutualista Israelita Argentina.

AMIA's roots go back to 1894, when the first Argentinean Jewish burial society—called a *chevra kadisha*, or sacred society—was organized in Buenos Aires. In 1935, reacting to the rise of strong Nazi sympathies, Argentina's Jews organized a political umbrella group called the Delegación de Asociaciones Israelitas Argentinas (DAIA). In 1945 a seven-story brick and granite building was constructed at 633 Pasteur Street, in the Once district, to accommodate the community's major institutions. By 1994 the AMIA headquarters was described as "the brains, the nerve center of the organized Jewish community." In addition to the headquarters of AMIA and DAIA, the building housed social service agencies where elderly Jews picked up their pensions, the headquarters of the chief rabbinate, hundreds of thousands of rare Yiddish books rescued from Russia, a theater, art collections, and the entire historical records of the Jewish community. At the time it was built, the designer was criticized by members of the community as extravagant for including the strong, bronze front doors and granite façade. He was not allowed to include in the design his plan for yet another set of iron gates.

"Someday," he said in his defense, "they will come and get us."

He was right. They did come. A century after the Jewish community first organized itself in Buenos Aires with the formation of its sacred burial society, master bomber Imad Mugniyah and his Iranian big brothers fixed their eyes on the building at 633 Pasteur. After more than a decade of practice, they knew precisely what they wanted to do and how to do it.

On the morning of July 18, 1994, a beautiful young woman named Paola Sara Czyzewski went to 633 Pasteur with her parents, Luis and Ana, to help them with their work as accountants. The twenty-one-year-old law student was determined to make her own way in life. She was quietly moonlighting to raise money for a trip to Europe, a celebratory indulgence to mark her having completed half the course of her legal studies. Paola had originally intended to follow her parents' footsteps into accounting. But after a period of studying economics, she found her real passion in the rights embodied in the law and changed her course of studies. She was a diminutive woman. Her parents compared her in a commemorative statement to *una hormiguita*, a tiny little ant, resolutely lifting above her head a weight of life far heavier than her size would seem to allow. She was also a meticulous planner, and announced in advance that she intended to have two male children. They would be named Kevin and José, she said.

"No pudo ser," her parents' commemoration of her life says simply—It could not be.

Shortly before 10:00 A.M. Paola went to the front door of the AMIA building to take a delivery of coffee the family had ordered. As she stood there, at exactly 9:53 A.M., a truck bomb exploded. In a thunderous flash it destroyed the AMIA building and killed Paola and 84 others. More than 240 were wounded. Irreplaceable books and records were destroyed. A suicide bomber had demonstrated that Hezbollah can strike where and when it chooses, even halfway around the world.

The skein of events that led to Paola Czyzewski's death winds back to the first of a series of bloody events that illustrate the difficulties that the United States faces in dealing forcefully and preemptively with terrorist organizations like Hezbollah. According to the 9/11 Commission Report, "The U.S. government . . . is working through intelligence, law enforcement, military, financial, and diplomatic channels to identify, disrupt, capture, or kill individual terrorists." As the following stories from Israel's experience show, capturing and killing terrorists preemptively may well result in retaliation. At the most superficial level of analysis these events are mere "tit for tat" exchanges from equally defensible moral positions. Yet few Americans would agree that the attacks of September 11, 2001, can be justified as appropriately equivalent responses, for example, to U.S. attacks on Osama bin Laden and his infrastructure. The real lesson is that rooting out and eliminating terrorist leaders necessarily carries with it the potential cost of further bloody attacks in revenge, until the group in question is effectively disabled or destroyed.

Yaakov Dubinsky, 30, and Yuri Preda, 33, were different from most recruits in the Israeli army. Russian Jews who had recently arrived from the ruins of the fallen Soviet Empire, the two were older men and therefore slated for noncombat reserve duty. On the night of Friday, February 14, 1992, they were among fewer than ten soldiers sleeping in their tents at a basic training camp in north-central Israel. They had been in the army only three weeks, and were part of a cadre readying the post for a larger class of recruits. They and the handful of recruits sleeping in the tents around them barely knew how to load their rifles. Most of the soldiers had gone home on weekend leave.

A small band of four Palestinian Arabs slipped through the night toward the post, armed with knives, axes, and a pitchfork. There was no fence around the camp, which was well within the Israeli borders. Just before midnight, the raiders fell upon the sleeping soldiers with a flurry of slashing blows. Dubinsky and Preda were hacked to death. A corporal who attempted to come to their aid was run through with a pitchfork and killed. The raiders slipped back into the night, taking four assault rifles with them. It was the most deadly terror attack on the military inside Israel since 1987, when a Palestinian had flown a hang glider across the border from Lebanon, landed near an outpost in northern Israel, and killed six soldiers with hand grenades and a machine gun before being killed himself.

News of the midnight attack created an immense uproar in Israel, which had already been lacerated with the surge in terror attacks that always accompanies the possibility of peace—another round of talks was pending, to follow up on a 1991 Madrid peace conference. Demands were made that the government "do something" to stop the attacks. In fact, the innermost councils of the Israeli government had already secretly set in motion an action that, although aimed at Hezbollah in particular, was intended to send a message to all terrorists, including the Al Fatah terror arm of the PLO, which had carried out the savage raid. The action was to be a "targeted killing" (a transparent euphemism for assassination) of Hezbollah's secretary-general, its most senior official.

Sheik Abbas Musawi was a cautious man. He clouded his travel with secrecy and used decoy cars to confuse his enemies. Musawi, 39, had good reason to be careful. Israel has a well-known history of tracking down and executing the leaders of its terrorist opponents, something the United States is only now learning to do. The Israeli security services began in 1956 by delivering book bombs to several high-ranking Egyptian military officers who had been sending *fedayeen* terrorists into Israel from Gaza and Jordan. They sent similar explosive volumes in the 1960s to former Nazi scientists working in Egypt to develop advanced weapons. Perhaps the best-known effort followed Prime Minister Golda Meir's order that the Mossad track down and kill the members of the PLO Black September (Fatah) group who kidnapped and murdered eleven Israeli athletes at the 1972 Munich Olympics. That project ultimately eliminated all of the known participants, save one who died of natural causes and the mastermind, Abu Daoud.* The Israeli record was tarred in 1973, however, when Mossad gunmen killed an innocent Moroccan waiter in Lillehammer, Norway, mistakenly identifying him as Ali Hassan Salameh, believed to be one of the principal architects of the Munich attack (and the man with whom the CIA's Robert Ames, killed in the 1983 bombing of the U.S. embassy in Beirut, had negotiated). By 1992, however, the Israelis had graduated to

---

* Daoud admitted his role in the Munich massacre in his 1999 autobiography, *Memoirs of a Palestinian Terrorist.*

using Apache helicopters and Hellfire missiles to eliminate terrorist leaders within striking distance of Israel.

The Israelis had noted a sharp increase in cross-border attacks
since May 1991, when Musawi took office as Hezbollah's secretary-
general. These included Katyusha rocket attacks on northern Israeli villages near the Lebanese border (the same kind of
short-range missiles are regularly fired at U.S. forces in Iraq). Well
before the midnight knife attack, Musawi's name had been for-
warded from the Mossad list of targets, called the "bank," to the
special "X Committee" of the Israeli Knesset. The X Committee
consulted with the attorney general who, acting in effect as a one-
man court, sentenced Musawi to death. An operation then was
mounted to find and eliminate the elusive target.

That was easier said than done, given Musawi's caution, but
the quarry was eventually brought to bay. On the afternoon of
Sunday, February 16, 1992, two AH-64A Apache attack helicopters
lifted off from an Israeli Air Force (IAF) base and headed north,
crossing the border into Lebanon.* Intelligence had been received
that Sheik Musawi was visiting the south Lebanese village of Jibchit. A team of an elite Israeli special forces unit, Sayeret Shaldag,
was operating within Lebanon, in the area Musawi planned to
visit. Among the supersecret unit's specialties is designating
ground targets for air strikes—an infiltrated ground team of its
members guided a dramatic 1981 IAF air strike that disabled Iraq's
almost-completed nuclear reactor at Osirak. Sayeret Shaldag
members were prepared to identify Musawi's vehicle for the helicopters.

Musawi attended a morning memorial service in Jibchit for
Ragheb Harb, an early Hezbollah activist who, after instigating
numerous attacks against Israeli forces in south Lebanon, was
mysteriously assassinated in 1983. In the early afternoon, Musawi
and his family got into an armored Mercedes limousine and set
out for Beirut with his security detail and others in an accompanying convoy of Range Rovers. Somewhere near the village of Kfar
Tufakta, about 20 miles southeast of Beirut, the Israeli Apache helicopters fell in behind the convoy.

---

* The IAF calls the Apache the Peten, Hebrew for "adder."

The Apache helicopter is an all-weather flying tank, designed to inflict terrific punishment on armored targets and on ground forces holed up in bunkers. An electric chain gun under the nose of the cockpit can fire 600 rounds of 30mm ammunition a minute, shredding its targets. The grand punch of the Israeli Apaches rested in their stubby wings, laser-guided Hellfire missiles designed to blast through the heaviest-known tank armor. At 4:30 P.M., the Musawi convoy having been identified and his Mercedes designated, the helicopter gunships opened fire.

At least half a dozen Hellfire rockets slammed into the vehicles. Musawi, his wife, and his son were incinerated in the back of the Mercedes. The explosions peeled the Range Rover escorts open like tin cans and set them afire. The two helicopters made a return pass to strafe with their cannons survivors crawling from the burning wreckage, then headed back to their base in Israel. The whole action had taken only a few minutes.

Israeli Defense Minister Moshe Ahrens made no apologies for the attack. He called Musawi "a man with a lot of blood on his hands." Yes, one official said, it was "a tragedy" that Musawi's wife and young son were with him. Nevertheless, said Ahrens, "This is a message to all the terrorist organizations that whoever opens an account with us, we will be the ones to close the account. This is true for all the bands, all the terrorist organizations, for all the leaders.

"We have learned," said Ahrens, "that terrorist organizations like Hezbollah know only one language—the language of force."

Americans who are repelled by this action—as were many Israelis—might do well to consider that the United States has engaged, or attempted to engage, in similar "targeted killing" against terrorists. In April 1986 President Ronald Reagan ordered an air strike targeting Libya's leader Muammar Qaddafi. Although Qaddafi survived the strike, an eighteen-month-old girl, alleged to be his adopted daughter, was killed and other members of his family were injured. Islamists retaliated by, among other things, killing Western hostages then being held in Beirut. More recently, the 9/11 Commission Report stated, "Policymakers in the Clinton administration, including the President and his national security adviser, told us that the President's intent regarding covert action against Bin Ladin was clear: he wanted him dead."

Musawi's death ignited Hezbollah. Tens of thousands of angry Shiites marched and chanted in Musawi's funeral procession through south Beirut, on the way to his place of rest in the Bekaa Valley. Orators at the funeral proclaimed Musawi a martyr, comparing his death to that of Hussein at Karbala, an end that Musawi had often professed to desire. Hassan Naserallah, promptly elected Musawi's successor as secretary-general, made it clear in his well-known teachings that if the Israelis knew something about force, so did Hezbollah. A fighter's strength did not lie in his weapons, but in his attitude toward death. The difference between them and us, he taught, was the willingness, indeed the eagerness, of Hezbollah's members to die on behalf of their cause. The Israelis' "point of departure is the preservation of life," he said, while "our point of departure is the preservation of principle and sacrifice." Naserallah's distinction is peculiar neither to Hezbollah nor to the Israelis. It informs broadly the radical Islamists' view that the West will retreat rather than suffer loss of life—as the United States, for example, did in Lebanon and Somalia—and accounts for the grisly practice of videotaping beheadings and mutilations, which are thought to be exceptionally frightening reminders of mortality to Westerners.

At 3:00 P.M. on March 17, 1992, Naserallah's point was driven home in Argentina. A Ford F-100 truck, loaded with 220 pounds of Semtex plastic explosive, was driven into the front of the Israeli embassy at the corner of Arroyo and Suipacha streets in downtown Buenos Aires. The resulting explosion leveled much of the embassy, shredded trees for blocks, and left a grisly debris of building materials and body parts strewn for hundreds of yards around the usually quiet area. Three nearby buildings were also destroyed, including a Catholic church and its attached school. Twenty-nine people were killed and more than 220 were wounded, including more than a dozen children lacerated by flying glass at the Catholic school.

The next day, Hezbollah took credit for the blast in a statement issued from Beirut, using the name of Islamic Jihad, Imad Mugniyah's special terror corps: "We proudly announce that the operation is one of our continuous strikes against the criminal Israeli enemy in an open war that we will not finish until Israel is wiped out of existence." When another Islamist terror group tried to take credit for the blast, Hezbollah released a surveillance video it had taken of the embassy before the blast. Hezbollah operatives have taken similar surveillance videos of government facilities in the United States, including FBI headquarters and the White House.

No one has ever been brought to trial for the Israeli embassy bombing. The resulting Argentinean investigation was a masterpiece of corruption, inefficiency, and incompetence. Only years later, largely as a result of the defection of a member of the Iranian intelligence service and the work of American and Israeli intelligence services—including communications intercepts from the Iranian embassy in Buenos Aires—has it become clear how Hezbollah was able to strike such a ferocious blow thousands of miles from its headquarters in Lebanon. Given the complexity of the operation, it is apparent that planning must have taken place long before the Musawi assassination, even if it served as a propaganda excuse for the vicious attack on civilian life.

Hezbollah's principal sponsor, Iran, began building a network in Argentina in the early 1980s, exploiting the large Muslim community, particularly in the Tri-Border. This work was done by the Ministry of Culture and Islamic Guidance, through which the Ministry of Intelligence often operates. Originally, Iranian activity in the Tri-Border was part of a program to build worldwide support for the Islamic Revolution. But with the rise of Hezbollah, Iran saw a more directly productive use for Lebanese Shiites in the region and began to organize Hezbollah cells. Hezbollah operatives in the Tri-Border meet to coordinate their activities—just as they do in the United States—in private homes, community centers, and mosques.

The man directly responsible for this cell-building operation in Argentina was the cultural attaché of the Iranian embassy in Buenos Aires, Mohsen Rabbani. His job was supposedly to provide cultural and religious information. His real job, however—like that of the Iranian ambassador to Syria in 1983, Ali-Akbar Mohtashemi—was building the local terror network. A Shiite cleric, Rabbani gave a 1991 speech in a Buenos Aires convention hall before an audience of about 100 Argentinean right-wing advocates and Shiite Muslims. The front row was reserved for officials of the Iranian embassy, who beamed as Rabbani declared in schoolboy Spanish, "Israel must disappear from the face of the earth." Rabbani's blunt statement is an articulation of the bottom line Hezbollah shares with Iran—ultimate intentions regarding the West and America's democratic ally, Israel, that have nothing to do with diplomatic disputes over where lines on maps ought to be drawn delimiting Israel's borders. Their shared goal is the complete and total elimination of the state of Israel, by extermination of its Jewish citizens if necessary. A corollary of that goal is the elimination of American presence and influence in the region.

The puppet master at the other end of Rabbani's strings in Tehran was another Shiite cleric named Ali Fallahian, the longtime Iranian Minister of Intelligence. Fallahian earned the sobriquet of "hanging judge" during the early years of Ayatollah Khomeini's Islamic Revolution for his indiscriminate handing down of the death penalty to Iranians he found to be insufficiently committed to the new fundamentalist program. For several decades following he was up to his elbows in more blood, engineering assassinations of dissident Iranians abroad and instigating terrorist attacks through surrogates like Hezbollah's Imad Mugniyah. More recently, Fallahian directed the Hezbollah operatives in Saudi Arabia who bombed the American barracks at Khobar Towers in 1996, killing 19 U.S. military personnel and wounding 515 persons, including 240 Americans. After a German prosecutor demanded Fallahian's arrest in 1997 as a result of a trial that demonstrated his involvement in the 1992 murder of four Iranian Kurdish dissident leaders at the Café Mykonos, a restaurant in Berlin, Fallahian stepped aside as Minister of Intelligence. But he stayed on as an adviser to the president of Iran. In 2002 he ran unsuccessfully for the presidency of Iran.

The decision to bomb the Israeli embassy was made—like the decision to bomb the American embassy and barracks in Lebanon—at the highest levels of the Iranian government. The approval was transmitted through Fallahian, who gave Mugniyah the green light and, through Rabbani, activated the local Hezbollah network in Argentina and the Tri-Border. The Ford F-100 truck used in the bombing was bought in the Tri-Border city of Ciudad del Este with $100 bills traced to a currency exchange house in Lebanon affiliated with a known Hezbollah supporter in the Tri-

Border. There is evidence that government officials, including police, were bribed to ensure the success of the plan.

This first significant flexing of Hezbollah's muscles outside of
Lebanon, using in-place support cells, and the inept response of
Argentinean authorities, gave Hezbollah's leaders and their Iranian uncles confidence that the terrorist group could be used as a
surrogate club whenever and wherever an attack was in both their
interests. The extension of Hezbollah's power in the Western
Hemisphere struck "like a bolt from the blue," an American diplo-
mat was quoted at the time. A whole new and troubling dimension was added to the worries of U.S. officials charged with
monitoring Hezbollah's actions and intentions. But Hezbollah was
not yet finished in Argentina.

In August 1993 a fatwa, or religious ruling, was issued by Ayatollah Ali Khamenei, who succeeded Ayatollah Khomeini as
Iran's supreme spiritual leader upon the latter's death in 1989. The
fatwa implemented a decision that had been made at a meeting of
Iran's Supreme Council for National Security, attended by Intelligence Minister Fallahian, as well as Iran's president and foreign
minister. Hezbollah was to strike again in Argentina, this time at
the AMIA building at 633 Pasteur Street. As he had done in the
embassy bombing, Fallahian turned the project over to Imad Mugniyah. The support cells in Argentina were activated and a
Lebanese suicide bomber, Ibrahim Hussein Berro, was selected.
Berro's brother, Asad Hussein Berro, had blown himself up in a
1989 suicide attack on Israeli soldiers in southern Lebanon.

Mohsen Rabbani, Iran's "cultural attaché" in Buenos Aires,
made several trips to and from Iran in the period leading up the
bombing. He also inquired around Buenos Aires about the availability of a specific brand and model of truck—the Renault Trafic,
a popular utility van. Eventually, Berro and explosives were
smuggled into Argentina through the Tri-Border, again with the
assistance of "support" cells providing local documents, transportation, and safe houses. The comings and goings of Iranian
diplomatic couriers increased during this period also. Eventually,
the Trafic van was prepared, the explosives loaded, and ballast
specially arranged to project the blast into the building to do maximum damage.

In the meantime, the Israeli government had been planning two events in Lebanon that would give Hezbollah an excuse for the AMIA bombing operation, which was well under way before the Israeli actions.

Very early on the morning of May 21, 1994, two helicopters carrying Israeli commandos took off from their bases, headed out over the Mediterranean, and then banked eastward, crossing the coast of Lebanon. The aircraft landed near the village of Qasr Naba, about 50 miles north of Israel in the Bekaa Valley. On foot, the commandos then traveled overland a short distance to the home of a senior Hezbollah official, Mustafa Dirani. In less than seven minutes the commandos broke into the home, overpowered the occupants, and left with Dirani—still in his pajamas and too surprised to use the gun by his bed—and his papers. The Israelis hoped to extract information from Dirani about the fate of Capt. Ron Arad, an Israeli Air Force navigator shot down over Lebanon in 1986. Dirani reportedly at one time had custody of Arad, and then sold him to another group. Arad's fate is a perpetually emotional subject in Israel. The Dirani raid had been off and on for months. It was finally approved by the Israeli cabinet the week before only upon solemn assurances by Prime Minister Yitzhak Rabin that the kidnap could succeed without significant bloodshed. The cabinet wanted no repetition of the ghastly deaths of Musawi's wife and young son.

Less than two weeks after Dirani's kidnapping, on June 2, the IAF returned to the Bekaa Valley. Four helicopter gunships and six jet fighter-bombers raked a Hezbollah training camp near Baalbek with machine guns, rockets, and bombs. That raid inflicted scores of casualties. "In every place where there is a possibility to strike at terror organizations, at Hezbollah, without it causing injury to civilians," said Rabin, "we have done it, we are doing it, and we will continue to do so."

Hezbollah's public reaction to these events was blistering and bombastic—its leaders were well aware that the planned AMIA bombing was well in train. They took the occasion to emit angry threats because they were confident that their threats would soon be fulfilled in bloody events.

"Retaliation is coming, and by God it will be spectacular," one

Hezbollah official told Reuters news service after the Dirani kidnapping. "This operation was a great boost to the legend of 'the long arm of Israel.' But our own arm is long too. Israel will soon find out."

Secretary-General Hassan Naserallah stated, "A thousand suicide commandos are ready to strike Israel all over the world."

One such commando was more than enough for the elderly Jews picking up their pensions, the unemployed waiting in line, the innocent civilians walking down the street, the workmen renovating the building, ordinary office people, children, and Paola Sara Czyzewski on the morning of July 18, 1994. Very early that morning, Ibrahim Hussein Berro made a call to his family in Lebanon, informing them that he was "about to join" his brother. Then he was taken to the Renault Trafic van, slipped behind the wheel, and drove it into the AMIA building at 9:53 A.M.

As in the 1992 embassy bombing, no one has been convicted of the AMIA bombing, although Rabbani, Fallahian, other Iranian officials, and a changing cast of shady Argentine characters have been charged with the crime in various Argentinean indictments. The official Argentinean investigation into the AMIA has descended from bumbling incompetence through macabre farce into a Kafkaesque labyrinth of clumsy charges and countercharges. Vast amounts of physical evidence were simply thrown into the Rio de la Plata. Key documents and recordings have disappeared. Witnesses regularly recount their sworn statements or testimony. A former president of Syrian ancestry, Carlos Menem, has been accused of taking a $10 million bribe from Iran to cover things up. Judges and other officials have been accused of similar malefactions.

The Argentine Jewish community itself is divided on whom to blame. Some denounce accusations against the Iranians as merely a cynical attempt to cover up the responsibility of local right-wing neo-Nazi anti-Semites. Ten years later, a trial limps along in episodic lurching starts and long sodden recesses. The survivors of those killed and mutilated in the bombing meet every year to commemorate their losses.

. . .

Ultimately, the lesson that America must take from the Argentine bombings has nothing to do with the Gordian knot of the Middle East conflict or the inadequacies of Argentinean justice. It is quite a bit more simple and direct. Iran and Hezbollah demonstrated forcefully in 1992 and 1994 that they could carry out major operations in the Western Hemisphere, using infrastructure from support cells exactly like those in the United States. The 9/11 Commission explicitly suggested that the role of Iran and Hezbollah in terror attacks on the United States should be more closely examined. On the day that Iran and Hezbollah decide that such scrutiny or preemptive actions by the United States against either cross the line of what they are willing to tolerate, they have demonstrated the capability to do in America what they did in Argentina.

About one month after the 1992 embassy bombing, Mohammed Hammoud flew from Lebanon to the Venezuelan island of Isla Margarita, a Hezbollah stronghold, where he and his cousins got their phony visas to enter the United States. A number of Hezbollah operatives who left the Tri-Border area after the bombing are reported to have traveled to Isla Margarita at about the same time, where they also were furnished with fake travel documents. The timing is not likely mere coincidence, but a tangible artifact of Hezbollah's decision to project its power around the world through an existing infrastructure.

American and Israeli counterterror experts warn that power can be brought to bear in America just as it was in Argentina. "You can believe there are no Hezbollah sleeper cells like this in America if you wish," an Israeli army Hezbollah intelligence expert said recently. "But our experience is that they are here."

A senior FBI official echoed the worry in this observation about the potential for deeply undercover sleeper agents.

"We think we know who most of the Hezbollah people are in America," he said. "I worry about the ones we don't know about. But I worry most about the ones that even the Hezbollah people that we know about don't know about. They are the ones who keep me awake at night."

"LIKE A SOCCER GOALKEEPER . . ."

*We're like a soccer goalkeeper. We can block 99 shots and no one
wants to talk about any of those. The only thing anyone wants
to talk about is the one that gets through.*
                                    —Dale Watson, retired FBI agent,
                                    former head of counterterrorism

Bob Clifford is a seasoned FBI agent who has spent most of his
career making terrorists look over their shoulders. Some of them
looked back a minute too late and felt the cold steel of handcuffs.
Others are still looking back because he is still on their trail. In
1994 Clifford took over the FBI's headquarters unit responsible for
collecting intelligence on the terror operations of Iran and Hezbollah. He saw the growing national pattern of Hezbollah infiltration.
Determined to disrupt the threat, he became one of the architects
of an internal revolution in how the FBI approached terrorism investigations. In the course of helping to shape this new approach,
Clifford rocked the boat at headquarters and made some
deskbound senior FBI bureaucrats squirm.

In 1997 Clifford moved to Charlotte, North Carolina. There he
met Rick Schwein, another young agent with a similar background and aggressive outlook. He saw in Rick exactly what he
thought he needed to shake Hezbollah's tree. Clifford persuaded
Schwein to come to work for him. Together they played the lead
roles in busting the Charlotte Hezbollah cell. The course of Clifford's career illustrates the problems and successes of finding in-

ternational terrorists, thwarting their plans, and bringing them to justice. It's a complicated and challenging task. Hezbollah's play-callers operate from hostile foreign territory, and finding and ex-trading fugitive terrorists is the serious game of a relentless bloodhound chasing a clever and elusive foe.

The Argentine bombings and the Charlotte Hezbollah case have in common a thread that links Hezbollah operations all over the world, from the Marine Corps barracks through Khobar Towers to downtown Washington, D.C.—where Hezbollah operatives have made surveillance videos of the FBI headquarters, the White House, Congress, and other potential targets for the signature Hezbollah calling card of high explosives and suicide. That thread has the personal attention of Hezbollah's secretary-general Sheik Hassan Naserallah.

American and other Western counterterrorism experts describe Hezbollah as the best organized terror group in the world. They often compare its structure to that of a first-class professional mili-tary unit. Local operatives—and the unwitting dupes they exploit—are the expendable foot soldiers who do the on-the-ground work, whether it be the daily grind of raising money and recruiting oper-atives or carrying out a spectacular bombing attack. But there are in-variably links back to Hezbollah's leaders in Lebanon, and in the case of major operations with international ramifications, through them to senior Iranian government officials. These distant officials are the chiefs of staff of Hezbollah's terror operations. They desig-nate targets, coordinate the movement of resources like suicide drivers and explosives, oversee intelligence and counterintelli-gence, give the final orders and religious rulings that set specific acts into motion, and handle the escapes of hot operatives. Naserallah himself pays special personal attention to his overseas operatives, such as Mohammed Hammoud.

News videos of marching ranks of fist-waving, chanting mili-tiamen, scenes of angry mobs at rallies, and Naserallah's passion-ately rhetorical public speeches might lead one to believe that Hezbollah is an emotion-driven collection of more or less crazy re-ligious fanatics. Cultural differences between Western and Arab

norms of dress and public behavior may reinforce such a conde-
scending view, typified in the occasional stereotypical cartoon one
sees of bug-eyed men with hooked noses in flowing robes and tur-
bans, waving curved swords. There is no doubt that the moral cer-
tainty bred of fanatic religious conviction absolutely propels
Hezbollah's agenda. But the conclusion that Hezbollah's behavior
is therefore mindless would be mistaken. Hezbollah's leaders are
well-educated, sophisticated, thoughtful, and among the most deliberately calculating in the Middle East. The poor soul who actually drives a truck full of explosives into a building full of
Americans may be thought of as a religious fanatic in Western
terms. But he is not crazy within the terms of reference of his own
culture, and the people who put him there are not simpleminded.
Hezbollah's masters run an efficient international operation that
skillfully manipulates the devotion to martyrdom that is increasingly a "normal" psychological state among radical Shiite Islamists.

"Naserallah is a brilliant thinker," said an Israeli intelligence
officer who has spent a good part of his career in Lebanon and
knows Hezbollah intimately. "He reads all of the world's players
and he takes everything into consideration. Naserallah understands the contemporary world and history in a sophisticated way
that is far superior to that of other so-called leaders like Yasser
Arafat, Saddam Hussein, or [Syrian president] Bashar Assad."

Sheik Fadlallah, Hezbollah's spiritual mentor and the man
who gave his personal blessing to the American embassy and Marine Corps barracks suicide bombers, was writing poetry as a
teenager that was acclaimed for its insight, beauty, and literacy.

While there are tensions between Naserallah and Fadlallah,
they are both sophisticated people with a shared vision of radical
change. They also see the world in a different time frame than
most Americans, and certainly most American politicians. Americans flip impatiently through what passes for a marketplace of
ideas in the cultural clutter of cable channels, and argue national
priorities at least every four years during presidential elections,
usually more often. The leaders of Hezbollah simply adjust their
tactics to the realities of the moment without changing their ultimate goals—eradicate the Little Satan of Israel, expel the Great

Satan of the United States from any position of influence in the Muslim world, and spread the Islamic Revolution into every land.

"They have a lot of patience," the intelligence officer said. "So what if it takes fifty years? They think in the long-term."

This combination of worldly perspicacity and millenary constancy is a dangerous mix, especially in the context of Hezbollah sleeper cells known to exist in more than a dozen American cities.

"It's not a question of whether they will hit us, but when and where they will hit us," said an American terrorism expert who has watched Hezbollah since its birth and sees it as a gun pointed at America's head with two fingers on the trigger—one Hezbollah's and one Iran's. "Right now, Naserallah reads the cards as a time to keep Hezbollah's head down and stay off America's radar screen. He and his friends in Iran know that Hezbollah has an address that is as easy to find as Afghanistan. He's being very careful to keep Hezbollah's fingerprints off any direct action against Americans, while quietly providing help to other terror groups. But Hezbollah's leaders have no doubt in their minds that we do not have the national backbone for a long-term, and I mean a really long-term, struggle. And when they sense a time of weakness or loss of resolve, when they and Iran think the balance is in their favor, they will strike and they will strike hard."

The ultimate responsibility-in-fact of these distant officials for horrible acts of terror against Americans in the past is no secret to the intelligence and federal law enforcement agencies of the United States. Some operatives, like Mugniyah, have been indicted on specific criminal charges—in his case, more than once—and are legally classified as fugitives from justice. Five Hezbollah operatives are still sought by the United States on criminal charges of supporting terrorism in the Charlotte case alone. These fugitives include Sheik Abbas Harake, Hezbollah's military commander around Beirut and the principal contact of cell leader Mohammed Hammoud, and Hassan Hilu Laqis, Hezbollah's official in Lebanon in charge of smuggling high-tech military equipment from North America. Another of the five fugitives, Ali Amhaz, who acquired the military equipment to send to Lebanon, is living comfortably in Vancouver, British Columbia, immune under Canadian law from extradition to the United States. Others have fled to escape prosecution in New York, Detroit, and other American cities.

Two Hezbollah members on the FBI's list of most wanted terrorists for their roles in the aircraft hijacking in which navy diver Robert Stethem was murdered—Ali Atwa and Hassan Izz-Al-Din—now live in Lebanon. Another member of the same hijack crew, Mohammed Ali Hammadei, was arrested in 1987 carrying explosives in the Frankfurt, Germany, airport. Germany refused to hand him over to the United States, ostensibly because he might be subject to the death penalty but actually because it was worried about the fate of German hostages taken after Hammadei's arrest who were then being held in Lebanon. Even though the United States was willing to forgo the death penalty, it agreed to smooth things over with its ally and dropped its demand for Hammadei's extradition, on the condition that he be dealt with severely if convicted. He was tried and convicted in a German court and sentenced to life imprisonment in 1989. This list of fugitives continues to grow as Hezbollah operations in America are broken up and criminal charges brought.

Hezbollah's terror bosses, foot soldiers, and hit men have evaded American justice by running to and staying safely in Lebanon and Iran, or traveling carefully elsewhere, sticking to countries not likely to hand them over to the United States. Like the so-far fruitless search for Osama bin Laden, their cases illustrate that it is one thing for a government to know that someone is responsible for an act of terror; it is another to bring that person to justice. Meanwhile, memories fade, survivors age, and the imperatives of diplomacy soften the promises of vengeance uttered by every American president from Ronald Reagan to George W. Bush.

At the outset is the problem of defining a specific criminal offense with which to charge someone in the Hezbollah chain of command (or that of any other terrorist group). In spite of the hysterical hyperbole about the threat to civil liberties from some quarters, America's approach to fighting terrorism is fundamentally one of respect for the rule of law. Given the Constitution's protections for speech and political advocacy, America's laws against terrorism must be defined in terms of specific acts. There is no such thing in the United States as a federal crime of "terrorism," "thinking terrorist thoughts," or "being a terrorist." The federal law instead defines and makes criminal specific acts that terrorists do or conspire to do, like murder, hijacking, bombing, sometimes in connection with specific locations (e.g., federal buildings, aircraft, ships) or people (e.g., government officials). This list of crimes has been expanded and refined since the 1980s as terror attacks escalated against America, significantly including knowingly giving material support to a terrorist organization. The reach of American law has also been extended to cover attacks against Americans and American interests abroad. But even if federal prosecutors have evidence that a high-ranking foreign official has been involved in a specific attack, they sometimes decide not to use that evidence in a public indictment and trial, in order to protect intelligence sources and methods that are deemed more valuable than prosecuting the person in question,* or to keep an investigation open because it leads to bigger targets.

Assuming that an international terrorist has been charged, how does the United States get him before its courts? First he has to be found. The CIA is primarily responsible for gathering foreign intelligence, but the FBI is primarily responsible for investigating terrorism crimes. The Bureau has increased its presence overseas, in response to terrorism, narcotics trafficking, and the combination known as narcoterrorism. In practice, the CIA and FBI usually— but not always, to disastrous effect—work together to find and keep track of important fugitives until the net can be thrown over them. In fact, the United States knows an impressive amount from various intelligence sources about the locations and movements of its most wanted Hezbollah fugitives.

If the world of international law were perfect, the United States would follow the conventional diplomatic route of extradition—formally asking a country in which a charged terrorist is hiding to track him down and to turn him over to the United

---

* Two examples illustrate the problem of protecting intelligence sources and methods. Suppose the American *source* is a "mole" deep within a target government or terror organization. If information the mole has provided is made public, the foreign counterintelligence can narrow its search to persons who would have had access to that information. The fewer such persons, the greater the risk of revealing it. Or, suppose the American *method* is an interception of the target's communications by any of various means from wiretap to spy satellite. If the intercepted information is made public, the target is made aware that he is being listened to, and will take steps to avoid the eavesdropping, thus shutting off the flow of information.

States for criminal trial. But in the real world, extradition of terrorists is usually not going to happen. As a general rule, an extradition treaty covering the specific crime involved is a prerequisite. Most fugitive terrorists end up in countries that are hostile to the United States and won't cooperate in such manhunts in any case—like Lebanon, Iran, prewar Afghanistan and Iraq, and others. Even friendly countries may decline to get involved, as did France and Saudi Arabia when the United States wanted to snag Mugniyah, and Germany when it arrested Hezbollah hijacker Hammadei. Moreover, a country is not required to hand over a fugitive if the host country does not have the same criminal offense on its books as the requesting country—which is why Hezbollah fugitive Ali Amhaz can safely twiddle his thumbs in Vancouver. Providing material support to Hezbollah was not a crime in Canada when the United States indicted Amhaz. Finally, many countries simply refuse to extradite if the offense carries a death penalty.

That leaves four other courses of less-diplomatic action. One is "gunboat extradition," sending in the troops as the United States did in Afghanistan and Iraq.* The other three means—short of using military force—are collectively called "irregular renditions," to distinguish them from true extraditions with all the diplomatic niceties. The first irregular rendition method is kidnapping, or "transnational forcible abduction," in the polite language of the courts. The 1960 Israeli abduction of Nazi mass murderer Adolph Eichmann, who was hiding in Argentina under an assumed name, is perhaps the best-known example.†

---

* The U.S. invasion of Panama in 1989 was also a case of gunboat extradition, since one of the three major reasons for the invasion was to bring Panamanian strongman Manuel Antonio Noriega to trial on criminal charges. Noriega was convicted of cocaine trafficking, racketeering, and money laundering. The courts rejected his challenge to the extradition by invasion.

† The United States has been involved in several such kidnappings, the most prominent of which was the case of a Mexican physician, Dr. Humberto Alvarez-Machain, who was taken at gunpoint from his office in Guadalajara by a Mexican recruited by U.S. DEA agents and flown in a private plane to El Paso, Texas. There he was arrested on charges of participating in the 1985 torture/murder of DEA agent Enrique Camarena-Suarez. Alvarez-Machain was acquitted, sued the Mexican who abducted him under a U.S. federal law called the Alien Tort Statute, and won a $25,000 damage claim, upheld on June 29, 2004, by the U.S. Supreme Court, which rejected the Justice Department's opposition to the claim.

A second method is "informal surrender," or "disguised extradition," in which the host country either looks the other way and lets United States agents come in and get their man, or quietly cooperates and hands him over without the bother of formal paperwork. In either case, the country often wants to help the United States (whether for fear or favor) but is leery of the reaction of its own populace. Pakistan has cooperated in several such surrenders. Ramzi Ahmed Yousef, who masterminded the 1993 World Trade Center bombing and spun other terror schemes for al Qaeda elsewhere, was arrested in February 1995 by FBI agents and Pakistani police, then informally spirited out of the country to stand trial in America. Likewise, Khalid Sheik Mohammed, who claimed credit for planning the September 11, 2001 attacks, was tracked down and arrested by FBI and Pakistani security agents in March 2003, then hustled to a secret location for extensive interrogation by American agencies. In both cases, Pakistani officials sought to downplay American involvement.

The final means is luring the target out by some kind of subterfuge. In 1987 FBI agents of the elite Hostage Rescue Team enticed Fawaz Yunis, a fugitive Lebanese Amal terrorist, onto a yacht in the eastern Mediterranean, where he thought he was going to take part in a drug deal. Instead, the yacht was steered into international waters, he was arrested, transferred to a U.S. Navy ship, and later flown from an aircraft carrier back to Washington, D.C. There he stood trial and was convicted for his part in a 1985 Royal Jordanian Airline hijacking involving several U.S. citizens.

Bob Clifford is a genuine terrorist hunter who—with the Navy SEALs, the Naval Investigative Service, and the FBI—has participated in all of these methods of capture.

Johnny Justino Peralta Espinoza slept only fitfully in the deep dark of the fourth hour of Sunday morning, July 19, 1992, more tired than he had ever been in his life. He could not lose himself in the sweet sleep of rest, but tossed fitfully on the rude bed in his mother's house in Villa Nuevo Potosi, a suburb of La Paz, Bolivia. Johnny Peralta was a fugitive and a sick man. He was only vaguely conscious of the dogs barking in the distance. It is not an uncommon sound around La Paz, where more than 300,000 dogs roam freely.

It was freezing cold outside the house. July is midwinter in La Paz, and at an altitude of two miles, La Paz is the highest capital city in the world. Johnny was wracked by the symptoms of his tuberculosis—night sweats, a hacking cough that worsened in the morning, and a debilitating breathlessness compounded by the thin air. His kidneys were failing, a common consequence of the spread of tubercular infection throughout the body.

Peralta had been on the run for more than three years, hunted since May 24, 1989, when he had coldly machine-gunned to death two young American missionaries. The pair—Jeffrey Ball and Todd Wilson, twenty-year-olds from Utah—were shot down in front of their apartment in a poor La Paz neighborhood as they returned from a day of the door-to-door missionary work that is traditional to their faith, the Church of Jesus Christ of Latter-day Saints, popularly called the Mormon church. Peralta was one of the leaders of the Zarate Willka Armed Liberation Front, a Bolivian terrorist group. The Front—named after Pablo Zarate Willka, an Aymara Indian leader who led the fight against expropriation of Indian land in 1899—also set off a dynamite bomb near then-Secretary of State George Shultz's motorcade during his visit to La Paz in August 1988. To the extent the Zarate Willka Armed Liberation Front had a philosophy, it was an irrational combination of Maoism and nativism similar to that of the ultraviolent Sendero Luminoso of neighboring Peru and with whom it was suspected of having links.

The U.S. government responded forcefully to the murders. It posted a $500,000 reward for information leading to the capture of Johnny Peralta. The FBI sent a team of six experts to La Paz with lie detectors, ballistics laboratory equipment, and other technical tools to help track down the killers. By July 1989 eight members of the Zarate Willka Armed Liberation Front had been arrested. But triggerman Peralta and several other leaders remained at large. In January 1991 FBI agent Bob Clifford returned and took up residence in Bolivia. He brought his young wife with him. In spite of the obvious danger—several Bolivian judges resigned from the case after receiving death threats—the couple lived on the local economy and out in the open. Clifford, fluent in Spanish, created his own special unit of the Bolivian police to track down the fugitive terrorists.

The determined American and his Bolivian team kept Johnny Peralta on the run. Peralta's brother, Juan Domingo Peralta, was killed in a shoot-out in July 1990. But the coin had two sides. About the size of Texas and California combined and the poorest country in Latin America, Bolivia is a land of dramatic geographical contrasts—the high altitude aridity of the Altiplano plateau, two chains of the volcanic Andes Mountains, the semitropical northeastern flank of the Andes, and the jungles, savanna, and tropical rain forests of the lowlands. Peralta's trail led through them all. "We could be in the Altiplano one day, and the jungle the next," recalls Clifford, a bright-eyed and energetic man whose youthful face and cheerful demeanor belie a tough core and a creative vigor that has bedeviled a succession of the world's most ruthless terrorists.

What was worse, however, was that Peralta always seemed to be one step ahead of Clifford's team. "We would hit a house where we had gotten word Peralta was hiding," says Clifford. "Boom, we'd go in . . . and we'd miss him by just fifteen minutes. The bed would be warm, maybe food on the table. But no Johnny Peralta." Peralta's counterintelligence was trumping Clifford's intelligence. But Peralta's string of luck was about to run out. The dogs barking in the distance were heralds of a tight-lipped band of men creeping through the inky black of the night.

Convinced that Peralta had somehow penetrated his team, Clifford instituted a new procedure that night. When the unit assembled for its briefing before the raid, the FBI agent made an announcement. No one would go in or out of the building. No one would make a phone call. The lockdown worked. It later turned out that one of the officers of the elite team was related to one of the defense attorneys defending members of the Zarate Willka Armed Liberation Front. Unable to pass on a warning, he could only wait with the others. When the raiders surrounded the home of Johnny Peralta's mother and crashed through the door at 4:30 A.M., the fugitive was still sleeping restlessly in his bed.

The hunt for Johnny Peralta was neither the first nor the most spectacular U.S.-aided terrorist manhunt in Bolivian history. That was the successful 1967 hunt for the Argentine doctor-turned-revolutionary, Ernesto "Che" Guevara, who tried to transplant Fidel Castro's Cuban revolution onto Bolivian soil.* But the less-well-known pursuit and capture of Johnny Peralta reflects the determined character of Bob Clifford. It was one of many building blocks from which he devised a creatively dynamic approach to the problem of terrorists hiding in the open in America. That approach has been pivotal in quietly bringing down Hezbollah operatives all over the United States, including Mohammed Hammoud and his Charlotte cell. Most of this work has never been reported and much of it never will be in any but the most general terms—the FBI is keeping a tight lid on the story of a decade of terrorist disruptions in order not to hazard ongoing investigations.

Bob Clifford radiates an extraordinarily positive outlook. At the same time he is remarkably deferential about his life and his work, a combination Eagle Scout, altar boy, and sports team leader. His upbeat nature is a heartening reminder that there are good people dealing with the worst the world has to offer who refuse to lose their own values and sense of self. Like FBI agent Rick Schwein and federal prosecutor Ken Bell, Bob Clifford is a family man to the core, devoted to his wife, his children, and classic American family values.

Clifford has a lean frame, jet black hair, and a boyish face in which dark, intelligent eyes dance to life when he talks about terrorism. Some of Clifford's buoyancy is undoubtedly the result of

---

* There are some similarities between the hunts for Peralta and Guevara. A special battalion of the Bolivian army was created with the help of U.S. Green Berets to track down Guevara and his band. Guevara was asthmatic and so, like Peralta, had his troubles breathing in the Altiplano and humid jungle alike. But unlike Peralta, Guevara was betrayed by the Bolivian peasants among whom he moved. He was captured near the hamlet of Higuera and summarily executed by the Bolivian army. His hands were cut off so that fingerprints could prove that he had indeed been disposed of. He and his comrades were buried in an anonymous grave. Thirty years later, Guevara's mortal remains were dug up and entombed at a memorial site in Cuba—not in Havana, where his presence might have been a rebuke to the sullied purity of *La Revolución,* but tucked safely away in the provincial capital of Santa Clara.

growing up in the small town of Ojai, California, where his family moved after he was born on March 12, 1959, the third of eight children, in the surfer city of Oxnard. If ever there were an idyllic community that embodies the dream of California—not a sleepy burg like Mayfield, RFD, but a smartly progressive hamlet where the kids excel in sports and make straight A's, and the moms and dads excel in their careers and civic virtue—Ojai is it. About 65 miles northwest of Los Angeles, the town of some 8,000 residents lies snuggly within the Ojai Valley. Ten miles long and three miles wide, the valley is distinguished by its east–west orientation (as opposed to the usual north–south line of California's mountains). The result is spectacular sunrises and sunsets that paint the surrounding hills and mountains with a magic palette, known locally as the "pink moment." Hollywood director Frank Capra was so taken with Ojai's beautiful setting that he chose it as the film location of the mythical Tibetan valley, Shangri-La, in his 1937 adaptation of James Hilton's novel *Lost Horizon*. Any kid growing up in Ojai has to work hard to develop a negative attitude. Bob Clifford played varsity football (tailback and safety), ran the 400-meter relay, and hiked with the Boy Scouts in the nearby Los Padres National Forest.

Another influence on Clifford's life has been his Catholic faith. After attending eight years of public school, he finished his secondary education at a private Catholic high school, then went on to undergraduate study at Saint Mary's College of California. With a current enrollment of 3,000 students, Saint Mary's is another example of the best of California dreaming. Located in rolling foothills about 20 miles east of San Francisco, its California Spanish Mission architecture is dominated by St. Mary's chapel with its typical bell tower and accompanying plaza and green quadrangle. Cozy courtyards, shady arcades, and aromatic groves of redwood and eucalyptus provide quiet places for thought and study. Saint Mary's is California's Catholic counterpart of North Carolina's Baptist Wake Forest, where prosecutor Ken Bell grew up as a faculty brat and later studied law. The college's religious values fit nicely into Clifford's family background. His mother was born in the wealthy Mexican mining town of El Oro, near Mexico City, and was sent north to be educated at College of the Holy Names in

Oakland, California. His paternal uncle, Father Richard Clifford, is a Maryknoll missionary priest in Mérida, in the Yucatán Peninsula of Mexico.

Bob Clifford considered a life in the missionary priesthood—a calling that also tempted legendary FBI counterterrorism expert John O'Neill, who perished in the collapse of the World Trade Center towers.* Clifford was drawn alternatively to a diplomatic career in the foreign service. In the end, however, the influence of his father's experience as a navy Seabee proved strongest.† Clifford was accepted by the navy's Officer Candidate School in Newport, Rhode Island, and was commissioned a naval officer on October 1, 1981, his first assignment to the destroyer fleet.

After a period of service with the "greyhounds of the sea"—also known as the "tin cans"—he was assigned as an intelligence officer to Naval Special Warfare Group One (NSWG 1) at the Naval Amphibious Base (NAB) in Coronado, California. The navy's special operations forces are its elite SEAL (Sea, Air, Land) teams. NSWG 1 is the headquarters for the odd-numbered SEAL teams, and NSWG 2 at NAB Little Creek, Virginia, the even-numbered teams. Like fellow FBI agent Rick Schwein, Clifford was not an "operator," but was rather a staff officer responsible for preparing target folders and helping to plan what the SEALs call "direct action missions"—armed assaults of the bang-bang type most people envision when they think of special operations.‡ Although the SEALs are a naval unit, their direct action missions

---

* O'Neill warned of the threat from Osama bin Laden soon after becoming chief of the FBI's counterterrorism section in 1995. However, his forcefully blunt personality and the vigor with which he tried to wake up official Washington alienated key FBI executive bureaucrats. His career frustrated, after several raging altercations about his aggressive pursuit of terrorists, O'Neill retired from the FBI in 2001 after 30 years of service with the Bureau. He had begun work as chief of security for the World Trade Center the week before he was killed.

† "Seabee" or "CB" stands for "construction battalion." The navy's construction battalions were originally created in 1941, recruited mostly from civilians in the building trades. Their mottos, "We Fight, We Build," and "Can Do" capture their history of constructing under fire and fighting back through all of the nation's wars since then. The Naval Construction Forces are active today around the world, building such military infrastructure as airfields, barracks, and port facilities.

‡ Clifford's service with the SEALs is a link to his father's service—the earliest predecessors of today's SEALs were underwater demolition teams recruited from the ranks of the Seabees to clear obstacles from Second World War landing beaches.

take them to both land and water targets. They arrive by any variety of air, land, or water means from parachute to submarine. Among Clifford's duties was planning for operational details, such as how to get in, how to get out, and what kind of indigenous help was available for the execution of these missions.

The missions and their particulars, like most special operations, are classified. Clifford will only say that he "did a lot of deployments," the experience of planning for which he later found helpful in his FBI career. However, it is worth noting that this was during the period of Hezbollah's violent birth, a time when serious turmoil in the Middle East—including Hezbollah's widespread taking of American hostages—prompted a number of SEAL missions in the area.

In November 1985 Bob Clifford was released from active duty and became a special agent with the Naval Investigative Service (NIS), where he remained until he joined the FBI in mid-1988. The NIS has multiple roles, from investigating crimes involving the navy to counterintelligence operations. Clifford was involved in the latter when he met the woman who was to become his wife. It was Columbus Day, October 12, 1987, and he was in line at the San Diego International Airport waiting for a flight to Washington, D.C., where he was scheduled to attend "double agent training" at the CIA. He ended up sitting next to the cute girl he noticed in line in front of him, Deirdre Durkin, from Bedford, Westchester County, New York. Her first take on Clifford was disconcerting. The flight was delayed and when he opened his briefcase, she glimpsed a handgun and a rosary. What is this guy, she asked herself, Mafia? They chatted and she mentioned that she had worked with Maryknoll in the Yucatán, where she met a tall, blue-eyed priest. The priest was Bob's uncle, Father Richard Clifford. The two got along famously until it was announced that the flight had been canceled. She ended up on one plane to New York, he on another to Washington. They kept in touch and on July 2, 1989, were married in Saint Patrick's Church in Bedford. A year later she was living in Bolivia with a husband whose job was hunting down terrorists.

Clifford's next posting was in August 1992 to the FBI's Washington Field Office squad specializing in irregular renditions—

shortly after Mohammed Hammoud's arrival in America. Although neither Clifford nor anyone else knew of Hammoud at the time, he and others in the FBI were well aware of the March 1992 Hezbollah bombing of the Israeli embassy in Argentina. Clifford's focus for the time being was elsewhere, however. Clifford was handed the file on Omar Mohammed Rezaq, a brutal Abu Nidal hijacker and murderer who was about to get an obscenely early release from a Maltese prison. Designated the lead case agent, Clifford was told to find a way to bring Rezaq before the bar of American justice.

Rezaq's terror spree began shortly after EgyptAir Flight 648 lifted off at 9:06 P.M. from the runway at Athens International Airport on the night of November 23, 1985. The 98 passengers and crew aboard expected an uneventful three-hour flight over the Mediterranean to Cairo. With the exception of the pilot and some of the crew, no one on the aircraft knew that scarcely six weeks earlier American naval jet fighters had forced the same plane to land at a NATO air base in Sigonella, Sicily, in a breathtaking American attempt to use military force to capture terrorist fugitives.* Now the airplane, Boeing 737-200 No. 21191/450, was about to become the scene of one of the deadliest air hijackings in history.

About 45 minutes into the flight, three of the passengers—Rezaq and two armed companions—stood up, pulled firearms from plastic bags, and started shouting frenzied commands. (Greek authorities later insisted that the passengers had gone

---

* In October 1985 four members of the Palestine Liberation Front, an offshoot of Yasser Arafat's PLO, hijacked the Italian cruise ship *Achille Lauro*. They shot and killed Leon Klinghoffer, a wheelchair-bound American Jew, then threw his body overboard. The ship anchored off Egypt before a navy SEAL rescue mission could be carried out. Egyptian president Hosni Mubarak stiff-armed the American request that the terrorists be handed over. Falsely claiming that the hijackers were no longer in Egypt, Mubarak arranged for them and the hijacking's mastermind, PLF leader Mohammed (Abu) Abbas, to escape to Tunisia. The United States learned of the pending flight. F-14 Tomcat fighters intercepted the 737 and forced it to land at Sigonella. The plane was surrounded by U.S. Delta Force commandos, who were in turn surrounded by Italian paramilitary *carabinieri*. The Italians refused to hand Abu Abbas and his terror team over to the Americans. Washington ordered the Delta Force to stand down. The Italians took custody of the terrorists and immediately allowed Abu Abbas to flee. He thumbed his nose at the United States for the next eighteen years, eventually ending up a guest in Saddam Hussein's Iraq. Captured by U.S. forces on April 15, 2003, Abbas died of a heart ailment in a prison outside of Baghdad on March 8, 2004.

through five screenings before boarding the aircraft.) One of Rezaq's companions rushed the cockpit while the leader, a man called Salem, collected the passengers' travel documents. When Salem got to a plain-clothed Egyptian air marshal, a furious gunfight erupted. Salem was killed; the marshal and several flight attendants were wounded. Rezaq then took command of the operation and the hijacked plane landed at Luqa Airport in Malta for fuel. He separated out the Israeli and American passengers. When authorities stalled on his requests for fuel and a doctor, Rezaq announced that he was going to start shooting passengers. He threatened to kill one victim every fifteen minutes until his demands were met.

True to his word, Rezaq forced five passengers to the front door—two Israeli women, two American women, and an American man—then shot each of them in the head at intervals, throwing them out the door onto the tarmac. One Israeli woman, Nitzan Mendelson, and one American woman, Scarlett Rogenkamp, were killed. The other three recovered from their wounds. Each time he shot one of the hostages, Rezaq danced, sang, and told jokes. He placidly asked a flight attendant for a sandwich after one of the shootings.

Meanwhile, a team of 80 commandos from Egypt's supposedly elite 777 unit—not highly thought of by the U.S. Special Forces who had trained them—were airlifted to Malta in a C-130 Hercules. The Americans sent a crack aircraft breaching team from the Delta Force, but the Egyptians impetuously attacked before the team arrived. In an operation that a U.S. federal appeals court described as "singularly incompetent," the 777 commandos set off an excessive charge of explosives under the plane, then waded in, shooting indiscriminately. The plane burst into flames. At the end of the carnage, two crew members and 58 passengers were dead, most from smoke inhalation. Rezaq was shot in the chest and alone survived among the three hijackers.

The U.S. Justice Department wanted to try Rezaq, but reluctantly deferred to Malta. Rezaq pled guilty to nine charges, including murder and attempted murder, and was sentenced to 25 years in prison. But in 1992 American authorities learned that Malta, reacting to pressure from perennial troublemaker Libya, was considering an early release for Rezaq. Clifford was put on the trail. Working with partner Kevin Foust, fresh from the drug squad, and Justice Department lawyers, Clifford interviewed survivors, studied all the records, and made a case of air piracy against Rezaq. It was a charge that was completely different from Rezaq's murder convictions and thus avoided the potential legal defense of double jeopardy—being tried twice for the same offense, forbidden under American constitutional law.* Suddenly and without warning to the United States, Malta released Rezaq in February 1993, ostensibly as part of a general amnesty. Clifford scrambled and put out a "red notice" on the Interpol network, alerting authorities that Rezaq was at large and wanted. The FBI team found out by way of a tip from the Russians that Rezaq, using his mother's maiden name, had flown to Ghana. Clifford flew there hoping to get Rezaq, whom the Ghanaian government had taken into custody. But Ghana stalled the American request to hand him over for prosecution.

There followed several months of delicate negotiations, during which a plan was developed to put Rezaq in American hands. The Americans eventually learned that Rezaq was leaving Ghana and would make a stop in Lagos, Nigeria, en route to Sudan. The Nigerians were willing to cooperate in an informal extradition. On July 15, 1993, Clifford, Foust, and a team of seven other agents flew in an unmarked Gulfstream jet to Lagos accompanied by a doctor and an Arabic interpreter. The plane was immediately surrounded by armed Nigerian troops. Informal diplomacy being what it is, the agents feared that the Nigerians might have had a change of heart. Their tension was relieved when Clifford observed that the Nigerian soldiers were pointing their guns away from the airplane and not toward them. Shortly thereafter, the flight from Ghana, now with Rezaq and undercover U.S. intelligence agents on board, landed. At 10:24 P.M. Nigerian security officials hustled a bewildered Omar Mohammed Rezaq from the transient lounge over to the waiting FBI plane.

"We're taking you to the United States," Clifford informed Rezaq. "What is your name?"

---

* The Fifth Amendment provides: ". . . nor shall any person be subject for the same offence to be twice put in jeopardy of life or limb. . . ."

"Omar Mohammed Ali," Rezaq replied.

"Is there something more?" the translator asked.

"Rezaq," the terrorist replied. A quick check of fingerprints confirmed his identity. They had bagged their man.

"No harm will come to you," Clifford, an exceedingly courteous man, assured Rezaq. "You will be treated humanely and professionally."

Clifford is a man who regularly addresses others with the phrases "yes, sir" or "no, ma'am." A colleague once made fun of his courteous good-natured manner. Clifford's eyes hardened into a laser stare and he shot back, "Don't ever confuse kindness with weakness."

Rezaq was sentenced to life imprisonment by a federal judge in Washington on October 6, 1996. The judge took the unusual step at the end of the trial of complimenting Clifford and Foust on the public record for their professional work. In the meantime, the FBI had redirected the point of Bob Clifford's spear. It was now aimed directly at Hezbollah in the United States.

Clifford was transferred to FBI headquarters in November 1994 and put in charge of the Iran/Hezbollah Unit of the International Terrorism Section. Down in Charlotte, Mohammed Hammoud was in his first year of smuggling cigarettes. He would enter into the bonds of the first of his three phony marriages the following month. Hammoud was still successfully flying beneath the radar. Said Harb, his friend and more ostentatious coconspirator, would pop up briefly on the FBI's screen, unbeknownst to either. But the brief focus on Harb would fade without action until Clifford's later transfer to Charlotte.

Until his assignment to the Hezbollah unit, Bob Clifford had been a can-do, kick-down-doors, make-things-happen kind of guy. Now he found himself in the completely different and much more conservative culture of FBI headquarters. Spread out before him were the crown jewels, the intelligence that the FBI had on Hezbollah and its members in the United States. This closely held information was derived from a vast variety of sources. It included, among other things, confidential informants at home and abroad (including Lebanon), walk-in tips from disaffected members of the Lebanese community in the United States, CIA reports on activity and people overseas, communications intercepts by the sophisticated electronic ears of the National Security Agency and other agencies, domestic wiretaps, and plain old shoe-leather work by FBI field agents. A career FBI intelligence analyst named Mark Connor—whom Clifford called, among other things, "senior chief" and "the Druid"—helped Clifford correlate and make sense of it all. What they saw was that Hezbollah was clearly and deliberately infiltrating the United States, at the direction of Hassan Naserallah. At the time Hezbollah operatives were most active in New York City, but they were spreading out, popping up in new locations.

Knowing Hezbollah's violent history, conscious of a second major bombing in Argentina, and aware that a similar Hezbollah infrastructure was building up in the United States, the next question was obvious to a man who had chased terrorists through the jungle and flown halfway around the world to arrest a fugitive hijacker. What are we going to do about these guys? The answer at first was . . . not much.

"I saw that we had a tremendous number of cases," Clifford recalls. "But the unit's approach up until then was not proactive. It was in the old foreign counterintelligence mode. Penetrate them, find out what they are doing, keep track of who is talking to whom, figure out what they are planning. But basically we were just keeping a lot of records on Hezbollah. We weren't going after them aggressively."

Clifford had just run into the inevitable result of two big legal problems that plagued the FBI in those days, before the shock of September 11, 2001. These legal roadblocks had forced the Bureau into the passive approach of simply monitoring potential terrorists unless and until they could be caught in the act of blowing something up or other equally bad behavior. The influence of one of these legal obstacles was so strong that it affected the mind-set of a generation of FBI managers. Many of them stubbornly refused to allow the use of key intelligence information to prosecute terrorists on criminal charges for fear they would cross a line that could be dangerous to one's career. The result contributed to the failure to stop the al Qaeda attacks on America in 2001.

The first legal problem the action-oriented Clifford faced was that at that time there was no federal law prohibiting what many Hezbollah members in the United States were doing—milking the American cow to finance their terror schemes while at the same time organizing themselves into local cells. Talk, even angry anti-American demagoguery, is protected speech in America. And until 1996, it was perfectly legal to raise funds for Hezbollah and other foreign terrorist organizations, or even to give them other support like training or supplies. The issue was repeatedly brought to the attention of Congress, which for years refused to act. Vocal and well-organized opponents of banning fund-raising—many well intentioned—argued that the money sent abroad was intended for the social welfare programs that Hezbollah and other terror groups often operate to cultivate local support. Civil libertarians proclaimed that a fund-raising ban would violate the constitutional rights of the donors to express their support for Hezbollah's "political wing" with their pocketbooks. The opponents were by no means limited to Muslims—one of the strongest blocs in opposition was Irish American supporters of the Irish Republican Army (IRA).

In the meantime, millions of dollars ostensibly given in the name of charity and supporting "political expression" were in fact diverted by Hezbollah and other terrorist organizations to more lethal purposes—buying explosives and weapons, arming paramilitary militias, and underwriting violent operations like suicide bombings. As a practical matter, every dollar given to a terrorist group like Hezbollah is "fungible," or interchangeable with every other dollar. While a person in the United States might say (and even think) that he was giving a dollar for "widows and orphans" or donating to promote Hezbollah's political activity, in fact Naserallah and Hezbollah's leaders are free to use the money for whatever purpose they choose, including making bombs and buying guns. The asininity of this loophole finally persuaded Congress in 1996 to make it a crime to give "material support" to any foreign organization that is specifically "designated" as a terrorist group by the U.S. Department of State.* Hezbollah was among the

* The prohibition against providing material support was enacted into law when President Clinton signed the Antiterrorism and Effective Death Penalty Act on April 24, 1996.

first such groups designated in October 1997. Use of the law and a number of related laws aimed at cutting off the flow of terror funds has been greatly expanded as major tools in the global war against terrorism since September 11, 2001.

In 1994, however, there was no such law. The FBI could not interfere with Hezbollah's members unless it caught them committing crimes. And in fact, many of them were indeed committing conventional crimes, just as Mohammed Hammoud and his cell were secretly doing in Charlotte. And like Hammoud, they were not violent crimes that would attract the local police, and generally not big enough to interest federal prosecutors.

"We could see that a tremendous number of these Hezbollah people were involved in various forms of criminal fraud," says Clifford. "We could see that. But the prevailing view, the conventional wisdom, was that we could not act on that information. We could not go after these guys who were breaking the law right and left."

The major reason for this astounding immunity of lawbreakers was the existence of what came to be known colloquially as "the Chinese Wall." This notional wall in effect divided the FBI into two separate agencies that were allowed to talk to each other only under strictly controlled circumstances. Those circumstances were *specifically* designed to limit the amount of information and guidance exchanged from one side to the other. On one side of the wall were the intelligence units, like Clifford's Hezbollah unit. On the other side of the wall were the criminal units, the vast bulk of the FBI agents who were responsible for investigating crimes and working with federal prosecutors to put criminals in jail. If the intelligence side wanted to talk to the criminal investigation side about the details of a case, it had to go up through a special chain of command on its side to get permission to talk to the other side, and vice versa. The further up one got in the chain of command, the more cautious were the decision makers. The matter was actually even more complicated than this summary, because the Chinese Wall also affected the relationship between the FBI and the CIA, and their relationships with the Department of Justice—prosecutors could not see intelligence files or even talk to FBI or CIA intelligence agents without permission under tightly regulated ground rules—and so on throughout the entire official counterterrorism structure of Washington.

The Chinese Wall was the fastidious creation of desk-bound government lawyers and a handful of hypersensitive federal judges, who misinterpreted the law in their zeal to micromanage the way the federal law enforcement offices worked with intelligence offices. These guardians thought it was actually a good thing to make the process of sharing intelligence difficult and complicated, because they mistakenly believed that these measures were necessary to protect the purity of a 1978 law called the Foreign Intelligence Surveillance Act, known as FISA. Congress passed this law in response to the discovery of abuses by the FBI and other government intelligence agencies, who were found to be conducting "black bag" jobs (breaking into such places as embassies) and monitoring U.S. citizens without going through the federal court system to get warrants for the searches and wiretaps. The intelligence agencies were relying on what they argued was inherent authority within the executive branch to protect the nation against threats to national security. They professed the not unreasonable fear that having to reveal what they were up to in the regular court system inevitably would tip off targeted foreign governments and other foreign powers, like terrorist organizations, that they were being watched and spell out exactly how. On the other hand, the attempted use in some domestic criminal prosecutions of information gathered in such intrusions without judicially issued warrants raised civil liberties concerns. The Supreme Court ruled in a 1972 case, *United States v. United States District Court,* that surveillance in domestic matters requires some form of prior judicial review. But it also recognized that cases involving foreign powers might raise different questions. It suggested the Congress review the issue and decide whether different rules were appropriate for national security matters involving foreign powers.

To resolve the dilemma—protecting domestic civil rights while preserving the secrecy of intelligence and counterintelligence operations against foreign powers in the United States— Congress set up a special secret court, the Foreign Intelligence Surveillance Court (FISC). The FBI—by way of the U.S. Attorney General—could get from this court special warrants (FISA orders) for searches and wiretaps only when a "foreign power" was involved.* For all other criminal cases, the FBI would still go to ordinary federal district courts (called "Article III" courts) for traditional search warrants.

But the bureaucratic Lilliputians soon set about pinning the law enforcement Gulliver to the mat. "It is quite puzzling," wrote the Foreign Intelligence Surveillance Court of Review (FISCR)—a special court of appeals charged with reviewing the actions of the FISC—when it finally straightened the matter out in 2002, "that the Justice Department, at some point during the 1980s, began to read the statute as limiting the Department's ability to obtain FISA orders if it intended to prosecute the targeted agents." The issue that the Justice Department focused on was not protecting ordinary American citizens from the use of intelligence information, but the use of intelligence information in *any* criminal investigation and subsequent prosecution. In other words, information gained through FISA warrants could be used only for some vague information-gathering purpose in cloud cuckoo land, but not for the nitty-gritty job of putting people in prison—even though the statute itself and the record of its debate in Congress made clear that the very actions of the foreign powers being monitored were invariably criminal acts in and of themselves. Moreover, some of the lawyers at the Justice Department further confabulated that strict measures had to be taken to be sure that federal prosecutors and criminal investigators would not try to evade the rules by going to the FISC for FISA warrants instead of Article III courts for ordinary warrants in order to get information that they secretly intended to use in criminal prosecutions of U.S. citizens. The real enemy seemed to be not the terrorists who clearly relished killing Americans, but the FBI and federal prosecutors who devoted their lives to protecting Americans, often at great personal risk.

The "exact moment" when the first brick in the Chinese Wall was laid down is "shrouded in historical mist," wrote the FISCR appeals court. But the wall was built up, strengthened, and widened brick by brick until it was the high hurdle Bob Clifford

---

* In fact, the FISC consists of selected sitting Article III federal judges who are assigned to serve as an extra duty.

faced in 1994. The bigger tragedy of the Chinese Wall is that it undoubtedly prevented the FBI from effectively following up on two cases that probably would have led to the heart of the al Qaeda conspiracy that resulted in the attacks of September 11, 2001. Two examples make this point.

The first was the case of Khalid Almidhar and Nawaf Alhazmi, two of the September 11 aircraft hijackers. The CIA began collecting information that linked the two to al Qaeda terrorism as early as 1999. There is some dispute about exactly what information the CIA sent to the FBI and when—including a published allegation that the CIA deliberately held back some critical information in order to keep the case out of the hands of the FBI's bulldog, John O'Neill—but it is certain that by August 23, 2001, the CIA had informed the FBI that Almidhar and Alhazmi were on the loose in the United States. FBI headquarters directed the FBI New York field office to open an *intelligence* investigation to try to find Almidhar. A New York agent realized the alarming importance of the matter, given Almidhar's known terrorist background, and tried to convince headquarters to open a *criminal* investigation, which would have mobilized vastly greater resources. The reply from headquarters sums up the devastating effect of the Chinese Wall:

> If al-Midhar is located, the interview must be concluded by an intel [intelligence] agent. A criminal agent CAN NOT be present at the interview. This case, in its entirety, is based on intel. If at such time as information is developed indicating the existence of a substantial federal crime, that information will be passed over the wall according to the proper procedures and turned over for follow-up criminal investigation. [emphasis in original]

The frustrated New York agent replied with chilling foresight:

> Whatever has happened to this—someday someone will die—and wall or not—the public will understand why we were not more effective and throwing every resource we had at certain "problems." Let's hope the [FBI's] National

> Security Law Unit (NSLU) will stand behind their deci-
> sions [about the "wall"] then, especially since the biggest
> threat to us now, UBL, is getting the most protection.

FBI headquarters lamely replied that "we are all frustrated
with this issue" but "these are the rules. NSLU does not make
them up." It was the classic We're just following orders defense.

A second case involved the alleged accomplice and possibly
twentieth hijacker Zacarias Moussaoui, who was brought to the
FBI's attention in Minneapolis because of a flight school's suspicions, based on Moussaoui's interest in learning to fly jet airliners
on trans-Atlantic routes, but not to learn how to land them. Moussaoui became the Minneapolis unit's "number one priority"
through September 11, 2001—when it suddenly and obviously
was too late. But the Minneapolis field office could not get the
lawyers at FBI headquarters interested in or focused enough on
Moussaoui to allow a search of his property, including a laptop
computer, that would have led to the plot. The field office was instructed not to get a criminal search warrant. This was based on
the reasoning that if an Article III judge denied the FBI a criminal
warrant, it would be harder to get a FISA warrant, since it would
look like the FBI was trying to end-run the Article III court by
going to the FISC. On the other hand, the FBI legal unit flatly misinterpreted the law and advised that no application could be made
to the FISC for a FISA order because there was not enough evidence that Moussaoui was an agent of a "foreign power." At one
point it was even suggested that he be deported to France so that
the French, presumably less fastidious about searches, could poke
about in his belongings. Thus was the matter of Zacarias Moussaoui batted back and forth in the catch-22 of legalistic limbo until
it was too late.

The Chinese Wall was eventually swept away when it became
clear after September 11, 2001, that it had caused key information
to fall through the cracks and prevented the FBI and other agencies from "connecting the dots" of what they knew. Congress
amended the law in the Patriot Act to make it clear that the
prospect of eventual criminal prosecution was no barrier to getting a FISA order. And the FISCR handed down a scathing opinion

that took the hide off the bureaucrat lawyers and judges who had created the wall, politely but acidly ripping them for misunderstanding the law and the Constitution, and for overreaching in trying to tell the Justice Department how to run its investigations.

But in 1994 the Chinese Wall and the culture of its sanctity stood in the way of Bob Clifford in particular, and the entire FBI counterterrorism program in general. Clifford set about looking for cracks in the wall. If there was no way to prosecute Hezbollah's American infiltrators for terrorism crimes, he was determined to hit them for every criminal violation that could be proven.

"I realized that these criminal acts they were deeply involved in were their Achilles' heel," Clifford says. "I wanted us to find out everything they were doing that was against the law, even if it were jaywalking or parking in a space reserved for the handicapped."

Clifford determined that there was one limited way in which he could use what he was learning on the intelligence side to spark criminal investigations. It was the equivalent of the tip from the ordinary concerned citizen. If a credible law-abiding citizen walks into an FBI office and informs an agent there that he has good reason to believe that Joe Smith is committing bank fraud, the FBI is justified in at least making a visit to the bank and inquiring about Joe Smith's transactions. If the visit reveals there is enough smoke to justify a more formal look, the office can open a full-blown criminal investigation and seek warrants for more intrusive actions such as searches and wiretaps. In effect, this is what Clifford decided should be done with the Hezbollah intelligence information, using an internal "cutout." He could not share any intelligence details with the FBI's criminal investigators. But if he knew that a certain Hezbollah operative was engaged in credit card fraud, he could give the criminal side a simple factual nugget (a "cut") and suggest to them that they might want to take a look at that person's financial activities—without providing any specific information derived from intelligence sources. The criminal case had to be made on its steam after the tip or "cut" was delivered.

As a practical matter, the intelligence agent and the criminal agent were often members of the same squad. The "cut" would be delivered by the squad chief, who acted as a one-man Chinese

Wall. The two agents could not speak directly about any intelligence information, and the squad chief had to make sure that he cut out anything specifically derived from intelligence. Yes, it was an awkward and cumbersome Rube Goldberg system, but it was the best that could be done.

Clifford called his approach of disrupting Hezbollah terrorist cells by lowering the boom for criminal activity "deliberate aggressiveness."

"I wanted to take the fight to them," Clifford says. "Everybody was monitoring, monitoring. I wanted to do something."

It has since become standard doctrine in the Justice Department—hailed by some as a "new" approach—that disrupting and deporting terrorists is as important a tool in preventing terror plots from coming to fruition as is criminal prosecution.* But it was not easy for Clifford then and it is still not easy today. The level of crime involved seems to some field offices and to some federal prosecutors as "nickel-and-dime stuff," not worthy of scarce resources. The Clifford approach also made senior bureaucrats nervous, both in the FBI and the Justice Department.

"Don't make waves," Clifford recalls being told by old headquarters hands. "Don't rock the boat. This is not the way we do things here."

Fortunately, Clifford won the support of two key allies—John O'Neill, who had just become chief of the International Terrorism Section after a career in criminal investigations, and Robert M. ("Bear") Bryant, the assistant FBI director in charge of the National Security Division. Bryant had been the special agent in charge of the Washington field office during Clifford's tour there. Other senior officials in the FBI and the Justice Department blew hot or cold, depending on how the wind felt on their uplifted fingers.

"Everybody was there for us when things went well," says Clifford. "Nobody was there when things went badly."

---

* "Prosecutors will not be limited to information brought to them by criminal investigators . . . and . . . will not always be guided by the end-game of developing admissible proof of a criminal offense, and will instead be involved in the process of gathering information necessary to assess immediate public safety dangers and disrupt terrorist plots," reads a 2004 draft of a U.S. Justice Department counterterrorism guide for federal prosecutors.

Clifford first joined forces with the FBI's New York field office—until recently the lead office in all terrorism investigations—
which soon became an enthusiastic and valuable partner in
implementing his new approach. The New York office had been
monitoring Hezbollah activity since the 1980s. In 1988, for example, a young Lebanese Hezbollah member named Yassem Fares
entered the United States on a student visa, then jumped his visa
without bothering to enroll in any school. In 1989 Fares and his
brother Malik got into a confrontation with two New York City
employees outside of a municipal office. Malik slashed one of the
employees with a knife and Yassem beat the other unconscious
with a cane. While they were attacking the employees the brothers
shouted that they were members of Hezbollah and were not to be
taken lightly, as if they were strutting around Bourj al-Barajneh.
State criminal assault charges were dropped when the brothers
agreed to be voluntarily deported to Lebanon. (The government
specifically stipulated that they were not to go to Canada, well
known even then as a haven for terrorists.) But two years later, FBI
surveillance photos of certain locations revealed that Yassem Fares
was back in Brooklyn, New York. He was arrested and convicted
of unlawful reentry after deportation. In the course of his trial, a
New York City detective working with the FBI in a joint terrorism
task force swore in a classified affidavit—based on several intelligence sources, including confidential informants—that Fares had
participated in Hezbollah's terrorist activities.

The Fares case didn't rate a single word in the news media—
the front page of the next day's *New York Times* featured an article
about a pending settlement of Hezbollah-sponsor Iran's compen-
sation claim for military equipment the United States refused to
deliver after the Islamic Revolution, and one about the U.S. Senate's rebuke of five senators in a savings-and-loan lobbyist fund-
raising scandal. The Fares case was a rare public glimpse at the
tip of the growing iceberg of Hezbollah terror operatives in the
United States—but it was a story to which the news media, much
of the government, and the American public were blind. The Islamists were at war with us, but we still didn't get it.

Clifford and the intelligence side of the New York office soon
focused on Mohammed Gharib Makki and his clothing business,

Nadia Fashions. (Makki is the brother of Hassan Gharib Makki, the convicted terrorist and senior Hezbollah officer discussed in Chapter Four.) They knew that Mohammed Makki, born in Lebanon but a naturalized U.S. citizen since 1987, was not only the leader of Hezbollah's New York cell, with strong ties directly to Hezbollah's leadership in Lebanon, but he and his business were also up to their ears in insurance fraud and trademark counterfeiting. Others in the cell were violating immigration law, with sham marriages, and criminal schemes like credit card "bust-outs"— charging up fraudulently obtained cards to the credit limit and then walking away—in addition to insurance and trademark fraud.

"Makki was buying lots of clothing for his store," according to Clifford. "Then he was falsely reporting them lost or stolen and filing insurance claims."

Clifford decided that Makki was a perfect test case for the new approach. He compares his plan to that of a military sniper on the battlefield: "First you take out the platoon leader, then you watch to see who takes over next." Clifford smiles. "I wanted to put a round right through Makki's head, watch the scurrying around, and see who took over after him."

Mohammed Gharib Makki was arrested on February 22, 1995, after a Brooklyn federal grand jury indicted him on mail fraud and wire fraud charges. Makki posted a $100,000 bail bond the next day and his U.S. passport was confiscated. He never made it to trial, however, but fled the country using his Lebanese passport, forfeiting the bond. Mohammed Makki remains a fugitive, living today in Lebanon. Nevertheless, the case was a grand success in Clifford's eyes.

"We found out through various intelligence sources that Makki's takedown had created quite a stir in the New York Hezbollah cell," says Clifford. "So I said, let's give them the old one-two punch and go after another guy."

The other guy selected for the second punch was a big tough guy who the agents had nicknamed "the Enforcer."

"He was the cell's muscle," Clifford says. "His problem was that he was here illegally, so we started cooperating with the Immigration and Naturalization Service on him. Part of the "deliberate aggressiveness" strategy was to use all of the resources we had available. They checked up on him, and before long he was arrested and deported."

The result was soon clear.

"We knew from other information," says Clifford, using the circumlocution of the intelligence world for secretly gathered evidence, "that we had actual impacts on the cell; we had empirical evidence that it worked."

Clifford wanted to take his show on the road and start poking "fingers in the eyes" of other Hezbollah operatives in the United States. "I could see that we could make many other cases all over the United States. We could rattle them, make some of them turn on their own countrymen and become informants."

At this point, however, the pucker factor went sky-high among some of Clifford's superiors, whom he loyally declines to name. He concedes, however, that former FBI Director Louis Freeh was "concerned about blowback" from the new strategy.

"I was directed to write a memorandum to [then] Attorney General Janet Reno, explaining what we were doing, how it had worked, and what we proposed to do elsewhere."

The highly classified memorandum went up the chain early in 1995, but Clifford never got a response. It was a classic "cover your ass" memorandum. If anything ever blew up in the FBI's face, everybody up the line from Clifford could say, "Well, the attorney general knew what we were doing." But nobody would actually have signed off on the plan, so Clifford could have been hung out to dry. Nevertheless, not being told "no" was the equivalent of being told "yes" for hard-charging Bob Clifford. He and Mark Connor developed a rolling list—several pages long—of candidates for the new program all over the country. And beginning in mid-1995, strange and inexplicable things soon started happening in Hezbollah circles.

"I'd call Mark in and say, 'Hey, Senior Chief, who's next on our list?' " Clifford recalls, using the term for senior chief petty officer, the navy's top enlisted experts. " 'Who are we going to fuck with today?' "

Their biggest worry was transgressing the Chinese Wall procedural nightmare. "We had to be careful any time we had a FISA wiretap up on some guy to be sure that we never mixed the intelligence side with the criminal side."

But other qualms were sometimes expressed within the Bureau. For example, one of the early targets was a member of a Hezbollah cell in Boston who worked at Logan International Airport. The Boston cell was big and its members were active. The man had access to virtually every area of the airport. Given Hezbollah's violent record with aircraft, that fact—in the days well before September 11, 2001—raised alarms in Clifford's Hezbollah unit. Boston's Hezbollah cell also had a reputation for forwardness. When one of their members had been brought into federal court on criminal charges, a group of other members showed up and glowered at the assistant U.S. attorney trying the case. Like the Fares brothers in New York, these toughs acted as if they were still in Lebanon, preening around with AK-47s, and oozed a basic contempt for American authority. Clifford was furious when he heard about the incident.

"They were obviously trying to intimidate him," according to a person knowledgeable about the incident. "This annoyed the FBI agent who was there to testify, so he went right up to them and asked if they had a problem and would they like to discuss it outside. He basically 'called them out.' Then he informed the federal marshals and the muscle was ejected."

It was arranged for an FBI field agent from the Boston office to visit the Logan Airport authorities to inform them of what the Bureau knew about the employee. The airport officials then interviewed the Hezbollah member, who elected to resign his job. Clifford recalls seeing a notation by former director Freeh written in the margin of a memorandum reporting the incident—a "raised eyebrow" about the civil liberties aspect of the action. Clifford thought nothing more of it. But another FBI employee says that several months after the Boston agent visited the airport, the agent got an internal memorandum from within the FBI notifying him that he had been "cleared of any wrongdoing" in the matter. This startled the agent, who had no clue that he had been under investigation. Someone in authority apparently thought that warning airport officials about an employee who was a member of an international terrorist group was potential "wrongdoing."

One official estimates that Hezbollah members, not necessarily cells, were active in about 100 cities across America during this period. Over the next year and a half—1995 and 1996—Clifford and his team rolled up close to 50 Hezbollah members in the United States, using everything from immigration violations to middling criminal charges. Currently, there are active investigations of Hezbollah-related criminal activity in at least fourteen cities, discussed in the next chapter.

"We could see that it was working," says Clifford. "We were keeping records of how we were taking these guys out. I wanted to put these people in a box, so that no matter where they turned, I could nail them, even if it was for jaywalking."

Not every case turned out as successfully as the Makki case. One example was an investigation into massive theft and trademark fraud involving Levi jeans. Hezbollah members had a large organized operation stealing jeans or slapping Levi labels on cheap imitations in large quantities and shipping them to the Tri-Border. They were then moved on to Europe and the Middle East and sold at huge profits. At that time, Levis were a hot commodity in the Middle East and Eastern Europe. Local people offered to buy them directly from visiting Westerners. In the Middle East, the trademark duds were considered the height of fashion. Money-laundering and credit card fraud was also involved.

"Hezbollah is one of the best organized criminal operations on the planet," according to one FBI source familiar with the matter. "Hassan Naserallah at least has to know about these enterprises, if he's not directing them himself."

Clifford worked with Levi company officials and with the San Francisco and Los Angeles FBI field offices, trying to stem the multimillion-dollar criminal operation, which went on for several years. According to another source, however, Clifford could never get the FBI's Los Angeles field office worked up about the case—counterterrorism was not a priority for most offices in those days.

On the other hand, the CIA, which has liaison officers in joint counterterrorism task forces throughout the country and had an officer working in Clifford's unit, thought "deliberate aggressiveness" was a great idea. The agency generated a similar program in the Tri-Border, calling it "Operation Double Tap."* The CIA is said to have had some success with it.

After two years on the job, Clifford was having great fun, but he also wanted to become a field supervisor. His in-laws had moved to North Carolina, and Bob had been down to Charlotte in connection with a case involving the deportation of a Hezbollah member. He liked what he saw of the region.

"John O'Neill called me into his office one day late in 1996," Clifford recalls. "O'Neill was a lot like a Mafia don. If he liked you, he would take care of you. If he didn't, you were in trouble. He liked me. The special agent in charge of the Charlotte office was visiting. John told me to sit down and explain our strategy to the SAC, so I did. I guess I made a good impression."

It turned out that the Charlotte office had a vacancy for the supervisor of one of its squads. Clifford applied for the job and on December 7, 1997, his pager went off as he was sitting in an obstetrician's office with his wife, expecting their second child.

"Hey, Bob," O'Neill announced. "You're going to Charlotte."

The circle was now closing inexorably on Mohammed Hammoud.

---

* "Double Tap" is a term of art in special operations forces. It refers to the technique of placing two very well-aimed shots in succession on a target's head or torso to ensure immediate death or incapacitation.

"DOING SOMETHING ILLEGAL TO BE LEGAL . . ."

It's ironic because really what you're doing is you're doing something illegal to be legal.

—Said Mohammed Harb

Said Mohammed Harb was the bad boy of the Charlotte Hezbollah cell. At five feet, seven inches, he might be considered short, but the personality of the man who called himself "Sammy" around Americans towered above the rest of the cell's coconspirators.

"He swaggered into the first day of the criminal trial wearing a black cashmere suit and sweater," said Iredell County Deputy Sheriff Bob Fromme, whose dogged curiosity helped to convict the members of the Charlotte cell. "He looked like a Mafia don. He was completely self-confident."

In the special alternate universe of cops and perps, Harb came to be well-liked, even grudgingly admired in a peculiar way by the tough lawmen who quietly investigated him and eventually brought him to book.

"Harb is as engaging as can be," said federal prosecutor Ken Bell. "We spent hours talking about religion and politics. He is at one and the same time more secular than the others in the cell and yet able to talk seriously about his religion. He laid out for me the whole history and path of Islam in an intelligent way. He is definitely an interesting guy."

"Some people are naturals," Harb's lawyer, Chris Fialko, said in explaining why Harb is so captivating. "Like John Edwards, Bill Clinton—and Said Harb. Harb is like Damon Runyon. He is all-American. Mohammed Hammoud and the others are still Lebanese."

Like the conspiracy's financial whiz Angie Tsioumas, Harb had the natural assets for success in the world: a nimble brain, an incredible memory, a puckish smile, and a dynamically driven personality. But also like Angie, Harb had a character flaw. He attracted criminal schemes like a cheap suit picks up lint. They seemed to leap onto him when he walked by. It was no matter to Harb that the sleaziest of his schemes violated the tenets of Islam, his professed religion. The Teflon terrorist had a glib rationalization ready to deflect moral guilt and explain why each of his crimes wasn't really all that bad. In fact, when you thought about it from Sammy Harb's point of view, maybe each was even a good thing.

Cigarette smuggling? "I never viewed cigarettes to be a big deal. I mean, to me the way I look at it, if the law want to stop it, all they had to do was just stamp the cigarettes either in here or in Detroit," he said. "As far as I knew, it was just a part of the game. I didn't see myself doing anything illegal. As far I didn't hurt anybody so I'm fine, you know."

How about the many fake driver's licenses he had? "All the identities I got," he explained, "all the driver's license were legal in a sense. They were from the DMV."

The phony Social Security cards he acquired in other people's names? "As far as the Social Security, the ID, everything has to do with it was legal. Perfectly legal. I mean, the Social Security Administration issued Social Security to those names."

Immigration frauds and briberies? "It's ironic because really what you're doing is you're doing something illegal to be legal," he explains in the peculiar moral logic of Said "Sammy" Harb. "So again, I didn't see it's a big deal because it's better to me, it's better than you being illegal and working under the table. I might as well get papers and work, pay taxes, whatever, you know."

There was more. An Internet pornography business. Visits to prostitutes. Drinking and smoking. And so it went—not the ideal lifestyle of a seriously religious Muslim.

"As far as religiously, it's wrong," Harb said of his involvement in the Internet pornography website. His elaborate rationalization echoes the compartmentalized thinking of those who justify donating funds to terrorist bombers in the name of religion, politics, or social welfare. "Okay. But to me I was, you know, I convinced myself that I wasn't really—I'm not working in pornography. It's like you have a gas station, okay. If you're religious person—which I wasn't religious, but if you're religious person, you have a gas station but this gas station sell beer. You're not supposed to sell alcohol period. But you go ahead and have the alcohol in somebody else's name so you profit and everything will be from everything else beside the alcohol. So you can justify it like this to yourself, I guess."

Said Harb was flashy, manipulative, opportunistic, and—at least, according to Mohammed Hammoud and other members of the criminal enterprise that formed around him—an untrustworthy liar who cheated his best friends.

"I would tell you to go into Charlotte and ask every single one—not only Lebanese—every one who met Said for one day, just one day, and if he tells you he is not bad, if he tells you Said is 'okay,' I'll be surprised," snapped the devout Muslim Hammoud. "Just the word 'okay.' "

"If it's in his best interest, Said Harb would do anything," fumed Angie Tsioumas. "Lie, cheat, steal, whatever."

Drivers who worked for Harb on the cigarette-smuggling runs accused him of ripping them off. "I mean, what was I going to do, go to the local police?" said one. Another driver said that when she tried to quit, Harb threatened to "blow up" the restaurant where she worked and "kick everybody's ass who worked there." Instead he just showed up outside, had a few angry words with her boyfriend out in the parking lot, and then lamely drove off and out of her life—until the feds came knocking on her door.

On the other hand, Angie and the others aren't exactly impartial judges. Harb's insider testimony was the keystone of the government's case against the Hezbollah cell. When the chips were down and the federal indictments were on the table, Harb followed the maxim of the cynically hard-bitten journalist Damon Runyon, to whom his lawyer compares him. "It may be that the race is not always to the swift, nor the battle to the strong," wrote

Runyon. "But that is the way to bet." Sammy Harb bet on the government.

Harb was born in the same hardscrabble slum as Mohammed Hammoud—Bourj al-Barajneh—on August 5, 1970. In the United States on that day the judge in the Los Angeles murder trial of Charles Manson, infamous leader of the "family" charged with the so-called Tate-LaBianca murders, ruled that the interminably long trial could proceed. Manson had thrown the trial into pandemonium two days earlier when he held up a newspaper with a headline that quoted President Richard M. Nixon declaring that Manson was "guilty" of the gory Helter-Skelter murders, which Manson fantasized would precipitate an apocalyptic racial war.

Like Hammoud, Harb grew up in the bloody helter-skelter of real wars of one kind or another raging around him. Black September erupted in Jordan a month after Harb's birth, with all of its consequences for Lebanon. By the time he was in his middle teens, Harb saw the neighborhood armed militia gradually change from Amal to Hezbollah, and like most of the teenagers he knew, he joined the Hezbollah faction.

"Lot of people who were in Amal became Hezbollah members and we just grew up together," he says. "Most of the people in Bourj al-Barajneh belonged to some kind of militia, and Hezbollah was dominant, so lot of people were in Hezbollah." Although Harb has a mysterious bullet wound scar on his left shin, he claims not to have been an active combatant for Hezbollah.

His best friend as a teenager, however, was a young man named Mohammed Hassan Dbouk, about whom there is no doubt. Dbouk became a hard-core, full-blown international Hezbollah operative. He started out as a fighter, then became a producer of propaganda films for Hezbollah's Al-Manar satellite television network, an intelligence operative monitoring Israeli troops in southern Lebanon, and finally an overseas buyer of technology for the terror apparatus. Dbouk would pop up from time to time in Harb's life and played a pivotal role in forming a triangle in which illicit funds flowed from Charlotte and elsewhere to Hezbollah's coffers in Lebanon; from there he went to Canada to buy military-type hardware, which was then shipped to Lebanon for use in terrorist attacks. Dbouk is now under federal indictment, a fugitive living in Lebanon.

Dbouk spent about six months living in Detroit in 1988, illustrating the ease with which Hezbollah has taken advantage of America's porous borders to groom its operatives. A leading academic expert on Hezbollah, Magnus Ranstorp of the University of St. Andrews, Scotland, related to the *National Journal* an illuminating anecdote of his visit to Lebanon in 1998. Ranstorp was there to interview Hezbollah officials. One of them spoke flawless American English and wore a New York Yankees baseball cap.

"When I asked him if he'd learned English at the American University in Beirut, he just laughed and said he learned it in Washington, D.C.," Ranstorp told the *National Journal.* "He said that Americans may know the top leaders of Hezbollah, but the organization doesn't keep membership lists, and they don't get caught carrying identification cards."

As the September 11, 2001, hijackers demonstrated and this anecdote confirms, Islamist terrorists can blend in and live comfortably among us, ostensibly just another exotic thread in the American multicultural quilt.

Harb's cousin, Mustafa Harb, came to Charlotte in the mid-1980s to study at the University of North Carolina. Said followed on a student visa in 1988, when he was eighteen years old. Although he was later a one-man, full-service marriage fraud bureau, Harb entered into a legitimate marriage with an American-born woman, apparently never violated the immigration rules, and became a naturalized U.S. citizen. He studied at Central Piedmont Community College and, like many others of the Charlotte Lebanese Shiite community, got a job at Domino's Pizza, where he eventually became a manager.

On August 18, 1995, however, Said Harb's American idyll was interrupted. He watched a television documentary on ABC's *20/20* that by his account sent him spiraling down into becoming a one-man crime wave and terror financier. The show told a distressing tale of cultural conflict that ripped apart a family of Albanian Muslim émigrés living in Plano, Texas, located about 20 miles north of Dallas. It began on August 12, 1988, when Sadri "Sam" Krasniqi was arrested in a high school gymnasium. Krasniqi, owner of a pizza store, was there on a family outing to watch his son compete in a Tae Kwon Do tournament. It is hard to get more all-American than an Albanian pizza shop owner watching a Korean karate match in a Texas gymnasium. But Sam Krasniqi was holding his daughter, then four years old, in a way that distressed some of the homegrown Texans. A woman named Mary Lou Taylor reported that Krasniqi was fondling his daughter. All hell broke loose. Krasniqi was arrested and charged with child abuse. Although he was ultimately acquitted of the criminal offense, Texas authorities were persuaded that, his acquittal notwithstanding, Krasniqi and his wife were not fit parents.

Custody was awarded to a Christian family, who converted the children to their own faith. Mrs. Krasniqi, who had visitation privileges for a while, was shocked to see one of the kids wearing a cross on a necklace. Muslim American groups took up verbal arms on behalf of the Krasniqis, who spent hundreds of thousands of dollars trying to reclaim their children. The two children eventually sent word through a newspaper story asking their biological parents to leave them alone—they liked their new family.

The at least superficially apparent unfairness of the case inspired the *20/20* documentary. It scared the hell out of Said Harb, he says. Although his recollection of the facts in the Krasniqi case is jumbled, its impact on him is not.

"I was watching *20/20* and there was a show pretty much about two Muslims who had their son taken away from them because they were kissing them in the chin," he said. "So some lady said it's—called the police, said it was sexual harassment, which we do this in our country, you know. We do that, we kiss our sons or daughters in the mouth, or whatever. Just out of affection. So the son get—you know, he was taken away from them. So I pretty much got shook up and I decided to move to Lebanon."

Harb packed up his family and went back to Lebanon in 1996. But Beirut was no Charlotte, North Carolina. Its economy was in the toilet.

"There wasn't any jobs," Harb recalls. "And the money went down the drain and I started withdrawing money on my credit cards and I was about $65,000 in debt. And so I decide to come back."

When Harb got back into town, after six months in Lebanon,

he needed money badly. He made two fateful decisions. The first was to get into cigarette smuggling.

"I had about $65,000, you know, in debt. And when I came back, I saw that most of the Lebanese people were working in transferring cigarettes. So that's what I did." Mohammed Hammoud was the go-to man for the smuggling business, and Harb got himself cut in for a share of the business.

His second decision was to take advantage of the American system of easy credit.

"Pretty much my credit was ruined, so I decided, you know, since it's ruined, might as well ruin it all the way." That decision soon led Harb to set up an astonishingly complex system of credit card fraud.

By then, however, several different American law enforcement agencies, from a local deputy sheriff to the FBI, were peering into the Charlotte operation, trying to figure out who was doing what. Unbeknownst to one another, they were examining some of the members from different perspectives. The flashy Said Harb had been up on the FBI's radar screen once before, then faded out of sight. Now he was back on the screen to stay. His wanderings were being followed very closely.

The FBI's interest in Charlotte's Lebanese Shiites goes back at least to 1991 and the first Gulf War with Iraq, when agents dropped in on Mustafa Harb, Said's cousin. It was apparently a friendly visit with a sharper point. They told Mustafa Harb that the Bureau knew about the Thursday night prayer meetings that were going on even then. That was fine, no problem, the agents said. But all the same, the FBI agents made their point—We know you're here.

Most Americans had forgotten by then about Hezbollah's bombings—if they ever focused on them enough to learn or remember the name of the distant Lebanese group—but the FBI had not. An FBI bomb forensics expert named Danny A. Defenbaugh had supervised the investigation of the Marine Corps barracks and two U.S. embassy bombings in Beirut. (Defenbaugh was inspector-in-charge of the 1995 Oklahoma City bombing investigation.) A string of events at the turn of that decade focused the attention of the American counterterrorism apparatus on the alarming possibility that Hezbollah might attack inside the United States. In 1989 Hezbollah issued a warning that if the United States exercised its power to arrest suspected terrorists abroad, it would attack Americans all over the world. "We will kill ten Americans in case the life or freedom of one revolutionary struggler was threatened," it claimed in a statement to a Beirut newspaper. In the same year, FBI officials told congressional leaders that they were concerned that dozens of Islamic Revolutionary Guard operatives had slipped past the INS and into the country. The officials estimated that there were then a total of some 300 IRG and Hezbollah agents in the United States.

Saddam Hussein's invasion of Kuwait on August 2, 1990, ramped up American concerns. Iraqi security officials pillaged thousands of Kuwaiti passports during their sack of the country. It was feared these would be made available to terrorists. A grand conclave in Baghdad of more than 1,000 representatives of terrorist groups after the invasion and before the American liberation raised concerns that Iraq would unleash terrorist groups as its secret weapon in a war with the United States. A special task force of FBI, CIA, NSA, State Department and other counterterrorism officers met daily and coordinated U.S. protective actions with the National Security Council.

In light of all these concerns and the clearly pending first Gulf War with Iraq, FBI field offices intensified their focus on potential Islamist threats. But by the time Bob Clifford arrived in Charlotte in 1997, that interest had peaked, fallen off, and the field office had other priorities. The hottest cases in the field office at the time were an Outlaws motorcycle gang case, part of a war on violent drug gangs, high-profile public integrity investigations of corrupt public officials, and a spectacular armored-car robbery. None of those fit into Squad Five, the so-called white elephant squad that Bob Clifford took over in his first assignment as a field supervisor. The squad was responsible for civil rights, foreign counterintelligence, and domestic terrorism. Clifford also headed the local FBI SWAT (special weapons and tactics) team.

He found Squad Five in the doldrums. There were a few excellent agents, but others were tired and had "retired on the job." The squad lacked a motivating spark plug and seemed to be just going through the motions. In other words, it was perfect for Clifford.

"It was exciting," he says. "I like field operations. It wasn't a very big ship, but it was my ship. I had to change the whole way of thinking of Squad Five, so I called in all the agents and said, 'Okay, here are our priorities. I want us to go all out, 100 percent on each of them.' There were so many things we could do and break new ground."

Clifford energized his crew. An epidemic of church fires in the South, for example: There had been so many the year before that it had been called the "summer of smoke." The Bureau of Alcohol, Tobacco and Firearms was the lead agency for investigating arson, but Clifford's squad was responsible for the civil rights aspect. "I had the whole squad go out there when there was a church fire. I didn't want it to be just a turf thing with ATF where we went through the motions." Clifford and his squad got out and met the leaders of various religious communities, including Muslims. In 1999 the team investigated a spate of racist and anti-Semitic graffiti and flyers. His insistence on working with the several faith communities would pay off later. "And," he says, "we started busting Klansmen."

The squad also conducted several successful foreign counter-intelligence operations, the details of which Clifford will not discuss. "We have several large military bases in North Carolina," he notes cryptically. "Our enemies are interested in troop movements, weapons capabilities, and many other things associated with those bases."

When it came to the local aspects of international terrorism, however, Clifford found a skeptical audience among his peers. There was an "all agents conference" of the more than 100 FBI agents in North Carolina during Clifford's first year.

"I gave a slide presentation," he recalls. "I went through the whole thing with Hezbollah, starting from the beginning, through the bombings and hijackings and hostage-taking, and brought it right down to North Carolina, why it was important in Charlotte. 'We have people here who are members of Hezbollah,' I told them."

The reaction was less than enthusiastic.

"They were actually laughing," Clifford says. "The agent who coordinated the training session chuckled and joked, 'Well, Bob, after that presentation, I just won't feel right going into a 7-Eleven anymore.'"

"I wasn't discouraged," he recalls. "I knew what the potential was. I saw the issue across the board. And I had caught the attention of a few people."

Bob also had an ace in the hole by then. A local member of the Lebanese community, a person who knew Said Harb and Mohammed Hammoud and most of the others, had walked into the FBI office sometime in 1997. This person—the first of several confidential informants whose names are closely guarded to this day to protect their lives and the lives of their families and relatives—was not happy with what he saw going on in Charlotte. He had played by all the rules. He entered the country legally, struggled to get his green card, worked hard, and played straight. He wanted to leave the sectarian wars of Lebanon and the Middle East behind and build a new life in America. Now this pack of visa-jumping lawbreakers were living in the fast lane, laughing at American laws, and scoffing at everything he had sweated for. Worst of all, he knew that some of them had connections to Hezbollah.

Everything the man told the FBI in Charlotte fit into what Clifford knew from his tour in Washington. His general allegations—combined with intelligence from Washington and other field offices—were enough to open several intelligence files on different people, but not sufficient proof in and of themselves to start arresting any of them.

"Said Harb was the big one at that point," says Clifford. "He was rising to our attention. He was flagrant in his behavior and had bad tradecraft, not very cautious or careful. Mohammed Hammoud, on the other hand, was very cautious."*

The outlines of what was going on were still vague, and a definite foreign connection was yet to be proven, which meant Clifford could not yet get a FISA court order to wiretap or search. Besides, it was basically all intelligence information, which meant

---

* "Tradecraft" is the bundle of skills that spies, terrorists, and others who operate undercover learn in order to function effectively without being detected.

that the Chinese Wall prevented Clifford from simply mobilizing the larger resources of all the field office's criminal investigators— if he could interest them in the terrorist group's middling crime. Finally, the squad still had all of its other responsibilities to attend to. Starting in early 1998, that included the search for Atlanta Olympics and abortion clinic bomber Eric Rudolph, a most wanted fugitive who was living off the land in the mountain wilderness of western North Carolina.

Nevertheless it was a start and Clifford set about juicing up his squad, which until his arrival was still in the old foreign counter-intelligence mode of simply taking notes. Clifford wanted to use his "deliberate aggressiveness" model in Charlotte.

"The squad was doing things the traditional way," he says. "But there was no effort to link any of this activity to a cell. I wanted us to develop a plan to answer every question I could think of: Who is talking to whom? Is there a cell? Who is their leader? What is their organization? Are there any communications with other Hezbollah members in the United States?"

Clifford called in his troops and fired them up.

"Are we employing every technique we have?" he asked. "Do we do their trash? Do we know where they go for lunch? If they have a girlfriend, who is she? I want a dossier on every one of these guys we know about, I want to know everything you can find out about that person. When we have that, then we can start to see the connections."

Meanwhile, the confidential source had to be developed. Cultivating informants is a delicate dance. They have to be kept motivated, but what they report also has to be filtered critically for believability. It takes a special touch and Clifford found his man in veteran FBI agent Art McClendon, who was given the task of developing the confidential source. "Art was one of the good guys on the squad," Clifford says. "He was very analytical, very deliberate, and he was very good with our informant."

By the fall of 1997 Squad Five had learned enough to know that one of the subjects they were interested in was dealing in stolen computers. Acting as the one-man Chinese Wall, Clifford passed a "cut" to the criminal side, suggesting an investigation be opened.

"Nothing happened," he says. "Nothing ever got done. The criminal squad was dealing with things like the Loomis Fargo armored car robbery and I was telling them about a few stolen computers?"

The March 29, 1997, armed robbery of a Loomis Fargo armored truck in Jacksonville, Florida, was the biggest armored car heist in history. The robbery yielded $18,834,455 and change. The trail led to North Carolina, and in September of that year FBI agents found most of the loot in a storage building in a town called Mountain Home, near Asheville. "The only thing that moves around here is the streetlight when it flickers" is how one local resident described the town. The agents dragged more than 30 bags stuffed with currency out of the Mountain Home Mini Storage. The cash weighed more than 900 pounds. It was an old-line FBI meat-and-potatoes-type case, one of several that were then hot in the Charlotte office. It is perhaps understandable why Bob Clifford's hints about stolen computers went nowhere fast, but low visibility and unlikely prosecution of their crimes is exactly what Hezbollah intends.

"Art McClendon was getting discouraged, and I could see that we were not going to get the support we needed from the criminal side," Clifford recalls. "So I decided we were going to have to do it all by ourselves."

The hunt for Eric Rudolph sucked up a lot of Clifford's time as SWAT team leader, as did a similar hunt for a double murderer named James Andrew Finley Jr. In August 1998 Finley shot and killed two campers in the Pisgah National Forest, then took to the wilderness as Rudolph had done. Finley was flushed out in less than 48 hours, eventually pled guilty, and was sentenced to life imprisonment. Despite these other demands, by the spring of 1998 Squad Five had started to put things together on the Hezbollah cell. The flashy Said Harb was being watched, then the tobacco-smuggling scheme was uncovered, then the details of the Thursday-night meetings began to emerge. It eventually became clear that this was not just a handful of different individuals each doing their own thing, but an organized cell engaged in a broad criminal conspiracy, and Mohammed Hammoud was the leader.

Clifford realized that he needed an experienced agent who could pull this all together into a criminal case that could be successfully prosecuted. "I needed a respected and effective agent who could put together a case on an organized criminal network." The stars aligned and by good fortune Clifford found that man.

"It was late, late one night in December 1998," he recalls. "I had been working late and as I was leaving, I see this guy with a goatee sitting at his desk also working late. We were the only two left in the office, and we started talking. It turned out we had similar backgrounds in the military. He had just come off of a big success in a complicated criminal conspiracy case involving the Outlaws motorcycle gang, and expressed an interest in counterintelligence work. He was just what I needed. His name was Rick Schwein."

"God forgives. Outlaws don't." The motto of the Outlaws Motorcycle Club, also known as the American Outlaw Association, pretty well sums up the organization's character. It is one of the four major national motorcycle gangs in America, along with the Hell's Angels, Pagans, and Bandidos—with whom it has clashed in violent turf wars, marked by bombings and shootings. The Outlaws gang grew out of a local club founded near Chicago in 1935 and has had as many as 34 chapters in the United States, Canada, Australia, and Europe. It is said recently to have shrunk to as few as 20 chapters, probably because of concentrated law enforcement attention over the last decade. The association in the United States is organized into four regions.

Outlaws chapters supposedly operate independently, but for decades the national organization has controlled a nationwide consortium of criminal enterprises. Drug trafficking, including methamphetamine and cocaine, is the main source of income but the Outlaws have been involved in a criminal farrago of extortion, contract murders, motor vehicle thefts, gun and explosives running, armed robbery, prostitution, rape, and mail fraud. According to some motorcycle gang experts, members of the Outlaws are required to sell drugs and must own at least one handgun. They are also required to ride in pairs, in order to avoid situations in which a single Outlaw might be picked off by rival toughs, thus bringing the organization into shame. The gang's national website claims that it is nothing more sinister than a civic association whose members like to ride motorcycles and do good works all over America. It claims to be unfairly persecuted by law enforcement agencies. As a Connecticut Outlaws chapter member told a local paper in June 2004, "We're not about none of that. It's a new time. It's a new era."

Rick Schwein was immersed for three years—from 1995 to 1998—in Operation Speedball, a razor's-edge investigation of the Outlaws in North Carolina. The case had several close calls but resulted in the indictment and conviction on racketeering charges of 36 members and associates of Outlaws chapters in Lexington and Charlotte, including 22 so-called "patch-wearing" members.

When Schwein arrived in Charlotte in 1988, fresh from the FBI Academy, his first assignment was to the white-collar crime squad. He stayed there for about a year and then moved to the "reactive," or violent crime and major offenders, squad—the team that specialized in kidnappings, bank robberies, extortion, and fugitives.

"Of all the things I did, it was the most fun," Schwein recalls of his time on that squad. "I got a lot of immediate gratification. It was the good guys against the bad guys, old-fashioned whodunits, and putting handcuffs on people. I felt that by taking these people off the street, we were helping the community."

After two years of putting handcuffs on violent criminals, Schwein moved on to the squad responsible for organized crime and drugs. It was here that he got important experience in two aspects of criminal investigation that were keys to success in the Hezbollah case: complicated investigations involving lots of people doing different crimes, and a federal law known as RICO—the Racketeer Influenced and Corrupt Organization Act. Congress passed the RICO law in 1970 as a tool for federal prosecutors to go after mobsters like the Mafia. (There is an urban myth that the acronym was deliberately fashioned as a reference to "Rico," the name of a gangster played by Edward G. Robinson in the 1930 movie *Little Caesar*.) In brief, the RICO law provides severe penalties for people who associate themselves, even informally, in a pattern of various criminal activities. It was designed as a way to stand back, look at the entirety of a criminal operation bigger than any single crime its members commit, and lower the federal boom on the whole lot.

The Outlaws case was the capstone of Schwein's time on the squad. The investigation began in 1995. Schwein and Jim Corcoran, a marine veteran of Vietnam, worked the case with Marc Robson, a Charlotte police officer. In addition to having a lead role in the intensive FBI investigation of the Outlaws' complicated criminal and financial dealings, Schwein also went through a special FBI vetting process for undercover work with Robson, including psychological testing and a two-week school. Robson went undercover, infiltrating the Outlaws, and Schwein was his backup.

"I would go to swap meets or hang out at the topless nightclub the Outlaws ran when Marc or one of our sources was conducting business with bad guys," Schwein remembers. "My wife used to always know when I'd been to the topless club, which was called Twin Peaks, as I would come home smelling of smoke and cheap perfume."

The Outlaws were cagy and operated their own form of counterintelligence. (A senior member of a chapter in another state would slap a stress analyzer on people he suspected of being informants.) "Several of the Outlaws' 'old ladies' worked at the club," says Schwein, "and it was a common practice for them to solicit lap dances so they could surreptitiously search patrons that they didn't know for guns or wires."

In fact, however, Schwein spent most of his undercover time "sitting in a car half a block away freezing my rear end off while Marc lived the life." He recalls one amusing moment when Robson was in the living room of a biker named "Winkle," working on a motorcycle. Schwein was outside, listening to the wired conversation. Winkle was grilling Robson, as he often did, while Robson was steering the conversation in the direction of his own fictional "conviction" for securities fraud. The hope was that Winkle would take the bait and start talking about the Outlaws' money laundering.

"I really thought we were getting somewhere," Schwein said, "when the biker suddenly quipped, 'Man, that blue-collar crime is where it's at!' Oh, well. No one ever accused us of arresting the smart ones."

In spite of a few hair-raising moments—the undercover

slipped out of character inadvertently and had to be gracefully and convincingly extricated, wiretaps were compromised, and an informant turned into a problem—in the end the investigation was successful. After almost three years of hard work, the case went to trial.

"I was in the same courtroom Hammoud would later be found guilty in surrounded by dozens of stolen Harley Davidson motor-cycle parts, scores of confiscated weapons, and pounds of seized methamphetamine, cocaine, and marijuana," Schwein says. "After six weeks of trial the Outlaws capitulated and pled guilty to all counts in the indictment."

The experience was excellent preparation for Schwein's next big assignment, working for Bob Clifford. It required Schwein to master the techniques of a complicated financial investigation into the gang's criminal enterprises, prepare a persuasive case under the RICO statute, and make innovative use of search warrants to tie the gang into the RICO law's statutes.

"One of the tools we used is what is known as an 'indicia warrant,'" he says. "It allowed us to seize indicia such as distinctive colors, patches, T-shirts, jewelry, etc., relating to the Outlaws. Under the RICO statute you must prove persons are 'associated in fact' to be considered part of the criminal enterprise. While it is not illegal to possess these items, possession of them may be evidence of membership or affiliation with the criminal enterprise. We used the same theory to seize evidence of an association with Hezbollah, when we sought to seize literature, videotapes, audiotapes, and the like."

Schwein was in the office late, going over evidence for another round of indictments, the night Bob Clifford stopped by and struck up a conversation.

"It was perfect timing," Schwein says. "I was just beaten up by a six-weeks-long trial, and burned out after eight years on the drugs and organized crime squad. I was ready for a change when Bob suggested that I come down and talk."

It was not a hard sell. Schwein's request for transfer to Clifford's "white elephant" squad was granted. Clifford laid out what he expected in no uncertain terms, and Schwein responded with equal vigor. The two former special operations intelligence officers and their years of complementary FBI experience merged perfectly. Clifford would still be the Chinese Wall, but Schwein would take the tips he got and run with the ball, aggressively pursuing criminal investigations.

"Rick," Clifford said, "I want to start putting handcuffs on some of these Hezbollah members, and you're the man who can do it."

Schwein went to work. Early on, he found out that Harb, Hammoud, and the others regularly played a pickup game of soccer in a Charlotte park. Schwein still had the goatee he had grown for the Outlaws case and stopped by the park one day.

"They were down one guy and they asked me to play," he says. It was a fateful moment for Said Harb.

"After the game, I noticed that all of the rest of them went off together. Harb left on his own, went to a place called The Liquid Lounge. That's when I decided that he was different from the others. He was the man we were going to turn into our witness."

Schwein was present months later when Harb was interrogated after his arrest.

"You look familiar," Harb said.

"We played soccer together." Schwein smiled.

Clifford had another objective. There was no Joint Terrorism Task Force (JTTF) of combined federal and local agencies in Charlotte at the time. He had seen the idea in action and wanted Schwein to reach out to other agencies and put together the equivalent of a JTTF in Charlotte. So, in addition to his own investigative work, Schwein started developing contacts with a range of other state, local, and federal agencies, finding out what they knew about his subjects. That's when he discovered that another federal investigation of the cigarette smuggling scheme by Hammoud and his cell was up and running at the Bureau of Alcohol, Tobacco and Firearms (ATF).

The ATF case had been sparked by the excellent police work of an Iredell County deputy sheriff named Bob Fromme, moonlighting as a security guard. Their joint investigation was well done, had the smugglers cold, and filled in with great detail much of what the FBI had only in outline. But the cigarette-smuggling case had every prospect of derailing the FBI's counterterrorism investigation. Federal prosecutors—unaware of the terrorism connection—were about to ship the whole thing off to Detroit, on the theory that no tobacco-friendly North Carolina jury would convict the gang. After all, it was Michigan that lost the tax money. Something had to be done and done fast.

"Bob, they don't have a clue about the Hezbollah connections," Schwein reported to Clifford. "We better sit down with them."

Put six-foot-tall Bob Fromme in a set of chaps, leather vest, and a half-moon sheriff's badge and he could walk onto the set of any Western movie ever made as the poker-faced, rawboned, big-fisted local law west of the Pecos. He looks like the kind of man that even rattlesnakes avoid.

In person, however, Fromme is a nice guy, soft-spoken and thoughtful, with five children and two grandchildren. He is an exemplar of local law enforcement officers fighting terrorism. Fromme has devoted uncounted hours of his own time immersed in studying the Charlotte Hezbollah case and sharing his knowledge of its operations and investigation with other local police agencies all over the country.

Iredell County lies north of Charlotte, quartered by Interstates 77 and 40. The county seat, Statesville, sits on the junction of the two highways, about 45 miles north of Charlotte and 130 miles west of the state capital, Raleigh. According to the county's Internet website, the name means "a valley of flowing air." The county is overwhelmingly rural white, and of its 122,660 residents in 2000, 118,188 were native-born. More than half of the foreign-born are from Latin America. Only 189 residents claimed an Arab ancestry. The county sheriff's office operates out of a one-floor, brick-façade building on Tradd Street.

Statesville is the site of one of three JR Tobacco Warehouses along North Carolina's interstate highways. The emporium hires uniformed but off-duty sheriff's deputies to supplement its rent-a-cop security force. In 1995 Bob Fromme started moonlighting as a security guard at JR's. His job was mainly to be a visible deterrent to any two-bit criminals who might be tempted by the large amounts of cash that flowed through JR's daily. But even though he was theoretically off duty, Fromme could not turn off his experienced cop's powers of observation and instinct.

"Every time I was on duty there, I noticed a particular group of individuals come in," he recalls. "There would be three or four of them. Each of them would buy 299 cartons of cigarettes. One of them would have a couple of plastic grocery bags full of cash—we're talking about twenty or thirty thousand dollars, all stacked and wrapped up in rubber bands. As each one of the others checked out with his float full of cigarette cartons, the one with the grocery bags would reach into his bag, pull out a bundle of bills, and pay for the cigarettes."

Fromme admits he had no idea what was going on at the time. But something about the way the purchases were being made struck him as odd, and his experience told him what was going on was likely criminal. He knew that drug traffickers often structure their financial transactions in ways to avoid triggering federal bank reporting laws. They often break money exchanges down into amounts less than $10,000 to avoid mandatory reporting under federal laws designed to stop drug money laundering. Structuring as a part of a money-laundering scheme is itself a federal crime.

"I originally thought that they were Mexicans laundering drug money," he says. "I have never seen volumes of cash money like that except in connection with drugs."

He later found out that the purchase of 60,000 cigarettes triggers the operation of a federal law called the Jenkins Act. The law is intended to help states collect cigarette taxes. It requires anyone other than a licensed distributor who transports and sells 60,000 or more cigarettes to report the details of the sale to the state tobacco tax administrator. The Hezbollah smugglers were indeed structuring their purchases to come just under that threshold—there are 20 cigarettes in a pack, 10 packs to a carton, and 30 cartons to a case. In other words, ten cases equals 300 cartons and totals 60,000 cigarettes.

"They were buying ten cases per person, minus one carton," Fromme says. Even though he wasn't sure what they were doing, he decided to snoop.

"I started casually following them out, writing down license numbers, and running the tag numbers," he says. "Then I started coming in on my own time and set up my own surveillance system. I followed some of them to the Virginia and Tennessee state lines."

Convinced that he had stumbled onto some kind of organized crime, he called a friend of his, an ATF agent in Charlotte named John Lorick. The ATF and the FBI share authority over Jenkins Act violations. The FBI is responsible for investigating failures to follow the law's reporting requirements, and the ATF investigates tobacco smuggling operations.

"John came up and we did surveillance together. He confirmed my suspicions. They had a front business in Charlotte, and they were so arrogant that they thought we were too stupid to figure out what was going on," he says, his eyes narrowed.

On September 1, 1996, the ATF officially opened an investigation into the smuggling scheme, and Fromme was assigned by the sheriff to work full-time helping the ATF. He spent much of the next three years zeroing in on the criminal operation. That included crawling around in the weeds behind the group's front tobacco shops to take surveillance photographs, following the vans in helicopters, and traveling as far as Dearborn, Michigan, to collect evidence, including the statements of undercover agents and informants. Unbeknownst to her, Angie Tsioumas was recorded by an undercover agent, prattling happily on about the cigarette-smuggling operation and her phony marriage to Mohammed Hammoud. That end of the investigation later led to other Hezbollah operatives in the Detroit area. The heavily Arab area of Dearborn is known among law enforcement officers who worked on the Charlotte case as "Hezbollah Central."

Fromme and the ATF team also worked with the state highway patrols of neighboring states such as West Virginia and Kentucky the smugglers drove through on their way to Michigan. Those patrols obligingly stopped several of the transports, all of which helped provide more evidence. Said Harb was stopped once, pled guilty to a misdemeanor, and was let off on probation, a common consequence for cigarette smugglers. The Charlotte smugglers thought they were being stopped because of their appearance and started hiring white American females to drive the loads. Angie Tsioumas was one of them.

Consistent with Hezbollah's overall strategy, Hammoud seemed to understand that cigarette smuggling was not a high priority for law enforcement, and that the penalties would be low even if he was apprehended. One of the investigative tools Fromme and the ATF used was a surveillance device called a pole camera. Although usually unobtrusive, they can be spotted, and at one point in the investigation someone pointed out to Hammoud one of the pole cameras.

"Well, let them watch," Hammoud scoffed.

Thereafter, he took care to cover up his license plate—after he had already parked the vehicle in plain view of the camera. Law enforcement officers took the incident as a display of Hammoud's contempt for the American system.

Fromme also got a lesson in the power of King Tobacco in North Carolina. Tobacco is the United States' ninth-largest cash crop. With a farm value in 2001 of $1.9 billion, the United States is fourth behind China, Brazil, and India in world production, and second behind Brazil in exports. Within the United States, North Carolina ranks number one in the production of tobacco. In 2003 the weed produced an annual farm income of $564.4 million dollars in the state. In 1997 there were 89,706 tobacco farmers in the United States and 12,095 tobacco farmers in North Carolina. Tobacco-related employment was 662,400 in the United States and 255,000 in North Carolina.

"I called up the state attorney general's office and asked them if they wanted to be involved in the investigation," Fromme says, his jaw set firmly. "I also called the North Carolina State Bureau of Investigation. They both declined to get involved. The answer I got was, 'The State of North Carolina is a tobacco-friendly state and as far as we are concerned, there are no violations of law occurring.' "

Technically, they were right. Only the federal Jenkins Act and the Michigan tax laws were being violated. But Fromme notes, only a little bitterly, that when the terrorist ring was finally broken, "the State Bureau of Investigation was sure there on the day of the raids."

By the spring of 1999 the investigation was complete and ready for prosecution. The ATF had referred the matter to Mark Calloway, the U.S. attorney in Charlotte. The case had been assigned for prosecution to Karen Edie, an assistant U.S. attorney.

Ken Bell had risen through the ranks to the position of first assistant U.S. attorney in Charlotte. He had tried his share of high-profile cases, including some of the drug gang cases that Rick Schwein had investigated, and he knew Bob Clifford from civil rights cases, but he was most interested now in public corruption cases. As the principal assistant, he could pick the cases he wanted to try personally. He was also responsible for the day-to-day management and oversight of all the office's criminal prosecutions. In that capacity, he, Mark Calloway, and Bob Conrad, then head of the criminal division and now U.S. attorney in Charlotte, would sit down every three months and go through the files on current criminal cases.

"The ATF did a fine job on the tobacco-smuggling investigation," Bell says. "It was basically finished and ready for prosecution. The problem was the nature of the case. The real losers were Michigan taxpayers. But the case would have to be tried in Statesville. We had real doubts that a tobacco-friendly, rural North Carolina jury would be very interested in trying to vindicate the interests of the state of Michigan. So, at that point we had just about decided to refer the matter for prosecution to the United States attorney in Detroit."

Before a decision could be made, Mark Calloway got a call from the FBI.

"I've got a very serious case that I must speak to you about," Bob Clifford said. "We need to see you right away. When can we meet?"

The next afternoon, Bob Clifford and Rick Schwein met with Mark Calloway, Bob Conrad, and Ken Bell in the U.S. attorney's conference room.

"They came over with a little projector and a screen," Bell remembers.

Bob Clifford also handed each of the prosecutors a piece of paper.

"I made them sign nondisclosure agreements," Clifford says. "That right away gets your attention. You're in the big leagues now."

Then Clifford started the slide show. He took them through the history of Hezbollah, working his way down to North Carolina.

"They are here . . . here . . . and here in Charlotte," he said, bringing up a slide of Hammoud, Harb, and the other known cell members. "You have a Hezbollah cell right here in Charlotte."

The prosecutors were stunned.

"We looked at each other and said, 'That can't be,' " Bell says.

But once Clifford's dramatic message had sunk in, Ken Bell grasped the significance of what he had just heard.

"I knew this was the case of a lifetime," he says. "It was a career maker. I turned to Calloway and said, 'I believe I'll take this one.' "

"I believe I want you to," replied Calloway.

Now everybody involved had a delicate course to navigate. The immediate problem was to bring Fromme, the ATF, and other law enforcement agencies into the bigger terrorism case without bruising any egos. One danger was the prospect of sinking into the turf fight that sometimes happens among federal agencies and among local departments and federal agencies. Much more investigation had to be done, and other agencies would have to be brought into the case.

Another problem was that much of the information regarding the Charlotte Hezbollah cell was highly classified intelligence data. The Chinese Wall was still up in those days, so even Rick Schwein wasn't getting all of the information that Bob Clifford knew about. Moreover, not everybody among all the possible investigative players had been cleared yet to see even the information that the FBI had on the criminal side of the case.

"I couldn't even tell Karen Edie why I was taking her case away from her," Bell says. "And we had to do the same kind of briefing for the ATF guys and Bob Fromme."

As the federal prosecutor, Bell played the role of quarterback and coach all in one. He had to develop the overall prosecution strategy—what specific crimes could be charged and proven—

while at the same time calling specific plays, such as what subpoenas to ask for and which witnesses to interview when, all the while making sure that everyone was moving along the same track and at a lively speed. At the same time, Bob Clifford and Rick Schwein were the lead investigators of the overall case now, Clifford working the intelligence side and Schwein the criminal.

Another meeting was held, this time with all the investigative agencies.

"I knew we had one chance to get them all on the team," Clifford recalls. "We had one shot at making them our allies or our enemies. I was determined we would build a coalition and that they would be our allies."

So Clifford took the larger group through his slide show again.

"When we brought up the picture of the local cell, the ATF guys went, 'Whoa!' " Clifford says. "Jaws dropped all over the room. They had no idea who they were dealing with."

The meeting was, he says, "a home run."

From there on out, Ken Bell says, "it was a magnificent team effort."

"GOD KEEP OUR LAND GLORIOUS AND FREE! . . ."

God keep our land glorious and free!
O Canada, we stand on guard for thee.
                    —*Lyric from the Canadian National*
                    Anthem "O Canada!"

Said Harb may have been the most visible of the Charlotte Hezbollah cell, but the investigators were worried most about Mohammed Hammoud. It soon became clear that Hammoud was the spider at the center of the web—a quiet, intense, cautious, and committed leader. It was at Hammoud's house that the weekly Thursday-night cell meetings were held. They featured a few prayers, followed by propaganda videos from Hezbollah's Al-Manar satellite television network—ranting speeches of Sheik Fadlallah and Secretary-General Hassan Naserallah, films of Hezbollah operations, and marching militiamen chanting slogans— then discussions of various criminal enterprises and Hammoud's pitch for donation of funds to Hezbollah.

In one video typical of many seized later from the home, Naserallah is addressing a crowd. He shouts, "We are people whose slogan was, is, and will remain to be, 'Death to America!' " The crowd roars back three times, "Death to America!" In another video of a Hezbollah martyr's funeral, an offscreen voice shouts "Death to America!" The crowd shouts back three times, "Death to America!"

One of the more chilling tapes was a home video made in Lebanon of several of Hammoud's small nieces and nephews. Their ages are not known, but they are barely beyond the toddler stage. Adults wearing sweatshirts emblazoned with Hezbollah slogans can be seen in the background. The children are crying.

An adult female voice can be heard prompting the children to speak: "Who are you? Who are you?"

Other adult voices are urging the children: "Say 'Hezbollah.' "

Someone slaps one of the kids to prompt the appropriate response. The female again prompts the kids: "Who are you? Come on, go ahead and say it. Say it with a loud voice."

Finally, one of the kids says, "Hezbollah."

The female repeats, "Who are you?"

"Hezbollah," says a child.

"He said it. He said it!" exults the female. "Who are you?"

"Hezbollah."

"Who are you?"

"Hezbollah."

Uncle Hammouda, as the children call Mohammed Hammoud in the video, may have been warmed by his nephew's statement of allegiance to Hezbollah. But he warned others in the cell that if they dared to mention his own affiliation with Hezbollah, they or their relatives would suffer unpleasant consequences. "If somebody lie and say I'm with Hezbollah, I will deal with him in Lebanon." Angie Tsioumas insists that she never learned enough Arabic to get the drift of any of this—not even the envelope on the refrigerator door for donations to the "widows and orphans," i.e., survivors of Hezbollah suicide bombers. By her account, the women went off to another room and did womanly things while the menfolk bonded over videos of Hezbollah attacks and "Death to America!" chants.

The neighbors on Donnefield Drive—a typical quiet street in a typical quiet suburban Charlotte neighborhood of well-kept lawns and manicured shrubs—noticed the gatherings. According to them, some of the meetings went on all night. They also thought Hammoud and his friends were less than friendly. One said, "They didn't wave back or talk to anybody on the block." Not waving back is close to a capital social offense in the easy congeniality of the South. But no one thought Hammoud and his dour friends were "helping terrorists or anything." Theories on the block about the goings-on at the mysterious house ranged from drug trafficking, through shades-drawn organized sex partying, to the near miss of religious meetings. No one knew that another neighbor who moved onto the block also had a secret—the rented house was an FBI "safe house," set up for surveillance of the cell.*

"We put in an undercover operative with just the right legend [cover story] for the neighborhood," says Bob Clifford. Eventually FBI investigators were also going through the trash and noting the addresses of all incoming and outgoing mail.

"We wanted the cell, and we knew he was the leader," Ken Bell says. "It was kind of odd, because he was the youngest of the Hammoud brothers. His position was unusual. We had to assume that for him to be given so much deference and respect, he had done something in Lebanon to 'make his stripes.' "

There was more to be concerned about than just that inference. The FBI's first secret informant had told them that the Hammoud brothers and their cousins, the Darwiches, were "100 percent Hezbollah." Two other witnesses testified that Ali Fayez Darwiche assured Mohammed Hammoud that he would "take care" of anybody who ratted them out by dealing with their relatives in Lebanon. Mohammed Hammoud had bragged to his associates that while on a trip back to the Middle East he had traveled to Damascus with the top Hezbollah political representatives to Iran and Syria. These were not the actions of a mere pizza delivery driver who had been corrupted into making a fast buck smuggling cigarettes. They were those of a person well connected to an established terrorism support network. Moreover, warned the FBI's inside source, if Hezbollah issued an order to carry out a terrorist attack within the United States, Mohammed Hammoud in particular would not hesitate to carry it out. It was not comforting to learn during the course of the investigation that Hammoud also went out to a rustic makeshift shooting range in the woods near

---

* The term "safe house" is often used to refer to a place for hiding persons under government protection. However, it also means a secure location from which undercover operations can be conducted or coordinated.

Charlotte and practiced military-style maneuvers with an AK-47 assault rifle and other weapons.*

"Mohammed Hammoud was the true believer," says Bob Clifford. "He was very serious, very disciplined, and very focused. He was the perfect sleeper. We had to find the flaw in his 'legend'—the story he had constructed of who he was."

Clifford—who of all the investigative team probably had the most comprehensive picture of the potential danger—saw that the risk was more than just the possibility of an isolated lashing out by a single intense fanatic and a handful of his sympathetic friends.

"If you know the history of Hezbollah, you know that it has an established modus operandi," he says. "It creates an infrastructure, as it did in Argentina, to support its terrorist attacks. Then it brings in the specialists. Everybody in America is now aware, after 9/11, that you can have committed terrorists living around you who look and act like they are assimilated, but who would act to commit violent acts against Americans if and when they are instructed to do so."

He pauses to let the point settle. "Well, we knew even before then that Hezbollah is more committed and better organized than al Qaeda."

Other experts agree. Some note for instructive comparison that, despite the urgings of people like FBI expert John O'Neill, the threat from al Qaeda was not taken seriously enough by American authorities for almost ten years after the first attack on the World Trade Center—an Islamist attack that many traditional experts dismissed at the time as an anomaly, the random act of a handful of inept local fanatics. The conventional wisdom among many "experts" was that no organized terrorist group would dare

---

* It is interesting to note that a six-page pamphlet titled *How Can I Train Myself for Jihad*, which was posted before September 11, 2001, on a radical Islamist Internet website and also was reported to have been found in terrorist safe houses in Kabul, Afghanistan, lectured that "military training is an obligation in Islam upon every sane, male, mature Muslim, whether rich or poor, whether studying or working and whether living in a Muslim or non-Muslim country." The pamphlet also discussed the relative availability of firearms and firearms training around the world. It described strict restrictions in some countries but noted that "In other countries, e.g. some states of USA, South Africa, it is perfectly legal for members of the public to own certain types of firearms. If you live in such a country, obtain an assault rifle legally, preferably AK-47 or variations, learn how to use it properly and go and practice in the areas allowed for such training."

launch a large-scale attack within the United States, since there were safer and easier-to-hit American targets abroad. Thus, as late as August 1, 1999, in a lengthy article surveying al Qaeda, *The Washington Post* could report with some evident skepticism that al Qaeda "looks less like a tight-knit group under one man's command than a disjointed, shadowy confederation of extremists from all over the Islamic world," and that "from court records as well as interviews with government officials and terrorism experts, it remains unclear whether al Qaeda has managed to assemble a powerful and dangerous network inside the United States or merely a sprinkling of sympathizers whose links to one another, and to bin Laden, are often tenuous." Meanwhile, al Qaeda was burrowing into the heart and sinew of America, planting operatives who were supported by a far-flung, well-developed, fully financed, and carefully concealed support network.

Hezbollah has been doing the same thing for an even longer period. In addition to its own structure, it gets a vast amount of funding from Iran and enjoys the sophisticated support of the Iranian intelligence and diplomatic apparatus. Nevertheless, there are skeptics who believe that Hezbollah would not attack within the United States. Some argue that Hezbollah has backed off from attacking U.S. interests since the 1980s. The former argument is unacceptably risky—it relies on indefinitely continued restraint by both Hezbollah and its major patron, Iran. That in turn depends on the United States never having to confront Hezbollah or Iran. That is not likely, given the outstanding indictments of Hezbollah operatives, and American concern about Iran's nuclear program and its continued arming of terrorists around the globe. If anything, a collision of interests with one or both foreign powers is more likely inevitable than not.

The argument that Hezbollah has backed off is just not true. Consider the following list of known hostile actions by Hezbollah, including attacks and planned attacks on American interests, which continue long past the bombings and hijackings of the 1980s:

- **2004—Iraq.** Hezbollah has at least two offices in Iraq. Although Hezbollah's leaders have been careful not to leave fingerprints that might prove that Hezbollah is directly involved in attacks on Americans, intelligence and counterterrorism sources say that Hezbollah is providing training and other expertise to the resistance forces battling Americans in Iraq. It is almost impossible to imagine otherwise, given the centuries of Shiite history in the belt across Iraq from Iran to Lebanon, Iran's intimate interest in Iraq and its dispatch to the country of Islamic Revolutionary Guards, and Hezbollah's inseparable connection with the IRG's Al Quds elite terror force through its master planner, Imad Mugniyah.

- **October 17, 2003—Lebanon.** Gunmen identifying themselves as members of Hezbollah stopped an official U.S. embassy motorcade on a routine trip in south Lebanon. The United States protested the action to the Lebanese government. This use of Hezbollah muscle demonstrates the contempt the organization still has for the United States, its willingness to use force to send the message that it is a force to be contended with, and its ability to operate as an independent entity even within a nominally sovereign nation.

- **1999—Paraguay.** Sobhi Mahmoud Fayad, a weapons expert serving as Hezbollah's military leader in the Tri-Border, was arrested in Asunción, Paraguay, for conducting surveillance of the U.S. embassy there. (In 2002, Fayad, whose brother is a senior Hezbollah official in Lebanon, was arrested again, convicted of tax evasion, and sentenced to six and a half years in a Paraguayan prison.)

- **1997—Cyprus.** A Hezbollah unit was discovered collecting operational intelligence on the U.S. embassy in Cyprus. Such surveillance is a necessary prelude to bombing attacks like the one described in the next item.

- **June 26, 1996—Khobar Towers, Dhahran, Saudi Arabia.** Lebanese Hezbollah terror operatives and senior Iranian officials played a major role in the bombing of Khobar Towers in Dhahran, Saudi Arabia. The eight-story building, part of a larger complex, housed personnel of the U.S. Air Force's 4404th Fighter Wing. Iran sponsored the creation of a Hezbollah wing in Saudi Arabia to carry out the attack, supplied the funds, and coordinated the planning and logistics for the bombing. Lebanese Hezbollah assisted in recruiting the Saudi terrorists, and trained them in Lebanon and elsewhere. It also sent an explosives expert to advise and assist in making the bomb. Several potential targets where large numbers of Americans could be killed were scouted before Khobar Towers was selected. The bomb was a classic Hezbollah product—a tanker truck that was converted to hold the equivalent of about 5,000 pounds of TNT. At 10:00 P.M. on June 26, 1996, the bomb went off with enormous force, killing 19 U.S. airmen and wounding another 372. The explosion blasted out a crater 85 feet wide and 25 feet deep. It blew out windows for blocks around and was felt 20 miles away in Bahrain. The Lebanese Hezbollah explosives expert stayed at a nearby farm during the two weeks preceding the blast and assisted the terrorists in converting the tank truck into a rolling bomb.

- **1990s—Singapore.** Singapore's Internal Security Department (ISD) reported in 2002 that during the 1990s Hezbollah operatives were recruiting members and collecting intelligence on U.S. and Israeli ships in the Strait of Malacca, and other targets in Singapore and nearby Malaysia. The Hezbollah operatives also planned a speedboat attack on U.S. ships. The attack would have been similar to one that an al Qaeda group planned to make against U.S. and British ships in the Strait of Gibraltar. The ISD did not reveal how Hezbollah's planned attack was foiled.

- **1990s—Russia.** Hezbollah recruited Palestinian students in Russia to carry out surveillance of American targets in Russia.

- **November 1989—Valencia, Spain.** Police busted a Hezbollah cell in Valencia, Spain, that had imported at least 440 pounds of plastic explosives for use in Europe against U.S. targets. The cell included three Hezbollah operatives and five supporters. The explosives were hidden in a shipment of canned fruit from Sidon, Lebanon, a Hezbollah hotbed. Arms were found in the homes of some of the cell members, who admitted planning attacks on U.S. interests. Another shipment of explosives from

Lebanon was later found on a ship in Cyprus. Additional arms and explosives were also discovered to have been cached in Europe.

- **March 1989—Germany.** German authorities arrested and convicted Hezbollah operative Bassam Gharib Makki—described in Chapter Four—on charges of possessing explosives and planning attacks on U.S. and Jewish targets in Germany.

It was for good reason that federal prosecutor Ken Bell considered Hezbollah to be "the most dangerous terrorist organization in the world." Given Hezbollah's violent record, its continuing animosity toward the United States, and Mohammed Hammoud's intense commitment to its cause, the investigators wanted to be able to act quickly if needed.

"We wanted to have indictable criminal offenses on the shelf, ready to go if we needed them, while we continued the investigation to make the terrorism charges," Bell says. "We wanted to be able to pick the cell members up immediately on criminal charges if we thought that they were going to leave the country or do something violent."

Overall, the investigation had two goals.

"We wanted to disrupt them, imprison them, and deport them," according to Bell. "And we wanted to send a message to Hezbollah. We wanted to show them, 'We are on to you, and we know what you are.'"

With Bell's guidance, the investigative team began shaping the case against the Hezbollah cell. The cigarette-smuggling case was solid and "on the shelf." The cell's rampant criminality also made it an ideal candidate for the tough federal RICO law, which provides longer-than-usual sentences for the crimes it covers.

"RICO allowed us to call them what they are—terrorists—and send a clear message to their leaders that this is not a friendly environment in which to operate," says the FBI's Rick Schwein. "In order to use RICO, we had to prove two basic things: that there was an 'ongoing pattern of criminality' and that those engaged in it were 'associated in fact.'"

"There was clearly an ongoing pattern of criminality," says

Schwein. "We had racketeering predicates falling out of the sky. That was their major vulnerability."*

There were a number of ways to show that the players were all associated in fact—their cooperative criminal acts like smuggling cigarettes and credit card fraud, the businesses and business relationships they built from the smuggling proceeds, and their family ties. But one association that became the cornerstone of the RICO case was Hezbollah.

"These were all either members of, sympathetic to, or affiliated with Hezbollah," according to Schwein. "And that is no different from a motorcycle gang that wears distinctive colors and gets together to advance the club's criminal businesses."

Using Hezbollah as one of the indicators of the cell members' association in fact would have an important advantage—when search warrants were eventually executed to collect evidence on the RICO charges, anything related to Hezbollah would be a legitimate target of the search—just as gang "indicia" had been in the Outlaws Motorcycle Club case that Schwein had worked on. "It allowed us to go in and collect evidence of their relationship to a designated foreign terrorist organization." This evidence could then be used in turn to support the terrorism charges.

The number of different law enforcement agencies that worked on the team illustrates the range of the cell's criminal activity. In addition to the FBI and ATF, the joint investigation included federal agents from the Immigration and Naturalization Service, the Internal Revenue Service, and the Diplomatic Security Service of the U.S. Department of State, as well as local officers of the Charlotte-Mecklenburg police department and the Iredell County sheriff's office. The work of filling out the details of the investigation was divided among these agencies according to their respective expertise and jurisdictions. "We didn't have a joint terrorism task force," says Bell. "But we functioned as if we did."

In July 1999 the FBI's Charlotte field office got a new special agent in charge, Chris Swecker. Bell and Swecker knew each other

---

* "Racketeering predicates" are a list of some 27 state and federal crimes that the RICO law allows to be cited as part of a pattern of racketeering. In addition to cigarette smuggling, some of the federal offenses include certain types of gambling, prostitution, obscenity, theft, fraud, extortion, bribery, and obstruction of justice.

in unusual ways. They had overlapped at Wake Forest law school (Bell was two years ahead of Swecker). Bell and Swecker's wife went to high school together, and Swecker and Bell's wife went to college together. Swecker had no previous experience in terrorism cases but, says Bob Clifford, "he grasped what we were doing quickly and was a big supporter."

The team's biggest challenge was investigating and proving a terrorism charge against the Hezbollah cell. One problem was timing. The federal law barring material support for any group officially designated by the secretary of state as a "foreign terrorist organization" was passed in April 1996. But the Clinton State Department did not issue its first list of designated terrorism organizations, including Hezbollah, until sixteen months later, on October 8, 1997—only after Congress threatened to reduce the agency's budget if it continued to delay. This meant that no one could be charged for any act of sending funds or other aid to Hezbollah before October 8, 1997. Thereafter, however, sending funds, equipment, or practically any other form of support to Hezbollah was a serious felony under federal law.

A second problem was that the crime of material support, and the designations of the specific terrorist groups, broke new legal ground across perilous constitutional territory. The Charlotte case would be the first criminal case to go to trial under the new law, and no one wanted to make a mistake that would cripple the law its first time out of the blocks. So, Bell and his local backup, Assistant U.S. Attorney Scott Broyles, asked for help from the legal experts in the terrorism section of the Justice Department in Washington. They sent a brilliant, vivacious young lawyer, Martha Rubio, who had successfully defended the material support law against several constitutional challenges raised by civil rights groups who wanted to strangle the new law before it even went into effect. Even though these preenforcement lawsuits failed to block the new law, serious legal challenges could still be mounted to a real prosecution. Rubio would come to be a valued player in many aspects of the case during the investigation and trial.

The final and biggest problem was the basic one of proving the facts. Clifford had intelligence information that showed the outlines of the funding pipeline from the Charlotte cell to Hezbollah's leaders in Lebanon. But most of it could not be used in a criminal prosecution. It came from confidential informants who would never testify in open court for fear of violent retaliation or from intelligence sources that would be compromised by a public trial. Until Clifford got better evidence of a clear connection to a foreign power, he could not even get a FISA order to conduct wiretaps and searches. Unless something or someone broke the legal logjam and opened up a new line of evidence that could be brought into a courtroom, no terrorism charge could be made. Meanwhile, the clock was ticking—there were rumors that Hammoud and perhaps some of the others were thinking of packing up and moving back to Lebanon.

The curious journeys of Said Harb finally led to exactly the opening the team needed.

Harb got involved in most of his criminal behavior—like the quip about why dogs behave the way they do—just because he could. The American way of life was like the Big Rock Candy Mountain to a man with Harb's larcenous instincts. The system made it easy for him. Credit card companies, government agencies, and obliging Americans who were willing to commit a few "little" crimes to make some tax-free money all greased the skids. But the reemergence of Mohammed Dbouk, Harb's boyhood best friend, dragged the happy-go-lucky con man firmly into Hezbollah's international web. Ironically, Harb's friendship with Dbouk evolved into perhaps the most serious terrorism-related criminal offenses in the Charlotte case. It could have put him in prison for a very long time. But it ended up giving the opportunistic Harb a get-out-of-jail-free pass.

Anyone can run his personal credit cards to the limit and then walk away without paying them off—if he is willing to ruin his credit record and be hounded for years by collection agencies and legal maneuvers. But Said Harb was not just anyone. He created an entire rogues' gallery of phony identities, got credit cards in those names, and went through a patient cycle of first paying cards off to build up his credit limit on each before finally "busting out" the card when the credit limit was high enough. By the time

Harb was himself busted, he was using so many different identities that he needed a bank of telephones that rang a different tone for each identity. He kept a notebook with the critical information about each fake identity so he could quickly refer to the basic facts about who he was pretending to be at any given moment.

Harb got as many as fourteen credit cards in his own name, then branched out and got his first fake identity when his cousin Mustafa left the United States. "My cousin, me and him were supposed to split that," Harb explained matter-of-factly. "I bought his identity from him. I established credit, at about around $45,000."

Harb got at least ten credit cards in Mustafa Harb's name. He found it amazingly easy to parlay Mustafa's driver's license into three new licenses—in the names of Said Harb, Harb Mustapha, and Ahmad Al al-Qam—by simply visiting the North Carolina Department of Motor Vehicles, whose employees apparently thought Arabic names were all pretty much the same.

"I went to the DMV and I told them I want to change an address or whatever. I just make up an excuse," Harb explained. In the process of changing an address, he also changed the name. No one seemed to notice or care. Harb kept the old license and walked out with what was essentially a new license in a different name. "You know, I didn't have a machine that is going to invent cards or anything like that. It was from the DMV. It was the real ID."

Then Harb added several new personalities—Ali Jaber, his old friend Mohammed Dbouk, and others—and continued harvesting plastic from the American system of easy personal credit.

"It worked pretty much the same way," Harb said, describing his system of scamming the willing credit card issuers. "What I'll do is I'll go to the bank. I'll open a thousand-dollar CD [certificate of deposit]. And then I'll withdraw a loan for a thousand dollars secured by that CD. And when the credit report shows up, okay, it's going to show up on the credit report as you have a loan, but it won't say it's a secured loan. It doesn't show up that way in the credit bureau. So when somebody pull up your credit after six months, well, this guy is already established. So you apply for a credit card, they send you a credit card."

It was simplicity itself.

"And then you just wait," Harb continued. "Every two, three

months, you know, you pick up which credit cards you want to apply for. Because they start sending you—I mean, you know how credit card companies are—they send you all these applications. You just pick up the right ones and pretty much get credit."

The inability of the United States government to keep track of the aliens among us—who comes in, where they live, and who goes out—opened up another vein Harb mined for fake identities he could use for credit card fraud. When Arab friends of Harb left the country, he bought their Social Security numbers from them.

"Let's say, you know, my friend is leaving to Lebanon," Harb explained. "He say, 'Okay, Said, you know I have no credit whatever. You know how to establish credit. Let's work something out.' Then, either I'll buy it for, let's say, $5,000, or $10,000, or whatever. Or I'll say, 'Well, when it generates enough money, then, we'll split it half, half.' That's pretty much it. I never went and made a fake Social Security. I had no way of making fake stuff. I wasn't interested in that."

The United States couldn't keep track of all these people Harb pretended to be, but he could, with his system of different phone rings and his little green notebook.

"You know, every time the phone would ring, I'd know which one was which. I never answered with my name. So I'll be like, 'Hello?' And then, you know, they would ask for who they were looking for." Harb would then turn to his notebook of multiple personalities, which contained, "Peoples' names I was building credit for, all their Social Securities, IDs, everything like that. So in case a credit card company called, I'd just flip the page and all the information was there. So I'm on the phone, they can ask me anything because everything is there."

Fake credit cards were not Harb's only major scam. He was also a one-man marriage factory. "When you're a foreigner," says Harb, "you know that in order for you to stay in this country, the safest way is to get married." And when his relatives needed to get married, Harb and his friends at Domino's Pizza delivered.

The first two fake marriages were those of his brother, Haissam Harb, and his brother-in-law, Samir Debk. Said sent the two money to buy 90-day visitor's visas from a corrupt foreign national employed by the U.S. embassy in Cyprus at $8,000 apiece, and airfare to get to the United States. Once the two were in Charlotte, "So they won't be illegal or out of status, I had them married to some girls I knew."

The girls were Terri Pish and Tonia Moore—Domino's Pizza employees. "Terri was a friend of mine," he said. "I didn't know Tonia, but Terri was a friend of mine for some years. And I asked it as a favor. I didn't want to put it as, well, you do this, I'll give you the money because I felt between friends it shouldn't be that way. But the understanding was, I'm going to help you out, you help me out. So favor for a favor."

Terri's recollection is a little different, but she doesn't dispute the basic facts: "At first I said no, I wasn't interested in doing it. About six months later, he called me on the phone and he was really upset and he just said can you please do this favor for me. And I finally just gave in and said yeah, I would do it."

Harb then took over all of the paperwork. "I did all of that. I filled out the applications. Took them to court to get married. Everything."

There was one big problem—Terri Pish and Tonia Moore were lesbian companions. The marriages were never even close to real. Neither was the marriage Harb arranged for his sister, Fatme Harb. She was actually married to Samir Debk, who complained to Harb that he was lonely and wanted his wife to come to America. So Harb obligingly enlisted Wayne Swaringen, an African American driver for Domino's Pizza. He gave Swaringen $10,000 and travel expenses to fly to Lebanon and "marry" Fatme. The happy couple ultimately had to get married on Cyprus. Because Swaringen was not a Muslim, no one would marry them in Lebanon. Two months after the marriage, Harb flew to Cyprus and went to the U.S. embassy with his sister for her visa interview. For a con man like Harb, the interview was disappointingly superficial. It clearly took the fun out of the game for him.

"Well, it was very short, number one. I mean, they didn't even take three minutes. Okay. There wasn't any personal questions. And the consulate who interviewed her, I assume he doesn't speak any Arabic because, number one, it is in Cyprus so if he speaks anything, it will be Greek. So I told my sister, 'I'm going to ask you whatever I ask you, just, you know, say whatever you want to say.

I'm going to answer it anyway.' So he asked her did she know that Wayne had a kid. I asked her, 'What did you eat today?' Pretty much that's how it went. I answered a couple of questions and then that was it. I mean, the weird thing for me was that I was expecting—you know, he's Christian, she's Muslim—so I expected some questions along these lines. He's black; she's not. I expected some questions along these lines. None of it was asked. And that's it."

Harb's next stop was the Internet pornography business with a friend named Mohit Behl. Because pornography is usually legal under American law—so long as it does not involve children—Harb claims to have seen the lucrative website as a way to get away from his life of crime. He was soon averaging about $10,000 a month for what he convinced himself were purely business duties. As long as he was not actually doing any of the dirty work, buying and taking pictures or working on the Internet website, he wasn't really in the pornography business. He saw himself as a clean-hands bean counter.

"I justify it to myself as, okay, I'm not working in pornography. Okay. But I'm getting money from Mohit. So I'm like getting money from Mohit, not from pornography. That's how I was looking at it." In fact, the money came from pornography, and pornography in any case was not a way out of crime for Harb but a way into even more—he and Behl set up a bogus bank account through which they double-billed their porno customers.

Harb was now riding a bicycle on a high wire, juggling new criminal schemes as they fell into his arms. But he was losing his balance and started to make big mistakes. His brother, Haissam Harb, went to visit friends in Ohio in late 1999. They persuaded him to visit the casinos in nearby Windsor, Canada—a violation of his immigrant status in the United States. When Haissam tried to get back in, he was caught and deported to Lebanon.* Unaware that he was already under intense FBI scrutiny, Said Harb tried in 2000 to bribe an INS official, David Howell, to get his brother back

---

* It may be that the INS didn't "catch" Haissam at all. According to Said Harb, the agency had issued two green cards with the same number, one to a woman and one to Haissam. When border agents checked Haissam's card on his attempted reentry, its number was returned as in the woman's name. The fluke led to discovery of Haissam's illegal exit and return, then to his detention and ultimate deportation.

into the country. The FBI set up an elaborate sting to record Harb's acts. Agent Howell took $10,000 from Harb, pretending to go along with the bribe. It was all watched and taped by the FBI.

By then, Harb had made an even more fateful choice. He had decided to help his old friend Mohammed Dbouk, the Hezbollah operative with whom he had been in regular contact since leaving Lebanon. Dbouk followed Harb to the United States in 1988, and lived in Detroit for about a year and a half. He returned to Lebanon after his parents were killed in an automobile accident. Because the Beirut airport was closed at the time, Harb flew to Yugoslavia to meet and comfort his old friend. The two drove together down to Lebanon. They stayed in touch over the following years. Meanwhile Dbouk's sister moved to Vancouver, British Columbia. In 1998 Dbouk told Harb that he wanted to come back West, but was having a hard time getting a visa. When opportunity presented itself, Harb was ready with a typically clever solution.

"His sister get into a bad accident and I was talking to him," Harb recalled. "I said, 'Why don't you let me call your sister, see if she can talk to the doctor. The doctor will fax some papers, or whatever, saying she was in pretty bad shape and you need to come and see her.' And that's what happened. He went to the Canadian embassy based on that and he came. And when he came in, he applied for political asylum in Canada."

When Dbouk's own wife and children joined him shortly thereafter, Harb sent him $4,000, allegedly as a friendly gesture of help. "When his wife came, he had to move from his sister's house," Harb claims. "I convinced him that he should take money from me so he can move and rent an apartment and so forth."

Harb made two trips to Vancouver in March and August 1999. FBI agent Rick Schwein knew of Harb's journeys. He also knew Harb was involved in some kind of criminal scheme, but he did not know exactly why he was going to Vancouver. Bob Clifford soon found out. But he couldn't tell Schwein what he had found out because of the Chinese Wall—his information came from a friendly foreign intelligence service. Dbouk's real role in Canada was as a procurement agent for Hezbollah. He was working with another Hezbollah operative, his brother-in-law Ali Adham Amhaz. The pair were taking orders from Hassan Hilu Laqis, a senior Hezbollah official in Lebanon responsible for overseeing procurement of military equipment from North America, who was himself working under the direction of master plotter Imad Mugniyah. Harb had been drawn into their operation. His friendly gesture—which Dbouk soon converted with Harb's consent into a contribution to the cause of Hezbollah—lit up like a rocket on the radar screen of the Canadian Security Intelligence Service, which had begun to watch Hezbollah with great interest by the time Harb decided to help out his childhood buddy. Harb didn't know it yet, but he had gotten himself into a jam from which there would be only one way out.

The Canadian Security Intelligence Service (CSIS) was born in 1984, the child of a scandal that arose from a job too well done.

For the 120 years before CSIS was created, Canada's federal police force—the Royal Canadian Mounted Police (RCMP) and its predecessors—had been responsible both for enforcing the law and for collecting intelligence on threats to Canada's security. The security intelligence function was tiny until the Second World War. In 1939 it consisted of three agents and two stenographers. But wartime espionage and the revelation by a Soviet defector in 1945 of a vast Soviet espionage network inside Canada made it clear the nation needed to devote more resources to monitoring threats to its security.

The threat was not only espionage from outside the country. In the 1960s Canada was rocked by the terrorist activities of a violent separatist group that called itself the Front de Libération du Québec (FLQ). The FLQ was founded by George Schoeters, a Belgian émigré who admired Che Guevara. Between its founding in 1963 and 1970, its members committed more than 200 acts of terrorism, including bank robberies, setting off a massive blast at the Montreal Stock Exchange that injured 27 people, other bombings that resulted in three deaths, and two shooting deaths. At least two FLQ members were trained in assassination techniques by the PLO in Jordan. An affiliated American cell, which included a Canadian woman and American Black Muslims, also had contact with Cuban diplomats in New York. The cell, some of whose members had been on goodwill visits to Castro's Cuba, acquired dynamite and plotted to blow up the Statue of Liberty in 1965. Infiltrated by a young New York City undercover police officer, the cell's members were rolled up after they brought the dynamite in from Canada, and were tried and convicted.

In October 1970—one month after the PLO's "Black September" in Jordan—the FLQ erupted in a wave of terrorism that shook the Canadian government and became known as the "October Crisis." The group's acts of terror included the kidnappings of James Richard Cross, the British trade commissioner, and Pierre LaPorte, the Quebec vice premier and minister of labor. Cross was eventually released, but LaPorte was strangled to death. These violent events stunned ordinary Canadians and enraged the government. Prime Minister Pierre Trudeau invoked the War Measures Act, declared martial law, and told the RCMP to take care of the problem. The RCMP took the prime minister at his word and went all out after the FLQ.

At the time, these aggressive measures were popular. As so often happens, however, once the threat was suppressed and things calmed down the public had second thoughts—just as in the United States criticism of CIA and FBI actions during the 1970s inspired the FISA law and eventually led to the erection of the Chinese Wall. Stories surfaced in Canada about abuses by the RCMP's security service during its scourging of the FLQ. The secret 1981 report of the McDonald Commission, later made public, confirmed that RCMP agents had used methods that ranged from poor judgment to out and out illegality, including scare tactics, false arrests on trumped-up charges, assault, extortion, intimidation, and illegal entries. The commission recommended that a security intelligence service be established that would be completely separate from the law enforcement function, and in 1984 CSIS was created.

CSIS has increasingly focused on counterterrorism since then. The agency says that in 1984 it devoted 80 percent of its resources to counterintelligence and only 20 percent to counterterrorism, but that it has now "tilted substantially" to counterterrorism. The CSIS explains why in careful, diplomatic language: "Our borders are long and unique among developed countries—we have a common border with the United States, one of the world's preeminent terrorist targets. Our openness and respect for human rights and freedoms make Canada an attractive place to live and do business, not just for the hundreds of thousands of legitimate immigrants who come here each year, but also for members of terrorist and criminal organizations." David Harris, the former chief of strategic planning at CSIS, put things bluntly to a U.S. congressional subcommittee. "Canada is sought out as a haven by terrorists. Fifty international terrorist organizations are represented on our soil. Some of our laws are, frankly, terrorist-friendly in inadvertently establishing immigration, refugee, and financial mechanisms that are vulnerable to exploitation by violence-prone groups."

American experts have been concerned for years about Canada's role as a "passive enabler of terrorism." The two countries share the longest international border in the world, over 4,000 miles, much of it through remote rural or wilderness areas. Worry about Canada being used as a launching pad for attacks on the United States has become sharper since September 11, 2001. A recent CSIS report stated "with the possible exception of the United States, there are more terrorist organizations active in Canada than anywhere in the world." The report added that terrorists in Canada have moved "from significant support roles, such as fundraising and procurement, to actually planning and preparing terrorist acts from Canadian territory." Such a move from support cells to active attack cells is what Hezbollah did in the Tri-Border and what U.S. authorities fear Hezbollah could do in the United States.

The case of an Algerian named Ahmed Ressam is a notorious example of an attempted cross-border attack from Canada. It would have a major impact on the Charlotte Hezbollah case. Ressam's attack plan was thwarted only by the vigilance of a single border patrol agent. Ressam belonged to a Montreal cell that was linked both to al Qaeda and the Armed Islamic Group, an Algerian Islamist terror organization. American experts regard Montreal as a particularly weak spot in the defensive wall against terrorists. On December 14, 1999, Ressam attempted to enter the United States, traveling by car from Canada on a ferry. A U.S. Border Patrol agent at Port Angeles, Washington, became suspicious

of Ressam's demeanor and searched the trunk of his rented
Chrysler. He tried to flee on foot, but was apprehended and arrested. The trunk contained fertilizer, chemicals, batteries, and
timers for making bombs. Ressam intended to bomb the Los Angeles International Airport as part of a millennium attack on the
United States.

It is no coincidence that just weeks before Ressam was apprehended, a police raid in Paraguay reportedly disrupted plans by
Hezbollah and al Qaeda to make simultaneous bomb attacks on
Jewish targets in Buenos Aires, Ciudad del Este, and Ottawa. U.S.
intelligence officials have seen an increase in such "ad hoc" or
"tactical" cooperation between Hezbollah and al Qaeda.

The CSIS will not say when it began to monitor Hezbollah's
activities in Canada, but it was certainly doing so when Said Harb
sent $4,000 to his friend Mohammed Dbouk in early 1999. The in-
telligence agency then and now operates in a manner like that of
the "foreign intelligence mode" that so irritated Bob Clifford when
he took over the FBI's Hezbollah unit—it watches, collects, and
documents the activities of its targets, but generally does not seek
to actively disrupt their operations. CSIS knew that Ali Amhaz
and Mohammed Dbouk were buying high-tech equipment in
Canada that had various useful military applications. They
bought the matériel partly out of funds sent to them from Hezbollah in Lebanon, and partly out of monies friends derived from
criminal schemes, such as credit card fraud.

CSIS had mounted wiretaps and other communication intercepts to collect intelligence on the Hezbollah cell. The intelligence
agency was reading the Canadian cell's communications with its
superiors in Lebanon. The intercepts included clear references to
Imad Mugniyah's role as overlord of the terror support operation.
They also revealed Harb's contacts with Dbouk. The RCMP was
investigating separately the Canadian cell's criminal operations. It
knew that Harb was up to his usual tricks, working credit card and
bank scams with Dbouk. Taking the two agencies' information together, it is clear that Harb was involved both for his own enrich-
ment and to help Dbouk's mission for Hezbollah.

Dbouk and Amhaz were buying what is known in the national
security world as "dual-use equipment," then shipping it to

Lebanon. James Campbell—a retired U.S. Navy commander and former supervisory intelligence officer with the Office for Counterterrorism Analysis at the Defense Intelligence Agency— explained the term. "Dual-use equipment is that which can be used certainly for civilian application, a business application, this sort of thing," he said. "But it also has a secondary application, for military or terrorist purposes."

Dbouk regularly received instructions from Lebanon to buy specific brands and models of dual-use equipment. The list included, among other things, night-vision devices, surveying equipment, global positioning systems, sophisticated video and digital photography equipment, advanced computers, stun guns, naval equipment, nitrogen cutters, and laser range finders.*

Commander Campbell explained at the trial of the Charlotte Hezbollah cell members exactly how some examples of the equipment could be used by Hezbollah in its terror operations.

"The Garmin Navtalk VHS 720," he explained, "is a GPS/cell phone combination system. So you've got a GPS and a cell phone in one nice little portable package so that you can navigate and talk. That particular system could be used as designed for identifying precisely the location of fixed targets. It could also be modified for use as a very sophisticated remote control improvised explosive device. In other words, you could modify this system and then use it to set off a bomb."

Another device was a Kenwood VC-H1 transceiver. "This particular item incorporates a digital camera feature so that an individual could take up to ten digital images and transmit those images using a handheld transceiver," he said. "It lends itself nicely to conducting preoperational surveillance against a target, then immediately transmits these images back to a headquarters element."

The stun guns? "Hezbollah has perfected the tactic of hostage taking. The stun guns would lend themselves well to hostage-taking operations."

---

* The Hezbollah operatives even explored the possibility of taking out life insurance policies on suicide bombers. The proceeds could be used to further Hezbollah's work. It is not clear whether any such policies were ever purchased.

At the time, these procurement operations were legal in Canada. However, CSIS knew of other troublesome Hezbollah activities in Canada. It operates car theft rings to raise funds, recruits operatives, and has agents in every major Canadian city who have videotaped potential targets for bombing.

Until recently, however, the Canadian government has taken a benign view of Hezbollah. In spite of pressure from the United States and from its own Jewish citizens—who are worried by the Argentine example of Hezbollah's wrath being unleashed against Jews worldwide—the Canadian government officially distinguished between Hezbollah's so-called "social" wing and its "military" wing. Even after al Qaeda's attacks on the United States prompted Canada to enact its first Anti-Terrorism Act in 2001, Canada refused to follow the U.S. example and list Hezbollah as a terrorist organization to whom it was forbidden to give support.

This finally changed in December 2002. One reason was a secret CSIS report that documented Hezbollah's long record of terror and its specific activities in Canada. Leaked news of the report brought pressure on the government to act against Hezbollah. The international terror group itself did not help its cause during the month of December 2002. Several speeches by Hezbollah secretary-general Hassan Naserallah, in which he reportedly urged Palestinians "to take suicide bombing worldwide—don't be shy about it" and threatened that Hezbollah would "act everywhere in the world," contributed to Canadian concern. And there was the image of children wearing Hezbollah headbands and suicide-bomb belts leading a demonstration before the American consulate in Cape Town, South Africa, during which the mob shouted "Death to America!" and "One American, One Bullet!"

In 1999, however, when CSIS learned from its intercepts of Said Harb's appearance on the stage of the Canadian buying scheme, it could not arrest him. But it did the next best thing in March of that year. It told the FBI in Washington what it knew about Harb. His connection to the Hezbollah procurement ring was a clear violation of American criminal law and it provided documentation of the Charlotte cell's link to a foreign power. At last, Bob Clifford could go to court and ask for a FISA order to start intercepting the cell's communications.

"I knew with that information we could get over the hump," Clifford says. "It showed a direct connection with Hezbollah operatives in Canada, and from them to Hezbollah in Lebanon."

But there was still a hurdle for the criminal side of the investigation—unless Canada was willing to allow its CSIS intercepts to be used as evidence in an open trial, there was no way the damning record of hundreds of conversations could get over the Chinese Wall and into the courtroom. Even then there would be major problems with federal rules of evidence.

On the other hand, Said Harb could connect all the dots—if he could be flipped to the government side. He could testify firsthand about the Canadian operations and about Mohammed Hammoud and the operations of the Charlotte cell. Everything Ken Bell, Bob Clifford, and Rick Schwein knew about Harb suggested he could be flipped. But they needed a way to squeeze him into a corner so that he had no choice but to turn on his friends. The only way to do that took them right back to the Canadian problem—if they could convince CSIS to let them use the communications intercepts, Harb could be made to see that he was nailed cold and would be facing a long term in prison.

An intricate dance thus commenced in the spring of 1999. A rolling American team of FBI investigators and Justice Department lawyers shuttled to Canada to court the Canadians. By the summer of 2000, the dance turned into a tense race against time.

Bob Clifford drafted requests for FISA wiretaps on Said Harb and Mohammed Hammoud as soon as he learned of the Canadian tip in March 1999. However, his requests languished without action—along with similar requests from dozens of other cases—in the Clinton Justice Department for almost a year. The Chinese Wall had been a problem for Clifford when he took over the Hezbollah unit in 1994. By 1999 it had become a fortress. Requests like Clifford's disappeared through the gates of the Justice Department, where they either came back with nitpicks or simply sat without action or explanation.

"It was like pulling teeth to get things out of OIPR," Clifford recalls.

The new fortress had been erected by two key Clinton political appointees: the Justice Department's number two official, Deputy Attorney General Jamie Gorelick, and a politically connected lawyer named Richard Scruggs. Brought up from Miami by Attorney General Janet Reno, Scruggs directed for a crucial time under Gorelick an obscure but extremely powerful office called the Office of Intelligence Policy and Review (OIPR).* All of the government's requests for FISA orders must be cleared through OIPR—it is the gatekeeper to the FISC, its chief the attorney general's principal adviser on national security legal matters. It was precisely in the OIPR that Clifford's requests sat gathering dust.

Jamie Gorelick, a graduate of Harvard and Harvard Law, is a high-powered Washington lawyer and Democratic party political operative. A partner in the influential law firm of Wilmer, Cutler & Pickering, she was appointed as a Democratic member to the national commission investigating the government's role in the attack of September 11, 2001.† Her service on the panel and a perception within the Bush administration that it was being blamed for the success of the terrorist attacks in a partisan manner prompted dramatic testimony by Attorney General John Ashcroft on April 13, 2004.

"We did not know an attack was coming because for nearly a decade our government had blinded itself to its enemies," Ashcroft said. "Our agents were isolated by government-imposed walls, handcuffed by government-imposed restrictions, and starved for basic information technology."

Then Ashcroft lobbed a bombshell—Commissioner Gorelick was herself the author of a secret 1995 memorandum that so institutionalized, strengthened, and broadened the Chinese Wall that it crippled counterterrorism investigations. "In 1995 the Justice Department embraced flawed legal reasoning, imposing a series of restrictions on the FBI that went beyond what the law required," Ashcroft said. He announced that he had declassified the memo-

---

* To avoid confusion it should be noted that there is another well-known Richard Scruggs, a successful plaintiff's trial lawyer from Pascagoula, Mississippi. That Richard Scruggs is best known for his leading role in lawsuits against the tobacco industry.
† The commission's formal title is the National Commission on Terrorist Attacks Upon the United States.

randum, titled "Instructions on Separation of Certain Foreign Counterintelligence and Criminal Investigations," so that the commission could see for itself what had been done in Gorelick's name as deputy attorney general.

The uncomprehending news media largely buried Ashcroft's revelation in a flurry of "he said, she said" stories dismissing the matter as political squabbling, typified by *The Washington Post*'s observation that "Ashcroft's pointed remarks capped a day of finger-pointing." Gorelick's defenders correctly but incompletely pointed out that there had been a wall even before her 1995 memorandum. However, there is no question that Gorelick's memorandum imposed severe new stringencies—Mary Jo White, the tough, highly respected, and Clinton-appointed United States attorney in New York, strongly criticized the new procedures in a protest memorandum to Gorelick. White had gained prominence in the successful prosecution of a number of high-profile organized crime and terrorism cases and well understood the adverse impact that the new restrictions would have.

Moreover, the same memorandum and its effect had been described by the independent and nonpartisan FISCR in its landmark ruling issued nearly two years *before* Ashcroft's testimony. The 1995 memorandum was then still highly classified and the appeals court referred to it circumspectly, but FISCR's ruling was the same as Ashcroft's criticism—namely—that the Gorelick procedures went far beyond what the law required. In its lengthy opinion tearing down the wall, the FISCR described Gorelick's edict (without naming her) as the touchstone of greatly increased Chinese Wall restrictions. Her memo, the FISCR wrote, recommended "limited contacts between the FBI and the Criminal Division in cases where FISA surveillance or searches were being conducted by the FBI" and "eventually came to be narrowly interpreted within the Department of Justice, and most particularly by OIPR, as requiring OIPR to act as a 'wall' to prevent the FBI intelligence officials from communicating with the Criminal Division regarding ongoing FCI or FCI investigations.

"Thus, the focus became the nature of the underlying investigation, rather than the general purpose of the surveillance," the court continued. "Once prosecution of the target was being considered, the procedures, as interpreted by OIPR in light of the case law, prevented the Criminal Division from providing any meaningful advice to the FBI."

It was no accident that the OIPR subsequently "narrowly interpreted" Gorelick's memo to prevent "any meaningful advice to the FBI." Nor was the slowdown in FISA requests accidental. These were the result of the forceful wishes of Richard Scruggs, who was an assistant federal prosecutor in Miami at the same time that Janet Reno was making a name for herself as the Florida state prosecutor for Dade County. The two came to know each other, and when Bill Clinton named Reno attorney general, she brought Scruggs to Washington as a special assistant. His first prominent role was directing the Justice Department's defense of Reno's actions during the siege at the Branch Davidian compound in Waco, Texas, and the resulting fiery deaths of about 80 members on April 19, 1993.*

In October 1993, Mary C. Lawton, a career government lawyer who had been the head of OIPR since 1982 and who helped write the FISA law, died suddenly of a pulmonary embolism. Reno subsequently appointed Scruggs Counsel for Intelligence Policy and Review, the federal government's top lawyer on national security policy. He was the first political appointee to hold the job. Lawton was beloved within the intelligence community, whose agents she called her "nuns." They felt she was tough but fair, thoroughly understood national security law, and in the words of retired FBI agent and former Hezbollah/Iran unit chief Ken Piernik, "She wanted to get the job done." Scruggs, who had a distinguished career as a federal criminal prosecutor but no significant experience in national security matters, began rooting through Lawton's old files. He decided that she had been lax in handling FISA requests and let far too much through OIPR and over the Chinese Wall. The handling of the successful 1994 prosecution of CIA turncoat

---

* Coauthor Tom Diaz was Democratic counsel to the U.S. House of Representatives Subcommittee on Crime and did the staff work for Democratic committee members during hearings on Waco in the summer of 1995. In this capacity he worked with a number of officials from the Clinton administration. He had some limited contact with Scruggs at the time, but dealt primarily with other administration staff from the Justice and Treasury Departments who were responsible for congressional relations.

Aldrich Ames especially alarmed Scruggs. He raised his concerns with Reno, inspired the Gorelick memorandum and monitored its enforcement with a gimlet eye once it was issued. Scruggs was no longer head of OIPR in March 1999 when Clifford submitted his FISA requests in the Hezbollah case. But the formalistic fortress he and Gorelick built remained in place, guarded by enthusiastic and faceless minions of their policies.

Interestingly enough, Scruggs was himself the subject of a formal inquiry by the Justice Department after he admitted having leaked to two reporters writing a book in 1995. He said he merely "indirectly confirmed" and "corrected" sensitive and highly classified information about the FBI's surveillance of the Aum Shinrikyo terrorist group in New York. "This was more than an ordinary leak," John L. Martin, who headed espionage investigations in the Justice Department at the time, said. "This was a horribly egregious offense."

Scruggs—who had blocked a FISA request by the FBI's New York office to monitor the terrorist cult's New York members after a Tokyo subway poison gas attack—was ultimately given a letter admonishing him for "bad judgment" in giving information about the New York matter to reporters Jim McGee and Brian Duffy. "It was not a reprimand," Scruggs claimed of the letter. The reporters ultimately painted Scruggs as the White Knight who had cleaned up the civil liberties mess that Mary C. Lawton—who was dead and could not defend herself—left behind in OIPR.

The logjam in OIPR broke with the arrest of would-be millennium bomber Ahmed Ressam in December 1999, when it suddenly became clear to even the most obtuse of the gatekeepers that there really are people who want to blow up Americans inside the United States.

Nerves were already on edge as millennium 2000 and potential terror attacks neared. Clifford helped things along when he was recalled to Washington on Christmas Day 1999 to be on hand in the FBI operations center at the turn of the new year and the new millennium. He found himself there—with Janet Reno, Louis Freeh, and other high-ranking officials—anxiously watching the countdown roll with the midnight hour across the world. He managed to get his request moved up in the stack of backlogged OIPR requests. By January 2000 the FBI had its FISA orders, first on Mohammed Hammoud and then on Said Harb.

By spring 2000, the criminal investigative files on the Charlotte conspirators were fat with evidence. All that remained was to swoop down with search and arrest warrants and roll up the cell. Making the terrorism case would still depend on turning Harb, but that had to be balanced against the chance that Mohammed Hammoud would bolt and go back to Lebanon.

" 'When is this guy going to be taken down?' people kept asking me," says Clifford. "So I made the decision to do it in late spring or early summer. The date was completely arbitrary. We agreed to do it on July 19."

The die was cast but the Canadians were not yet in the game.

"We started really pushing the Canadians in June," Clifford says.

Virtually everybody who was anybody on the American side of the case made a trip or two to Canada, trying to persuade CSIS to do something it had never done before, even in Canada—let its intelligence intercepts be used in open court.

"Our Department of Justice thought it was a great idea," says prosecutor Ken Bell. "But they said, 'It's not going to happen. CSIS will never do it.' "

The Canadians themselves were less sure. "They said at first, 'We'd like to help, but we doubt that we can. But we'll hear you out,' " Bell recalls. He put Justice Department lawyer Martha Rubio to work, figuring out how to meet each of the Canadians' worries and concerns, and how to overcome problems of American law in admitting what was essentially secondhand evidence.

Rubio is a dark-haired beauty, intense, but quick to smile. The young lawyer, from a big family in California, was up to the task. She has a résumé that could have been parlayed into big bucks at a high-rolling law firm. But she chose instead the less lucrative but more rewarding path of quiet public service. As a legal policy wonk, she finds herself working long hours, nights, and weekends, often out of a personal choice to pursue perfection. The Justice Department also puts her Spanish language ability to work as a liaison with Spain and other countries in sensitive matters. In a series of carefully crafted and detailed legal memoranda, Rubio provided Bell and the others with the legal ammunition they needed to assure the Canadians and ensure that their evidence could be used in an American court.

Formal at first, the two sides began to bond over long turns at various taverns and sharing war stories. It was clear to Bell that everything hinged on one man, a broad-shouldered, hearty Canadian named Mike Wright, who headed the Canadian team and was senior adviser to the head of CSIS.

In the middle of one long and trying session of legal point and counterpoint early on in the process, Wright suddenly stood up and pointedly announced, "I need to go outside for a smoke. Anyone want to go with me?"

No one else stood up. Wright repeated himself.

"I'm going out for a smoke. Anyone else want to come along?"

FBI agent Rick Schwein poked Ken Bell, who was leading the U.S. team and was focused on a document.

"Ken," Schwein muttered under his breath, "go out and smoke with him."

Bell took the hint and followed Wright out into the biting Canadian winter air.

"So, Ken, tell me," the burly Wright said through a cloud of frosty smoke. "What is it exactly you fuckers really want?"

Bell knew it was no time for dancing.

"We want your crown jewels," he said bluntly. "We want to take your intelligence holdings into our courtroom and convict some terrorists."

Wright didn't flinch.

"Okay," he said. "I think we can help you."

The negotiations went on for months, with more than one close call. But Bell knew the team would ultimately get what it wanted.

"The decision had to go up to the director of CSIS," he says. "But it was clear that if Mike told the director it should happen, it would happen. And, at that point, I knew that he would recommend that it should happen, and it would. Our job was to work out the details."

Negotiations continued with the Canadians as the Charlotte team drafted what would ultimately be a 93-page affidavit—

signed by FBI agent Rick Schwein, INS agent David Howell, the man Said Harb tried to bribe, and ATF agent Kent J. Hallsten—in support of requests for search and arrest warrants to be executed on July 19. Then the team found itself in the middle of new negotiations as the clock ticked. With several hundred agents marshaled for the scheduled raid, Janet Reno herself had taken a sudden interest in the case and was concerned about the Hezbollah aspects. The matter became a cliffhanger as Chris Swecker, the special agent in charge of the Charlotte office, and various other lawyers and agents, flew to Washington to work out problems that Reno and her staff saw in the case. Reno in particular was concerned about the use of the RICO law in a terrorism case and potential violations of the constitutional rights of the Hezbollah suspects. The discussion occasionally got heated, according to one of those who was present, but eventually Reno and her staff signed off on the warrant request and the affidavit. The delay kicked the raid back to July 20.

The warrants were finally issued—seventeen arrest warrants and nineteen search warrants—and preparations were made for a massive raid to hit the cell and its members early on the morning of July 20, 2000.

The ringing phone woke Angie Tsioumas at exactly 6:00 A.M. It was the first time that she and Hammoud had not gone to work at the BP gas station they had bought using proceeds from their cigarette-smuggling operations and a loan from the U.S. Small Business Administration. Hammoud had worried about the loan application to the government agency, wondering whether they would do a background check. According to Angie, when she asked why he was worried, he said cryptically, "There are some things it's better for you not to know."

Angie thought the phone call would be from the employee opening the station, asking for the alarm code.

"Mohammed," she asked sleepily as she reached for the phone. "What's the alarm code at the station?"

The voice was one she did not recognize. It was a man and he was blunt.

"Do what they say," he said.

"What?" she asked.

"Do what they say," he repeated, and then started speaking in Arabic. At that moment there was a loud crash and the thud of running feet as the front door downstairs was smashed open.

"I threw the phone down and picked up a Smith and Wesson handgun I had bought," Angie recalls. "I thought we were being robbed. I threw the gun to Hammoud, so he was sitting there in the bed with the gun in his hand when I heard people yelling, 'ATF! ATF!' "

By now, Tsioumas was at the head of the stairs and could see the ATF raid team coming up the stairs.

"I yelled at Mohammed, 'Throw the gun down, throw the gun down! It's the ATF!' "

Hammoud complied, a move that no doubt saved his life. Over the next few minutes, 250 federal, state, and local law enforcement agents spread out over the city of Charlotte and its suburbs and swept up the Hezbollah cell and its various criminal coconspirators. Clifford, who had directed the raid's planning and oversaw its execution, listened with growing relief as team after team reported success without violence.

"Our biggest fear was the danger of a shoot-out," he said. "Only one of our targets was not immediately scooped up." It was Mohit Behl, Harb's partner in pornography, who was on a trip to California. "We arranged to have him picked up later in the day out there."

Clifford had also arranged to have female, Arabic-speaking agents present at every location where a female Muslim was to be arrested or confronted. He knew that they would need to be assured that they were safe and that if a body search were necessary, no man should be allowed to do it.

Said Harb knew the jig was up from the moment he was arrested. Ever the artful dodger, he soon started angling for a deal.

Scooped up at 6:15 A.M., he was allowed to get dressed, speak briefly with his wife, and smoke a cigarette. He was then taken in a Charlotte-Mecklenburg Police Department cruiser to the U.S.

Army Reserve Center, which had been converted into a processing center for the raid. There he was read his rights and grilled until about 1:30 in the afternoon by Rick Schwein and Eric Stocky, an agent of the Diplomatic Security Service.

"Why the SWAT team?" he asked. "It's not like I'm a terrorist or anything."

Harb sang like a canary, except about his attempt to bribe INS agent Howell and the details of the Hezbollah connection.

"Harb talked and talked and talked about his criminal activity," says Schwein. "Then at one point he asked me to put my pen down. 'I know why you've done this to me,' he said. 'You want Dbouk and you want Hezbollah. I can't talk about that now. Let me talk to my lawyer. But if I do help you, I want my family taken out of Lebanon.' "

Harb hired Chris Fialko, a rising star in the North Carolina criminal defense bar. Fialko had been one of the defense lawyers in the Loomis-Wells Fargo armored car robbery, and was just getting ready to go to trial in defense of Rae Carruth, a Carolina Panther wide receiver charged with capital murder in the alleged contract killing of the woman pregnant with his child. (Carruth eventually was found not guilty of murder in the case.)

"I understood quickly that Harb was not their target," Fialko said. "And I know what to do when my client is not the target. I also knew that they needed the Canadian stuff to prove any material support against Harb."

Thus began what Fialko describes as "a long dance" of negotiations.

"I knew my phones were tapped and I assume they still are," says Fialko. "So I did everything in person with Ken Bell and Rick Schwein. My deal was Harb's family had to be taken safely out of Lebanon and he could not be charged with any material support offense."

Assured that they could pull the plug and withdraw from the case at any moment they felt that use of their evidence would imperil Canada's security, the Canadians finally agreed to the American request. In February 2001 the deal was cut secretly with Harb and put under court seal.

Machinery was set in motion to get a dozen members of his family out of Lebanon, five of whom were children.

"That was a bureaucratic nightmare," recalls Bell. "It was not entirely clear who had the authority to issue the visas. Then when they did get the visas, there were problems with which airports they could travel through."

The family had to be taken secretly from Lebanon to Damascus, then flown to the United States. To make matters worse, the move was made on Easter Sunday. Fialko and Bell were on a round-robin of phone calls, trying to untie the visa knots with the bureaucratic machinery in Washington and Europe to get the family safely into the United States. Eventually things fell into place and Said Harb was able to greet his family out of the reach of retaliation from Hezbollah.

The trial of the Charlotte Hezbollah cell began on May 23, 2002. The government's case was solid on the criminal counts—its main problem was knowing when to stop layering on the evidence. Ken Bell hammered away, a master craftsman at the peak of his career. Said Harb carried out his end of the deal and told the story of the Hezbollah connections and his own involvement in the purchase of dual-use equipment. On Friday, June 21, 2002, the jury came back with its verdict: guilty on all counts.

Said Harb was sentenced to three and a half years in prison. With the time he had already spent in jail awaiting trial and the usual reductions for good behavior, he is out on the street, a free man.

Mohammed Hammoud was sentenced to 150 years in prison. He has appealed his conviction and his sentence, which he is currently serving in a federal maximum security prison in Texas.

"If this can happen in Charlotte, North Carolina," said U.S. Attorney Bob Conrad, "it can happen anywhere in America."

In fact, it is happening all over the United States.

"RISE FOR JIHAD! . . ."

Rise for Jihad! Rise for Jihad!
I offer you, Hezbollah, my blood in my hand.
                            —*Excerpt from Hezbollah tape seized*
                                in Dearborn, Michigan

On the morning of Wednesday, June 5, 2002, the front page of *The New York Times* informed readers that the Justice Department was preparing new regulations that would require thousands of Muslim and Middle Eastern visa holders to be registered and fingerprinted. There was a paroxysm of indignant reaction. Professional civil libertarians and Arab American groups frothed that the plan was a "blatant example of racial and ethnic profiling."

"The message it sends," said James J. Zogby, president of the Arab American Institute, "is that we're becoming like the Soviet Union, with people registering at the police station." Zogby might as well have used as an example any number of Arab states that treat their subjects with as minute and oppressive detail as the former Soviet Union—including most prominently at the time the brutal regime of Saddam Hussein in Iraq.

Later that morning, jurors in Charlotte, North Carolina—646 miles south of New York—listened to a tape seized from the home of Mohammed Hammoud.

"We're the lovers of martyrdom," shouted Hassan Naserallah.

"Death to America!" roared the crowd, repeating the angry phrase six times.

"They accuse us of being terrorists," responded Naserallah. "Let Christopher, Clinton, and the State Department and the American Congress record that we the sons of Hezbollah are terrorists until we return our nation to our dignity."

Still later in the day, the emergency room at Scripps Memorial Hospital in Chula Vista, California—2,827 miles west of New York—received an unusual patient. The man was comatose and bleeding profusely from the mouth. Two men who identified themselves as construction workers claimed they found him wandering about their work site. The two were later found to have given false names, addresses, and telephone numbers. The moribund man was a Lebanese, Youssef Mohammed Balaghi.

Chula Vista ("beautiful view") is the home of the U.S. Olympic Training Center, the first such facility in the United States to be designed and built from the ground up for the purpose of developing world-class athletes. The city also happens to be located fifteen minutes south of San Diego and seven miles north of the Mexican border, which is why hospital authorities notified the U.S. Border Patrol when Balaghi died later in the day. The Border Patrol was immediately concerned because his symptoms were similar to those of radiation sickness. The nation's authorities were on edge about the prospect of a terrorist attack with a so-called dirty bomb, a massive conventional explosive device laced with radioactive material, the purpose of which would be to contaminate a broad area, spread panic, and disrupt the economy more than to cause immediate death and injury. Lithuanian government officials announced only four days earlier that they had broken up an attempted sale of highly radioactive material to a mysterious German national, for whom an international alert was put out. Less than a week later, Attorney General John Ashcroft would announce the arrest of Jose Padilla, a U.S. citizen and convert to Islam, charged with plotting to set off just such a bomb somewhere in the United States on behalf of al Qaeda.

Balaghi's corpse tested negative for radiation exposure. Medical authorities concluded that he had died from heat exhaustion. But Balaghi's death was the first thread pulled from a criminal enterprise that gradually unraveled and led authorities to a Mexican ring specializing in smuggling Lebanese into the United States, and from there to a man federal authorities accuse of being a hardened Hezbollah operative. The investigation got its first big break when Patricio Servano Valdez, a Mexican caught guiding illegal immigrants into California from Mexico, told immigration investigators that he was working with a restaurant owner in Tijuana named Salim Moughader Mucharrafille.

Mucharrafille's restaurant, Café La Libanesa, was located at 10 Calle Tapachula, in an upscale neighborhood of Tijuana named Colonia Hipodromo. The café specialized in Middle Eastern cuisine such as hummus and baklava. Two local landmarks are located near the restaurant—the Hipodromo racetrack, and the U.S. Consulate. The consulate is less than a block away, at the corner of Boulevard Agua Caliente and Calle Tapachula. La Libanesa was a favorite of many of the Americans, none of whom imagined that the charming and popular young host on the cell phone—the Mexican-born son of a Lebanese Druze father who fled the civil war—was fielding calls from clients of a smuggling ring that stretched from Tijuana to Beirut. Mucharrafille had applied for a special quick-entry business visa that would allow him to make multiple temporary visits to the United States, to buy supplies such as phyllo dough for Lebanese pastries and smuggle clients into the United States. He was arrested when he came over the border for an interview in connection with his visa application.

On March 18, 2003—the morning after President George W. Bush gave Saddam Hussein 48 hours to voluntarily go into exile or face war and told the Iraqi people, "The tyrant will soon be gone"—Mucharrafille pled guilty to immigration smuggling charges. Authorities say his operation had helped some 300 Lebanese sneak into the United States, most of them Muslims. The deals were made in Beirut, where the clients were sold Mexican visas by a corrupt Mexican foreign service officer, and given Mucharrafille's cell phone number as their contact in Tijuana. Because he cooperated with investigators, Mucharrafille was sentenced to a relatively light one year in prison. Among other things, he gave U.S. authorities a ledger and a list of names of those he had smuggled. Released ten months later and deported, he was promptly arrested again by Mexican authorities and faced a stiff prison term. His outraged American lawyer accused the Border Patrol of using the Mexicans to punish Mucharrafille with the long sentence he had avoided in the American court.

The thread continued. In July 2003 the Mexican government announced that it was conducting a broad investigation into the subject of lost visas and passports, and the sale of illegal visas from its consular offices. On November 12, 2003, Mexican authorities announced the arrest of Imelda Ortiz, a 25-year veteran Mexican foreign service officer. The career officer's full name, Imelda Ortiz Abdala, reflects the Hispanic naming tradition of using the father's surname (Ortiz) as the middle name and the mother's surname (Abdala) as the last. It also reveals her maternal Arabic origin—"Abdala" is the phonetic rendering into Spanish of the Arabic "abd Allah," which means "servant of Allah," and was the name of the Prophet Mohammed's father. Abdala is a common name among Latin Americans of Lebanese descent.

Imelda Ortiz Abdala had been fired in May 2003 after it was discovered that a number of Mexican passports had disappeared from the consular office in Mexico City during her tenure there as chief of the office. Before that she had been chief of the consular section at the Mexican embassy in Beirut, from May 1998 to October 2001. She was arrested because the trail of the Mucharrafille investigation ended at her desk. Ortiz Abdala had been selling Mexican visas at the Beirut end of the pipeline for as much as $4,500 each. The ongoing Mexican investigation revealed similar sales in an unspecified number of other consulates, including Cuba. The Mucharrafille-Ortiz Abdala case alarmed American officials, who had been concerned for some time about the growing Hezbollah presence in Mexico. So were some Mexican officials. On May 29, 2001, Adolfo Aguilar Zinser, then the Mexican president's national security adviser, said in a radio broadcast that "Spanish and Islamic terrorist groups are using Mexico as a refuge." Zinser refused to name specific groups, but Mexican newspapers reported the next day that he was referring specifically to Hezbollah.

Even so, the subject of immigration and terror remains a sensitive and complex subject between the two states and among powerful political constituencies within them. Any U.S. screw tightening is felt on a large scale in Mexico, whose long-term agenda is lessening economic pressures in part by increased immigration to the north, and among whose people an informal motto is "So far from God, so near to the United States." In 2003 Zinser himself was fired from his later post as Mexico's ambassador to the United Nations after he publicly blasted the United States for subordinating Mexico to the status of a "backyard," largely over the question of increased immigration controls in the wake of September 11, 2001. Proposals to restrict immigration from the south also invariably arouse the ire of organized groups of Hispanic Americans in the United States, whose growing political strength is focused on more rather than less accommodation of such immigration, legal or not.

For example, Hispanic groups have favored the growing trend among civil jurisdictions and businesses to recognize an identification card, called the *matricula consular,* issued by the Mexican government to its citizens in the United States, whether they are here legally or not. About one million are currently in circulation, issued by some 47 Mexican consular offices in the United States. Many counterterrorism officials are strongly opposed to the trend, which has been encouraged by Mexican officials,* and New York State among others has refused to recognize the cards. FBI intelligence officials and other critics of the cards point out that the only people who need them are in the country illegally to begin with, there is no coordinated system for controlling their issuance, and the documents themselves are easily forged. The cards are therefore neither reliable nor secure evidence of the holder's true identity. They also warn that the *matricula consular* is also a perfect "breeder document" with which to get other documents, such as a driver's license, and establish false identities like those used by Said Harb and others in the Hezbollah cell. In fact, a number of Latin Americans from countries other than Mexico and at least one Iranian have been arrested in possession of the Mexican identity card within the United States. Several other countries are considering following the Mexican example and issuing similar identity cards to their nationals in the United States.

It is also hard for American authorities to forget the case of Mahmud Abouhalima, mastermind of the first World Trade Center bombing. An unlawful Egyptian émigré turned New York City

---

* Robert Rodriguez, chief of consular affairs for the Mexican foreign ministry, and an aggressive promoter of expanded use abroad of the card, was suspended in July 2003 pending completion of the country's investigation into visa fraud and other irregularities in its visa and passport programs.

taxi driver, Abouhalima fraudulently took advantage of a general amnesty program for migrant farmworkers. "The amnesty program was a joke," according to a former INS spokesman. "Since documentation wasn't required, the burden was on the government to prove the aliens were not farmers. Fraud was widespread and enforcement virtually impossible." Abouhalima applied for amnesty in 1986, was awarded temporary legal residence in 1988, and got his green card two years later. There is no evidence that he ever worked as a migrant farmworker.

In any event, U.S. investigators mounted a massive effort to track down the people in Mucharrafille's ledger. One trail led them to Dearborn, Michigan—an appendage of Detroit that some law enforcement officers call "Hezbollah Central"—and the arrest of Mahmoud Youssef Kourani. According to federal prosecutors, Kourani is a well-trained and extremely dangerous operative, the most serious portent of potential Hezbollah terrorism they have yet seen in the United States.

A drive through the inner-city southwestern neighborhoods of Detroit is a tour of the worst of inner-city America. Litter and dilapidation compete with indifference and despair to shape block after block of trash-strewn grime. But if one makes a turn onto one of the several thoroughfares that crisscross the heart of the city of Dearborn, Michigan, one notices a remarkable transformation. The streets are clean, the storefronts and houses well kept, and there is throughout a general air of industrious commerce and social order. One other thing stands out—there are so many signs in Arabic and such a concentration of ethnically oriented businesses that one could easily imagine being in the Middle East. Restaurants, supermarkets, specialty shops, social and civic organizations all advertise their presence in the flowing Arabic script. Get out and walk around and one hears the distinctive sounds of the Middle East—music and language—and the scents of prepared food and produce.

The distinctive nature of Dearborn is no wonder. A third of the city's 100,000 legal residents claim Arab ethnicity, the second largest urban concentration of Arab Americans in the United

States after New York City. At least 3.5 million Americans of Arab descent live in the 50 states, but they are heavily concentrated— two-thirds live in ten states, and a third live in California, New York, and Michigan. The majority of Arab Americans are Christians—only about 23 percent are Muslims. They enjoy a lower level of unemployment, higher income, and a higher level of education than the average American. About 94 percent live in metropolitan areas—the top five areas of concentration are Los Angeles, Detroit, New York/New Jersey, Chicago, and Washington, D.C. Lebanese represent by far the greater part of Arab Americans—34 percent nationally—and are the majority in most states, except New Jersey, where the majority are Egyptian Americans, and Rhode Island, where those of Syrian descent are the majority.

Dearborn is the site of an Arab American museum scheduled to be opened in 2005. The city is largely a product of Henry Ford's automotive industry, and many of the city's Arab American families trace their origins in America to ancestors who came to work in the factories. Like most of the country, the greater portion of its Arab American population is of Lebanese descent. Clearly, not all of them are Shiites. Nor are all of the Shiites supporters of Hezbollah. Nevertheless, the concentration of Hezbollah sympathizers and activists among the more recent Shiite émigrés from Lebanon is such that the catch phrase of those who are watching Hezbollah in America is "Dearborn is where the action is."

"At one time, we had whole city blocks that were Hezbollah strongholds," said Ken Piernik, a retired FBI agent who supervised the Iran/Hezbollah unit at FBI headquarters until recently. "Some of the former South Lebanon Army people relocating to the United States were naturally attracted to the area. Well, it ended up that we literally had Hezbollah sympathizers chasing the SLA people around with guns."

The Israelis are known to have helped SLA members relocate to various Lebanese communities in the United States, where they keep tabs on Hezbollah for Israeli intelligence services. Israel's official position, of course, is that it does not collect intelligence within the borders of its friend and ally.

Hezbollah activity in Dearborn produced the first-ever indictment under the 1996 federal law banning material support to terrorist organizations. Naturalized citizen Fawzi Mustapha Assi was 38 years old when the FBI arrested him on July 23, 1998, on charges of attempting to illegally export high-technology dual-use equipment to Hezbollah in Lebanon. According to the indictment and other papers filed in his case, customs officials searched Assi's luggage when he attempted to board a flight to Lebanon on July 13, 1998. They found seven pairs of night-vision goggles, an infrared heat detection device, and a Boeing global positioning satellite module. Assi—an engineer at the Ford Motor Company's Dearborn assembly plant—had been under surveillance for some time prior to the Customs search. His phones had also been tapped under a FISA order. Interviewed after the airport search, he allegedly admitted to the FBI that he was attempting to export the high-technology items to a Hezbollah contact named "Hassan" in Lebanon, and said he had exported body armor and books and videotapes about security procedures to his Hezbollah contact. Agents observed him dump similar items into the trash after their interview with him. Among the items found in the bins was information about Israeli cabinet members and the locations of their offices.

A federal magistrate released Assi on bond over the strong objections of federal prosecutors, who appealed the decision to a federal trial judge. Five days later, Assi disappeared, even though he was wearing an electronic tether. Assi's tether was of the variety that reported by satellite his distance from a home unit, not his exact location. Its last report indicated that he left his home at 7:15 A.M., and his truck was later found in the Ford plant parking lot. What he did to or with the tether itself remains a minor mystery, at least publicly, although one FBI agent joked, "We found it in the middle of the Ambassador Bridge between Detroit and Canada." Assi was found to have fled to Lebanon, where he remained as a fugitive for almost six years until May 2004, when he voluntarily returned to Detroit to face trial on the charges against him. Federal prosecutors complain that the presence of a Lebanese consulate in Detroit has made it easy for some defendants to flee the country if they are released on bail, even after their Lebanese passports have been confiscated—several such suspects simply went to the consulate, got new passports, and fled.

Meanwhile, Ali Boumelhem of Detroit was convicted in September 2001 of conspiring to smuggle arms to Hezbollah in Lebanon. According to the government's sentencing memorandum, Boumelhem "illegally acquired and shipped firearms, ammunition, and weapons parts to Lebanon over a period of years." Federal agents intercepted one such shipment, a shipping container destined for Beirut that contained, among other things, two shotguns, 750 rounds of ammunition, parts for AR-15 semiautomatic rifles, and flash suppressors for AK-47 assault rifles. However, prosecutors say that Boumelhem was involved in a considerable amount of similar activity before that interception. The investigation began after agents got a tip from a confidential informant that Boumelhem had shipped arms to Lebanon in the past and might do so again. A cousin and a former spouse also helped as informants. Agents trailed Boumelhem and his brother, Mohammed, to gun shows in Michigan as part of the investigation. Mohammed was acquitted after trial. Ali was sentenced to 44 months in prison in March 2002.

At least thirteen people have been indicted in Michigan as a result of a continuing investigation stemming from the Charlotte Hezbollah case. The investigation uncovered another related cigarette-smuggling pipeline from the Cattaraugus Indian Reservation in New York to the conspirator's home base in Dearborn. In addition, from time to time members of the criminal enterprise took "fraud field trips" to defraud retail and wholesale merchants in Michigan, New York, and North Carolina with phony credit cards. One of the defendants, Hassan Moussa Makki, was stopped at the Canadian border with $500,000 of undeclared cash and checks. He eventually admitted that some of the funds were intended for Hezbollah, to whom he had sent earlier contributions. As of early 2004, nine of those indicted had pled guilty to various charges under the federal RICO law. Makki pled guilty to material support and RICO charges and was sentenced to 57 months in prison on December 18, 2003. Another of the conspirators, Elias Mohammed Akhdar, was sentenced on January 8, 2004, to 70 months in prison.

Federal prosecutors say, however, that the most serious of the Hezbollah cases is that of Mahmoud Youssef Kourani, the man

who got into the United States by way of the Beirut-Tijuana pipeline. "This is the case to watch," said a senior federal prosecutor in
Detroit. He is currently charged with fund-raising, and other activities deliberately not yet publicly specified by prosecutors, in violation of the federal law against providing material support to a
terrorist organization.

Mahmoud Kourani was born on April 22, 1971, in the village
of Yater in southern Lebanon. Yater was the scene of frequent
fighting and shelling in the conflict with the Israelis. Kourani
is one of five brothers, four of whom are alleged to be active
in Hezbollah. Two brothers—Hussein and Abdullah—are active
members and Hezbollah soldiers. Another, Haidar Kourani, is a
high-ranking official, chief of security for Hezbollah in southern
Lebanon. "He is basically the chief of staff of Hezbollah's military
wing," according to an assistant U. S. attorney supervising Kourani's case in Detroit. "He is very close to being the head." Mahmoud Kourani told an FBI informant that he and his brother
Haidar were members of the Hezbollah unit that in 1988 kidnapped and tortured to death U.S. Marine Corps Col. William
Higgins in Lebanon.

Mahmoud Kourani, prosecutors say, received specialized training
in Lebanon and Iran in weaponry, spy craft, and counterintelligence. While in Lebanon, he was a fund-raiser and an "operational
recruiter"—he recruited young men for operational, as opposed to
merely support, duties for Hezbollah—and oversaw the process of
the detailed background investigations and vetting that Hezbollah
uses to clear all potential operators. According to federal prosecutors, Kourani continued his fund-raising and recruiting activities
in the United States, under the direction of his brother Haidar. "He
was a Hezbollah recruiter in the United States," says a federal
prosecutor. Documents in the case state that more than nine informants have identified Kourani as a member, fighter, and fund-
raiser for Hezbollah. Kourani told an informant that Hezbollah
had sent him to train in Iran on multiple occasions.

Kourani allegedly flew to Mexico after paying $3,000 for a
Mexican visa in Beirut, leaving behind his wife, Wafa Kdouh

Kourani, and three children. Once in Mexico, he called Salim Moughader Mucharrafille at his restaurant in Tijuana, and was then taken across the border into the United States hiding in the trunk of a car. He went straight to Dearborn, where he hooked up with the conspirators in the Akhdar-Makki smuggling and racketeering enterprise, including coconspirators in nearby Canada. When federal investigators tracked Kourani down and arrested him on May 8, 2003, they found with him another Lebanese national, Ghaleb Youssef Kdouh. Kourani was charged with harboring an illegal alien, pled guilty, and was sentenced to six months in prison. During this time, the FBI and others continued their investigation into Kourani, and on January 25, 2004, he was indicted on the charges of providing material support to a terrorist organization, Hezbollah. Kourani is specifically charged with providing funds to Hezbollah, but federal prosecutors hint that they are investigating other activity.

The FBI flatly refuses to talk about any aspect of the Kourani case, or even to voluntarily provide public documents—possibly because the Detroit office and its chief have been publicly and uncomfortably on the griddle after a series of bungled moves involving informants who were feeding false information to agents, and an embarrassing dispute with a federal prosecutor.* These miscues resulted in the dismissal of charges against two Dearborn area men charged with material support, a case that inflamed the Arab community. Federal prosecutors are also careful, stressing that the Kourani case is still very much under active investigation. However, it is known that at least $13,000 in cash and checks was found in Kourani's closet when he was first arrested. Investigators also allegedly discovered that he sent $40,000 in cash to his brother Haidar, and that he also sold a home in the Detroit area and sent the proceeds from that sale to a brother in Lebanon.

Mahmoud Kourani explained to an FBI informant that he was running a mortgage fraud scam in the Detroit area. He bought

---

* The public affairs offices of federal agencies often cooperate with writers and journalists by providing copies of documents that have been filed in criminal cases, such as the affidavits of agents filed in support of search warrants. Although these documents can be obtained from courthouse files, it is usually quicker and easier to get them from a cooperative investigative agency once the case is public.

burned-out houses and made superficial exterior repairs. He then got inflated appraisals from a bribed appraiser. An associate took out and defaulted on loans based on the inflated appraisals, splitting the money with Mahmoud, who sent it on to Hezbollah in Lebanon. He said that he owned three more homes in the Detroit area, and added that he could send as much money as he wished back to Lebanon because a friend who was related to a "Sheik Hassan" (it's not clear who this is) worked at the Detroit airport and would help. The money was sent back on the person of a Lebanese courier.

Prosecutors say that Kourani practiced the Shiite doctrine of *taqiyya,* or concealment. When he thought it necessary, he shaved his beard and stayed away from mosques and other religious activity, keeping secret his religious beliefs while operating within enemy territory—the United States of America.

How many Hezbollah cells are there in the United States? Besides Charlotte and Dearborn, according to investigators and documents, Hezbollah supporters are actively involved in criminal conspiracies in New York City; Newark, New Jersey; Boston; Chicago; San Francisco; Louisville; Houston; the Miami-Fort Lauderdale metropolitan area; Los Angeles; Portland, Oregon; Atlanta, Georgia; and Tampa, Florida. Smaller and less organized clusters of sympathizers and fund-raisers are active in scores of other communities throughout the United States. Of course, it is possible that there are other unknown Hezbollah operatives hiding in deeper cover than Mohammed Hammoud, Mahmoud Kourani, and scores of others who entered the country illegally but were eventually detected.

Federal authorities will not discuss the known cells in any detail, since they are the subjects of ongoing investigations designed to bust them either by criminal prosecution or by means of the disruption and deportation tactics pioneered by Bob Clifford. Cigarette smuggling remains a staple of the organized conspiracies, as are credit card scams, fraudulent insurance claims, bank fraud, phony marriages, and other immigration violations.

Another popular scheme is known among investigators as the

"Enfamil scam," although it may involve other brand names of baby formula. Perpetrators of this fraud use a variety of means to profit by selling adulterated, fraudulent, or expired baby formula to retailers. By whatever means the fraudulent product is acquired, the criminals put counterfeit labels on it and profit either by selling it to unscrupulous third-party distributors and retailers, or by selling it themselves if a retail outlet is part of their criminal enterprise. Hezbollah cells are known to have operated Enfamil scams in Los Angeles and Houston.

A scheme under investigation in the Atlanta area is known as the "Lebanese Amway scam." It combines immigration fraud with retail extortion. The conspiracy brings Lebanese into the country illegally and requires them to work off their entry fee at convenience stores owned by the principals. Once the debt is paid off, the subjects are underwritten to open a new store, provided that they buy their stock from the criminal network.

The genius of Hezbollah's operation in the United States is its discipline in staying just beneath the law enforcement radar while relentlessly finding the crevices in America's defenses. It continually seeks out new schemes of fund-raising and new channels by which to infiltrate the United States, as evidenced by the Beirut–Tijuana smuggling ring. Hezbollah receives tremendous support from the Iranian government, which ultimately underwrites its global enterprises, including its infiltration of America. Iran provides not only funds, but diplomatic and intelligence resources to back up Hezbollah's own talents.

Unfortunately, the demands of other aspects of the war on terror have actually caused the FBI's Hezbollah/Iran unit to atrophy rather than grow, according to a knowledgeable insider. "It is not because the threat is perceived as any the less," he says. "It is simply a matter of having to draw resources away to put elsewhere."

The ultimate challenge in the war on terror is to effectively protect our society while at the same time preserving its distinctive civil liberties, social values, and economic structure. Having said that, the least helpful approach is the sort of civil libertarian dogmatism that reflexively poses all law enforcement measures as the greatest danger to our freedoms.

"I didn't work for the FBI for 32 years to undo the Constitution," is how Jim Kallstrom, the retired assistant director in charge of the New York FBI office puts it. "I did it to protect the Constitution. And I know that another major terrorist attack here, of proportions the American public has yet to imagine, would lead to demands for enormous restrictions on our liberties. What if 200,000 people die the next time? What if there are bombs going off in our shopping centers, fuel goes to five dollars a gallon, and kids are dying from botulism because our food supply has been contaminated? Then there will be a massive overreaction the other way. The biggest threat to our civil liberties is our continuing inability to deal with the threat in a reasonable time. Inaction is the bigger threat to our liberties. We have to develop systems that work before the problem becomes so big that it's unfixable."

How can we develop such systems?

First, we need to understand the true nature of our enemy and organize against him in the same way we have with other threats to our society. That requires the realization that although neither the religion of Islam, nor all Arabs, nor all Muslims are at war with the United States, a determined, radical, and substantial global army of radical Islamists long ago declared war on America. Hezbollah is in the front rank of that army of hostile combatants, by virtue of the depth of its hatred, the status it has earned among jihadists from past successes, its vast skills in the techniques of terror, its teaching those skills to other terrorists from all over the world, its role as a primary funnel of Iran's support of terrorism, its growing presence in neighboring countries, and—last but not least—its determined establishment of a broad presence within our own borders.

Second, we should stop the politically profitable game of making scapegoats of our law enforcement and intelligence agencies *as institutions.* Nothing is more distressing than the sight of ranks and panels of preening politicians—who in the years before September 11, 2001, absented themselves from dozens of hearings in which the threat was raised and the warning given, or failed to comprehend what they heard, or failed to take action—now pointing fingers at men and women who have devoted their lives to the service of our country. Yes, individuals make mistakes. Yes, systems are imperfect. And, yes, corrections should be made on the basis of experience. But the authors have seen the result of the relentless after-action finger-pointing and blame-laying: Decades of experience and acres of knowledge are fleeing our intelligence and law enforcement agencies because no one in their right mind wants to face the prospect of being pilloried before the sort of public inquisition that has become the current fashion. Many of the most talented people in our government are marking the days until they can retire and simply get the hell out.

"We didn't need a 9/11 Commission to tell us that the radios didn't work," said one frustrated former senior official. "We had been telling Congress that for twenty years. They ignored us, and when the radios didn't work, they blamed us."

Third, we should stop trying to put handcuffs on our law enforcement agencies and start trying to put them on terrorists. The infamous Chinese Wall is only one manifestation of the insidious attitude among radical libertarians that the greatest danger to America lies in its law enforcement agencies. The words "wiretap" and "search of business records" are treated as horrid icons of a police state, things inherently far worse than, say, the release of a deadly designer virus in downtown Chicago, the detonation of a dirty bomb in Los Angeles, or the explosion of a dozen backpack bombs on the Acela Express train between Washington and New York.

Fourth, we need as a nation to understand that—as the case of the Charlotte Hezbollah cell demonstrates—the agents of law enforcement who use these tools are good, solid people whose goal is not to harm the innocent but to catch and convict the guilty and protect us from the most terrible of schemes. Yes, abuses are not only theoretically possible, but bound to happen among mortal administrators of the law. The answer is not to deprive law enforcement of the tools it urgently needs in these times of unprecedented peril, but to punish the few who break the rules and abuse the processes of the law.

Fifth, we need to come to terms with the intertwined problems of our inability to control our borders and our lack of a consistent national form of secure identification. The cases we have described demonstrate over and over again that terrorists can cross our borders with ease—whether on a phony visa or in the trunk of a car—and once here can plunge into a cornucopia of easily obtained false identities. What is more astonishing than our national paralysis on looking this issue in the face and confronting it head-on is the fact that powerful interest groups exert relentless pressure for less, rather than more, immigration and document security. The simple, plain, and unavoidable fact is that we will never be secure from the terrorists among us—whether they be Hezbollah, al Qaeda, or some recombinant variant as yet unheard of—unless and until we control and know who comes across our borders, keep track of them while they are here, and know when they leave.

Sixth, we need to study the "trip wires" of organized terrorism in a free society and then take advantage of the informational means to find out when they have been triggered. That means first understanding in great depth of detail the patterns of how people like the hijackers of September 11, 2001, and the cigarette smugglers of Charlotte operate in their daily lives. How do they typically travel? Where do they typically live? What is the typical pattern of their financial transactions? How do they communicate with each other and when? And so forth. It is the analog of what credit card companies, supermarket chains, and Internet retailers already do to all of us—they know our patterns. The more controversial step is doing something about it. That requires taking advantage of this information to search out ongoing patterns and highlight those that fit the terrorists'.

Seventh, we must truly integrate into our national thinking the idea that everything changes in a world where terrorism is a fact of life. The most ordinary things that we take for granted are extraordinarily vulnerable—our food and water supply, our power systems, and our transportation networks, for example. Our enemies know that they can leverage our dependence on complex systems of technology into catastrophe. We need only to recall the economic, social, and psychological damage done on September 11, 2001, to understand what a few determined people striking at critical nodes can do. The FBI and others responsible for protecting our critical infrastructure—all the systems of commerce, finance, communication, transportation, and energy—understand this. Many believe that the best defense is rooting out the terrorists before they can strike.

Finally, our institutions need to honor and not punish those in our law enforcement and counterterrorism communities who push aggressively against the terrorists who would do us harm. John O'Neill labored against immense inertia, indifference, and even hostility within the established bureaucracy when he raised his clarion call warning of the dangers of al Qaeda. Americans need to learn from that experience and reward extraordinary men and women like him who refuse to accept the conventions of previous eras.

The story of the Charlotte Hezbollah cell is in the final measure a tale of an incredibly talented team of just such extraordinary people. Bob Clifford, Rick Schwein, Ken Bell, Bob Fromme, and Martha Rubio came together like an all-American constellation at just the right time and place. They led a team of many others too numerous to name. They are uniformly too modest to take credit, always pointing to other team members and other agencies that were part of the investigation. Yet, in our view, they were the heart of the matter. We are grateful for their efforts and are honored to have met them.

ENDNOTES

"You've Got to Be Taught . . ."

1. Hala Jaber, *Hezbollah: Born with a Vengeance* (New York: Columbia University Press, 1997), p. 1.

"For the Violence Done in Lebanon . . ."

2. Thomas W. Lippman, *Understanding Islam: An Introduction to the Muslim World* (New York: Meridian, 1995), p. 139.

3. "Shiite Muslim Holiday of Ashura," *All Things Considered*, National Public Radio, April 4, 2001.

4. "Shiite Moslems Mark Death of Saint," Associated Press, September 26, 1985.

5. Fouad Ajami, *The Vanished Imam: Musa al Sadr and the Shia of Lebanon* (Ithaca, New York: Cornell University Press, 1986), p. 48.

6. Martin Kramer, "The Oracle of Hizbullah," in *Spokesmen for the Despised*, ed. R. Scott Appleby (Chicago: University of Chicago Press, 1997), p. 94.

7. Ibid. pp. 90–91.

8. Ibid. p. 94.

9. *Deborah D. Peterson v. The Islamic Republic of Iran*, 264 F. Supp.2d 46 (D.D.C. 2003), at 50.

INDEX

ABOUT THE TYPE

The text of this book was set in Palatino, designed by the German typographer Hermann Zapf. It was named after the Renaissance calligrapher Giovanbattista Palatino. Zapf designed it between 1948–52, and it was his first typeface to be introduced in America. It is a face of unusual elegance.